THE
NEIL GAIMAN
READER

ALSO BY DARRELL SCHWEITZER

Exploring Fantasy Worlds
Discovering H.P. Lovecraft
The Thomas Ligotti Reader
The Robert E. Howard Reader (forthcoming)

FICTION

The Mask of the Sorcerer
The Shattered Goddess
We Are All Legends
The White Isle

THE NEIL GAIMAN READER

EDITED BY

DARRELL SCHWEITZER

WILDSIDE PRESS

THE NEIL GAIMAN READER

CONTENTS

INTRODUCTION TO
A VERY LARGE SUBJECT

This book is a pioneering effort, not quite the first book of Neil Gaiman criticism, but close to it. When Stephen Rauch proposed to submit a 50,000 word article to this book, I suggested he just approach Wildside Press about having it published as a book all by itself. The result was *The Sandman and Joseph Campbell, In Search of the Modern Myth,* which beat *The Neil Gaiman Reader* into print by a substantial amount of time and has been, deservedly, a notable success.

This one is, literally, years in the making, and has proven the most difficult of any such critical anthology I have ever edited, precisely because there is no established tradition of Gaiman criticism, the way there is for Lovecraft or Dunsany or even Thomas Ligotti. It was one thing to say, "Someone ought to do a Neil Gaiman Reader," and another to master the entire, and rapidly-growing Gaiman *oeuvre.* I won't claim to have done so. I am relying heavily on the expertise of others here, and I am grateful to them all.

What is most amazing about Gaiman, among many amazing things, is how *recently* he has come onto the scene. His first story, a humorous interview with Cthulhu, published in the British fanzine *Dagon* #16 only appeared in 1987. Gaiman, of course, is not a kid, but he has, in about a decade and a half, accomplished more than most writers do in a lifetime and continues to give the impression that he is only getting started. He's already redefined the universe in the *Sandman* series, creating a major work which I am sure will resonate throughout the fantasy of the twenty-first century. Maybe he is not the first to do so (he would doubtless modestly bow to Alan Moore), but he is *one of the first* to write comic books with the intensity of serious novels, to raise the form into High Literature. I mean that.

Then there are his dynamite short stories, and his novels, *Stardust, Neverwhere, American Gods,* and *Anansi Boys.* He is moving into film with *Mirrormask.* I do not doubt that it will have a long life ahead of it, at festivals, and as a rental.

Huge. The size of his imagination is huge. Clearly Neil Gaiman is not a flash in the pan, but perhaps the premier imaginative storyteller of our time, in whatever medium he choses.

This bears examination. Hence the book you hold in your hands.

—Darrell Schweitzer
Philadelphia, Pennsylvania

The Neil Gaiman Reader

CAMPBELL AND *THE SANDMAN:* REMINDING US OF THE SACRED

Stephen Rauch

Throughout humanity's existence, people have use myths to make sense of what the world is and how it was made, as well as how they should live their lives ethically and responsibly. Joseph Campbell and others have proposed that myths also function on a deeper level, manifesting what Mircea Eliade calls "an unquenchable thirst . . . for being" (Eliade, 64), an often universal representation of people's hopes, dreams, concerns, and fears. However, the underscoring of mythology as vital to the well-being of a people leads to an ominous view of today's society. Rapid technological advancements and cultural shifts have led to what Campbell calls a "demythologized world" (Campbell, 9). Eliade echoes these sentiments that modern man has become profane as the "result of a process of desacralization" (203). What is necessary, then, is to find a modern myth, one that features elements of the same timeless patterns evinced by ancient mythology and that is still appropriate to the world and social situations of today. One work that meets these criteria is Neil Gaiman's *The Sandman*, a monthly comic that has crossed over into serious literature, drawing from the mythologies and literature of many cultures throughout the years, as well as the world of today. *The Sandman* centers around seven beings, called the Endless, who are more than gods; they are anthropomorphic personifications of human consciousness. These beings include: Destiny, Death, Dream (the central character, hence the title), Destruction, Desire, Despair, and Delirium. Gaiman's stories serve as a mythology for the present world, combining cosmological explanations, instructive ethical teachings, and a profound feeling of wonder; they represent our dreams (in more ways than one) and our fears.

Before examining the place of mythology in today's society, the definition of mythology must be understood. Campbell begins by defining myths on a simple level as stories about gods. Then, he defines gods as "[personifications] of a motivating power or a value system that functions in human life and the universe" (22).

Later, he refers to "a profound sense of mystery" (209), and "the experience of being alive" (5). Also inherent in mythology is the sense of a "sacred space" (Campbell, 92). Eliade reflects this reasoning, citing "a sacred space, and hence a strong, significant space" that contrasts with the "nonreality of the vast surrounding expanse" (Eliade, 20-21). Eliade also refers to "the irruption of the sacred," when the sacred world manifests itself suddenly, creating communication between the profane world (what we think of as the physical) and the sacred (63). It is this world, according to Eliade, that is actually real; in fact, the "*eternal present* of the mythical event . . . makes possible the profane duration of historical events" (89). Campbell agrees with this, referring to "a plane that is behind the physical plane, and that is somehow supportive to the visible one to which we have to relate" (71). It is in this sacred, eternal world that many of the events of mythology are enacted.

In light of these descriptions of myth by Campbell and Eliade, we can begin to examine *The Sandman*'s place in mythology as a reflection of sacred space and a hidden, supporting plane of existence. The central character, Dream, also called Morpheus (after the Greek god of sleep and dreams), rules the Dreaming, a place where dreams become a reality, and which humans visit every night as they sleep. Here, the traditional rules of "reality" do not apply; rather, anything can happen according to the wishes of the Dream-king. Logical order, as is the case in actual dreams, is often secondary or even absent entirely. In the Dreaming, time is eternal; its inhabitants do not age (as we understand aging), although they do change over time as a result of experience. Each of the Endless has his or her own realm, and it is these realms, not the world as we know it, that are eternal. Time in the Dreaming is also cyclical in many ways; for example, Old Testament figures Cain and Abel both inhabit the Dreaming as servants of Morpheus. Here, the mythical act of Cain killing Abel is repeated over and over. A little while afterwards, Abel gets up, brushes himself off, and continues on his way as the cycle resumes (Sandman 2.15,22[1]). In addition, there are echoes of the physical world

---

1   References to *Sandman* issues will be in the form of (*Sandman*

lacking solidity and reality. At one point, Rose Walker, one of the many human protagonists, muses: "If my dream was true, then everything we know, everything we think we know is a lie. It means the world's about as solid and as reliable as a layer of scum on the top of a well of black water which goes down forever . . . We don't have a clue what's just really going down, we just kid ourselves that we're in control of our lives while a paper's thickness away" lies the "real" plane of existence (*Sandman* 16.18-9). Eliade's "irruption of the sacred" and Campbell's "invisible plane of support" are both present in Rose's speech, and in the greater world of *The Sandman*.

The next important mythological element of *The Sandman* is its treatment of gods. Gaiman populates the world not just with gods from one culture's mythology, but from many pantheons. Although Greek and Roman mythology are featured most frequently, "A Season of Mists," one of the longer plot-lines (issues run in plot-lines of 6-10 issues, with non-sequential "short story" issues in between), includes gods and mythological beings from Norse, Egyptian, Japanese, and Christian traditions, as well as the planes of faerie, order, and chaos. So many schemata of mythology are represented because they all share in the timeless themes and traditions that support mythology. In this way, the gods of different cultures can coexist, and all traditions are valid. The seven Endless function behind the scenes of other myths, since they are more than gods: as aspects of consciousness rather than powers in the universe. This situation echoes Campbell's idea that gods are "magnified dreams, and dreams are manifestations in image form of the energies of the body in conflict with each other" (39). This symbolism finds form in the intrigue that arises between the Endless, who often find themselves opposing each other in power struggles. Finally, gods themselves are featured as aspects of dreams. Gaiman's choice to set the series in the world of dreams further underscores the importance of dreams in mythology. Campbell notes this connection; "A dream is a personal experience of that deep, dark ground that is the support of our conscious lives, and a myth is the society's dream. The myth is the public dream and

Issue.Page Number). Information on the collected issues is found at the end.

the dream is the private myth" (Campbell 40). Gaiman continues this connection, as the goddess Ishtar says, "I know how gods begin. We start as dreams. Then we walk out of dreams into the land. We are worshipped and loved, and take power to ourselves. And then one day there's no one left to worship us. And in the end, each little god and goddess takes its last journey back into dreams . . . And what comes after, not even we know" (*Sandman* 45.20). In this characterization of gods as "magnified dreams," Gaiman has connected his world of the Dreaming to the greater world of mythology as a whole.

In addition to answering questions about the nature of the world, myths serve as examples of how (or how not) to live in the world. Indeed, ethical concerns must be present in some form in any culture's myths. Campbell says that "this is the [function] that I think everyone must try today to relate to—and that is the peda- gogical function, of how to live a human lifetime under any cir- cumstances" (31). However, in following ethical provisions, one must be careful that the precepts match the society in which one is living. Campbell rejects the idea of applying the ethics of one time and place to another:

> The models have to be appropriate to the time in which you are living, and our time has changed so fast that what was proper fifty years ago is not proper today. The virtues of the past are the vices of today. And many of what were thought to be the vices of the past are the necessities of today . . . The old-time religion be- longs to another age, another people, another set of human val- ues, another universe. By going back you throw yourself out of sync with history. (13)

In *Sandman*, Gaiman addresses many of the issues that face our modern society: AIDS, child abuse, depression, homophobia, and serial killers (perhaps the modern form of demons). There are several examples of both appropriate and inappropriate treatment of others in *Sandman*. The "old way" of religious intolerance is represented when Wanda, a preoperative transsexual living in New York (a modern analogue to the mythological search for identity), is killed in a hurricane. His/her mother refers to the event as "God's judgment on a city of sinners" (*Sandman* 37.16). The series is full of people applying the religious and ethical tradi- tions of a different time to the present, where they do not apply (if they ever truly applied at any time). In contrast to the intolerance shown by many, others are accepting of the state of the world. After a friend of Rose Walker's dies from AIDS, she is discussing her friend's "innocence" (she had contracted HIV from a kidney transplant) with another friend, Hal. He rejects such moral labels, replying, "Rosalita . . . there isn't any innocent. There isn't any guilty. There's just dead" (*Sandman* 69.18). However, at the same time, Gaiman addresses old and timeless issues. In "A Season of Mists," Lucifer decides that he has had enough of Hell, so he abdicates, locks up Hell, and gives the key to Morpheus. Later, he says, "I told [Dream] that there was always freedom, even the ultimate freedom. The freedom to leave. You don't have to stay anywhere forever" (*Sandman* 68.14). The theme of freedom and responsibility is echoed elsewhere: at one point, Destruction decides to abandon his realm and his responsibilities. In contrast, Dream and Destiny are very conscious of their responsibilities. While *The Sandman* presents an era-appropriate vision of ethical conduct, Gaiman's addition of problems like freedom and responsibility, the search for identity, and change emphasizes the idea that many "modern" issues are indeed timeless in their own way: old forces in new masks.

Another facet of the *Sandman* myth concerning ethical conduct occurs in what may be the central story (in a story about stories): Dream's relationship with his son, Orpheus. Orpheus, the great minstrel, follows the story of the Greek myths. His wife, Eurydice, dies soon after their wedding, and he journeys to the underworld to regain her, only to lose her again when he looks back on the return trip to earth only to see her pulled away from him forever. In the original story, Orpheus is later killed when a group of nymphs tear him to pieces because he, in his grief, will not join their dance. However, in Gaiman's version, Death will not take Orpheus, as he has already entered the underworld. So his head remains alive, and Morpheus finds it and establishes a local priesthood to protect it. In this way, he abandons his son to an eternity without rest, saying: "Your life is your own. Your death, likewise. Always, and forever, your own. Fare well. We shall not meet again" (*Sandman* 49.4). Later, Morpheus is forced to return to the island where his son's head is kept. In granting his son a boon (in return for help in a quest to find Destruction), Dream kills his son, giving him the death he has craved for thousands of years. Campbell speaks of the "great hero" myth, saying that "the hero's sphere of action is not the transcendent but here, now, in the field of time, of good and evil" (66). In mercifully killing his son, Morpheus takes responsibility for his actions and their consequences, for those he has hurt. Frank McConnell describes Dream as "[entering] time, choice, guilt, and regret—has entered the sphere of the human" (iii). Other plot-lines echo this theme of redemption (one involves his atonement for consigning a former lover to Hell). The central plot forms what has been called "a magnificent parable about the humanization of myth; about how the values of regret, responsibility and the awful duties of love outweigh even the power and majesty of the gods we invent and then worship" (McConnell v). For in killing his son, Morpheus knows that he is also bringing about his own death. Soon after, he is killed by the Furies, whose function it is to avenge blood-killings. In the end, Morpheus accepts responsibility and even his humanity, and it is only in the face of his impending demise that his role and instructive example as a mythological hero truly shows through.

In examining the mythology of a particular culture, one should look for the ways in which the myths reflect the characteristics and mood of that people; so if *The Sandman* is to be a myth for the modern world, it should address the concerns of people today. Eliade characterizes "modern man" as without religion, a condition "made possible by the desacralization of the cosmos accomplished by scientific thought and above all by the sensational discoveries of physics and chemistry" (51). Indeed, as religion has lost much of its sway on many people, the "world today" is often characterized by a sense of remoteness and aloneness in the universe. Gaiman takes steps toward reclaiming meaning by examining the worth and special qualities of individual people, what Campbell calls "the inner world . . . of your requirements and your energies and your structure and your possibilities" (57). If the modern world has made us feel small and alone, Gaiman reminds us of the richness of these inner worlds. At the grave of a friend, Barbie, the heroine of one of the story-lines, says, "Everybody has a secret world inside of them. I mean everybody. All of the people in the world—no matter how dull and boring they are on the outside. Inside them they've all got unimaginable, magnificent, wonderful, stupid, amazing worlds . . . not just one world, Hundreds of them. Thousands, maybe" (*Sandman* 37.19).

Dream's sister, Death, echoes these sentiments: "Nobody's creepy from the inside . . . Some of them are sad, and some of them hurt, and some of them think they're the only real thing in the world. But they're not creepy" (*Death* 42). In Death's and other statements, there is an overarching theme of comfort and acceptance of the problems of life. And in that acceptance, there is hope. Tori Amos (a friend of Gaiman's), says of lessons learned from the character of Death, that "she keeps reminding me there is change in the 'what is' but change cannot be made till you accept the 'what is' . . . She said if you allow yourself to feel the way you really feel, maybe you won't be afraid of that feeling anymore" (Amos 6). Above all, *Sandman* speaks of hope. After Morpheus' death, Matthew, a talking raven that served him, wants to die rather than serve the new Dream-king, but later changes his mind. In accepting the present situation, he says, "Funeral's over. Time to get on with our lives. Time to grow up" (*Sandman* 72.21). In this statement lies a hope that transcends depression and brings with it a promise of renewal. For the problems of our age that seem to leave each one of us alone, *The Sandman* offers guidance, encouragement, and hope.

In addition to addressing the problems of the modern world, *The Sandman* speaks to perhaps the paramount fear throughout human history: the fear of death. Campbell and Eliade both stress the eternal nature of mythological life, but behind this, there lies the central problem of mortality. In fact, perhaps the development of mythology was originally precipitated by these fears. For without mythology, we are conscious of only a few things: We're lost. We're cold. We hurt. And IT'S GOING TO END. If mythology has lost its grip on profane man, as Eliade suggests (113), then it is only natural for people to struggle with the meaning of it all. To answer this human need, Gaiman uses the character of Death. She is portrayed as a happy and positive presence (she has a penchant for saying things like "peachy keen!") who loves humanity (*Death* 73). Indeed, she is there for everyone when his or her time comes, assuaging the fears of the dying, reassuring them that death is a natural process and showing them the promise of eternal life in some form. To signify renewal, Dream is reincarnated after his death as another aspect of himself, who also contains the spirit of a child born in the dreaming. While the old Dream is always cloaked in shadows (even his word-balloons are black), the new

Dream is covered in white, offering a fresh start. However, these measures only address part of the issues surrounding death. Therefore, it is not surprising that Gaiman also provides examples of dealing with feelings of grief at the death of others. After the death of Eurydice, Dream advises Orpheus to say goodbye to his wife: "It is the mortal way. You attend the funeral, you bid the dead farewell. You grieve. Then you continue with your life. And at times the fact of her absence will hit you like a blow to the chest, and you will weep. But this will happen less and less as time goes on. She is dead. You are alive. So live" (*Sandman* 49.19). Another time, Barbie muses to herself at the end of the *A Game of You* story-line: "And if there's a moral there, I don't know what it is, save maybe that we should take our goodbyes whenever we can. And that's all" (*Sandman* 37.24). Even in the face of death, there is hope; for dreams always reflect hope.

In examining *The Sandman*, it appears that the work as a whole shows many of the characteristics of myth delineated by Campbell and Eliade. The Dreaming includes the ideas of sacred (and thus eternal) time and space, cyclical time, and the "irruption of the sacred" that Eliade discusses. So too does the myth include Campbell's sense of wonder and mystery. Also, the interrelation of gods, myths, and dreams is continually stressed throughout the series. Turning to the temporal world, it serves as an instructive myth, expressing how to treat others with respect and humanity in the modern world. In the wake of Campbell's characterization of the ethical precepts of "old-time religions" as no longer applicable, Gaiman has given us a myth for today that still encompasses the seemingly timeless issues that are also the province of mythology, beginning with the deeds of Morpheus himself and extending outward through the other characters. On a more individual level, Death and other characters serve to allay the fears that haunt modern people most directly: feelings of remoteness and loneliness in a "desacralized" world (to use Eliade's terminology), and feelings that are stirred up not only by fear of our own death, but also by our grief at the death of others. Finally, these issues are all pulled together in the central idea of *The Sandman*: the importance of stories. The *Sandman* stories as a whole reflect what Campbell calls the timeless "themes that have supported human life, built civilizations, and informed religions over the millennia" (4). Campbell also says that the true value of mythology is in recognizing these timeless themes, "to see life as a poem and yourself participating in a poem" (55). Eliade continues this idea, positing that in mythologically driven society, "the true sin is forgetting" (101). Perhaps this idea fits Gaiman's work as well as any. One of Morpheus' many titles is the Prince of Stories, and much of *The Sandman* is concerned with stories and story-telling (for what are myths if not the first literature?). Many characters: humans, gods, and many who are somewhere in-between, are carefully woven throughout the story, from the first issue to the last, giving the work as a whole a sense of unity and cohesion (as any good myth should). Indeed, some issues feature Morpheus' relationship with no less than William Shakespeare, one of the most acclaimed storytellers in history. A deal between the two, in which Shakespeare was given his inspiration and abilities in return for writing two plays for Morpheus (*A Midsummer Night's Dream* and *The Tempest*), forms the basis for their encounters. The comic's final issue focuses on one such meeting. Morpheus says "I am Prince of Stories, Will, but I have no story of my own. Nor shall I ever" (*Sandman* 76.37). Here, Gaiman is being ironic, but it is significant that he has chosen to end his story by talking about stories. For, on repeated readings, the aspect of these stories, both individually and as a whole, that shows the most clearly is their essential humanity. All the characters in *The Sandman* are woven throughout the tale in a way that we might empathize with them. Even the non-human characters share a certain humanity; we care for them as they become our lightposts on the often dark journey of life. For if the way has been "lost" in the modern world, then the final legacy of *The Sandman* may be the reclamation of our emotions in an "emotionless" age, by simultaneously addressing the heart, mind, and soul. More important, these stories provide a friend, and unlock the things that reside in us, for "all the gods are within us" (Campbell 39). And such a realization, of seeing yourself in the gods and the gods in you, can return the intensity of feeling that has perhaps been lost. And this is precisely what Campbell means when he refers to mythology as "the experience of being alive" (xvi).

The preceding paper was written several years ago, and would serve, later on, as a skeleton for what would follow, a book on *Sandman* as modern myth, seen through the teachings of Joseph

Campbell. And while I still agree with most of the things I said then, there is one point I wish to address:

The literature and theory that served as background for the idea of the "modern myth" was essentially pessimistic: the world has lost its meaning (if indeed it ever had any), people have lost their sense of wonder, and we have woken up to the fact that we are insignificant specks in a cold and empty universe. In short, existential *angst*. However, while the "high" culture—philosophy and literature—seem to have given up on meaning (which is probably a gross oversimplification), popular culture tells a far different story. For while some complain about the lack of meaning coming from the world's traditional sources, chiefly religion, but also family, country, and some others, many more people are searching frantically, and taking meaning anywhere we can find it. And if the ready-made sources aren't doing it anymore, then we'll just have to dig a little deeper. After all, we have to grow up sometime.

And so in the popular culture (which is, after all, where people *live*), we have seen the rise of artists taking the mythic impulse and grandeur, and fusing it with the emotional intimacy that we might miss in reading the stories filtered down through thousands of years and become fixed or stylized. To name a few: there is Garth Ennis' *Preacher*, which uses a fierce anger to call God to account for the suffering in the world—after all, it is he who serves *us*, and we who give *him* meaning. There is the work of fantasist Charles de Lint, in which the person sitting next to you in the café just might be a spirit . . . or a god, trying to live in the world with the rest of us. There is Grant Morrison's visionary comic series *The Invisibles*, which reveals the secrets of the universe. One of them is posed in the question: "We gods are only masks. Who wears us? Find it out!" (Morrison 172). The answer, of course, is: we do. And finally, there is Joss Whedon's *Buffy the Vampire Slayer*, in which the most horrible monsters can seek redemption, and find it in ordinary human feeling; for feeling is what makes us what we are. *Buffy*, above all, reminds me most of Gaiman's vision, for in the moments of greatest darkness, when all seems lost, we are filled and consumed by a great and burning love for the world.

Have these works been influenced by Neil Gaiman? Undoubtedly at least some of them have, to varying degrees. For once an idea enters the popular discussion, it begins to propagate itself. But to argue which came first, or is best, or who owes what to whom, is to miss the point, for we are talking about culture and meaning and wonder: everything that makes us human. In other words: life. And what makes *Sandman* truly mythic, beyond all the gods and goddesses, angels, and demons, faeries, even the Endless, is that it opens the way to life, or, as Campbell was so fond of saying, "the experience of being alive" (xvi). In other words, *we're doing just fine.*

Works Cited

Amos, Tori. "Introduction." *Death: the High Cost of Living.* New York: DC Comics, 1994. 4-7.

Campbell, Joseph with Bill Moyers. *The Power of Myth.* New York: Doubleday, 1988.

Eliade, Mircea. *The Sacred and the Profane: the Nature of Religion.* San Diego: Harcourt Brace and Company, 1957.

Gaiman, Neil. *Death: the Time of Your Life.* New York: DC Comics, 1997.

Gaiman, Neil. *The Sandman: Preludes and Nocturnes.* (Collected *Sandman* issues 1-8) New York: DC Comics, 1989.

Gaiman, Neil. *The Sandman: The Doll's House.* (Collected *Sandman* issues 8-16) New York: DC Comics, 1990.

Gaiman, Neil. *The Sandman: A Season of Mists.* (Collected *Sandman* issues 21-28) New York: DC Comics, 1992.

Gaiman, Neil. *The Sandman: A Game of You.* (Collected *Sandman* issues 32-37) New York: DC Comics, 1993.

Gaiman, Neil. *The Sandman: Brief Lives.* (Collected *Sandman* issues 41-49) New York: DC Comics, 1994.

Gaiman, Neil. *The Sandman: The Kindly Ones.* (Collected *Sandman* issues 57-69) New York: DC Comics, 1996.

Gaiman, Neil. *The Sandman: The Wake.* (Collected *Sandman* issues 70-75) New York: DC Comics, 1997.

McConnell, Frank. "Introduction." *The Sandman: The Kindly Ones.* New York: DC Comics, 1996. i-vi.

Morrison, Grant. *The Invisibles: Apocalipstick.* (Collected *Invisibles* Volume I, Issues 9-16). New York: DC Comics, 2001.

DREAMS AND FAIRY TALES: THEMES OF RATIONALITY AND LOVE IN *A MIDSUMMER NIGHT'S DREAM* AND THE SANDMAN

Julie Myers Saxton

In Issue #19 of Neil Gaiman's *Sandman* series of graphic novels, William Shakespeare and his company act out the first production of *A Midsummer Night's Dream* for an audience comprised of Auberon, Titania, and their fairy entourage. Shakespeare has written the play according to the terms of an earlier arrangement with Dream of the Endless, the title character of the *Sandman* series, who presents it to the Faerie to repay them for their gift of "entertainment and diversion" while outside of their realm.

Much like the play itself, *Sandman #19*, also entitled *A Midsummer Night's Dream*, plays upon themes of reality and truth in contrast to shadows and dreams, and at the center of Gaiman's story, like Shakespeare's, is a discussion of love, responsibility, and relationships. Although this issue of the graphic novel series makes the most transparent references to Shakespeare's play, elements of *A Midsummer Night's Dream* can be seen throughout the series, and not just for the backdrop or mythological context. The play exists as an argument to which *The Sandman* is Gaiman's response.

Shakespearean scholars have commented upon the dual realms set up in *A Midsummer Night's Dream*: the city of Athens and the forest of the Fairies. The city, with the Greek hero Theseus as its ruler, stands as an emblem of rationality, order and logic, evidenced by strict adherence to the law. In the opening scene, Theseus shows little sympathy in the case of Hermia and her lovers, stating that even as king, he is subject to the rules and he "by no means may extenuate" the law. Theseus, with his adherence to reason, also does not believe in Fairies, and is quick to discount the lovers' tale upon their return from the woods. He says their story is:

More strange than true, I never may believe

These antique fables, nor these fairy toys.
Lovers and madmen have such seething brains,
Such shaping fantasies, that apprehend
More than cool reason ever comprehends. (V.i.2-6)

Theseus is "preëminently the hero of a daylight world of practicalities" (Barton 8). His ways are not those of the poets and the lovers, and neither is Athens, under his control, the place where the irrational can occur.

That is left for the wood, under the rule of Oberon, the King of the Fairies. It is a night realm, as much as Athens is the city of the daylight. The "sublunary" activities of the fairies only take place at night, and they are described by the Athenians in terms of dreams. After spending the night in the woods, both Lysander and Demetrius have problems recounting the foregoing events, and it seems to Lysander that they must have been in a "half sleep half waking" state. He believes their visions were "dreams." Demetrius further questions whether they are awake at all when Theseus and his men enter the wood for the hunt. He says, "Are you sure that we are awake? It seems to me that we sleep yet, we dream" (IV.i. 201-203).

Their reactions aren't surprising. Oberon's mazed world is indeed a strange one, where the unusual and the unnatural occur. Lovers change affections willy-nilly, hobgoblins play tricks, and mythical and legendary creatures from Celtic, Anglo-Saxon, and Teutonic fairy stories all walk the same Greek forest. This is, as Catherine Belsey states, "a place of anarchy and anxiety where behavior becomes unpredictable and individual identity is transformed" (189).

Theseus calls it the world of the lover, the poet, and the lunatic, yet there is little doubt that this unpredictable realm is the place of creativity. It is imagination's domain, where stories are born. Northrop Frye in his work on *A Midsummer Night's Dream* says that:

> the wood-world has affinities with what we call the unconscious or subconscious part of the mind: a part below the reason's encounter with reality, and yet connected with the hidden creative powers of the mind. [. . .] It becomes the world in which those profound choices are made that decide the course of life, and also the world from which inspiration comes to the poet. (129)

Frye's description of the woods also characterizes The Dreaming, the home of Gaiman's Sandman, who is the King of Dreams. He is known by many names, Lord Morpheus and Dream are the most common, and given these names (which are in actuality descriptions of his function), it is not surprising that the heart of his realm is a place of imagination and creativity. Dream speaks about his home, saying, "The Dreamworld, the Dreamtime, the Unconscious" call it what you will "is as much part of me as I am part of it" (#2. p 17). It is not coincidence that he is also called Lord Shaper and the Prince of Stories, for he directs the poet's pen to shape unknown things, and in his realm, stories are made.

The Dreaming's library, "the largest library that never was," consists of "every story that has ever been dreamed," as well as "novels authors never wrote or never finished except in dreams" (#22. p 2). It boasts of millions of titles, including "The Bestselling Romantic Spy Thriller I Used to Think About on the Bus That Would Sell a Billion Copies and Mean I'd Never Have to Work Again" (#57. p 2).

The Dreaming is also the place of concepts and premises. "You want ideas?" the Sandman questions Richard Madoc in disgust when he learns that he has captured and abused the muse Calliope to further his career. "You want dreams? You want stories? Then ideas you will have. Ideas in abundance" (#17. p 17). Story premises then bombard Madoc's mind, and the onslaught becomes torture. The ideas come so quickly that Madoc, trying to get them all down but having no pen or paper, uses the wall and the blood from his own fingertips. The plays, stories, and songs rush at him, as Madoc says, "so fast, swamping, overwhelming," that he must be treated by a doctor within hours of meeting the Sandman. Dream releases his mind at Calliope's request, but leaves Madoc completely bereft of ideas for the rest of his life. Dream, as the Prince of Stories, is also the controller of the creative force of fiction.

It is interesting to note also that in Gaiman's series William Shakespeare finds his inspiration for *A Midsummer Night's Dream* and *The Tempest*, his only original works, through his contact with the Dream Lord. More than simply giving Shakespeare a commission, Dream has given him the words to write. He has "opened a door" inside of Shakespeare that will allow him to write works that will pass into immortality. Dream implies that he has done this for other writers, as well. He speaks the truth when he says "poets and dreamers are my people" (#31. p. 19). Like the Fairy wood, The Dreaming is a place of inspiration.

It also possesses the strangeness of Oberon's forest, and it too is a place in which the impossible can happen. Men can become ravens, places can become people, and pumpkin-headed scarecrows can create and remove entire sections of buildings. But the Dreaming is not wild and uncontrolled, and it operates under strict rules that are largely absent in the Fairy realm. In his Shakespeare's play, Oberon is king, and he has the power of command, but it doesn't appear that his will is supreme. Titania has defied him, to the point that their fighting disrupts the weather, yet she still refuses to surrender her Indian boy, despite Oberon's demands. And since he resorts to trickery to get what he wants, it appears that he cannot force her to obey.

Also, for the fairies, there are few repercussions for the meddling in the lives of the mortals. When Puck confuses the Athenian men and anoints Demetrius' eyes with the nectar, he is chided by Oberon and told to correct his mistake, but the episode is more amusing than anything else, especially to Puck. The fact that Demetrius is still under the influence of the love potion even at the end is of little consequence to the Fairies. They have no responsibilities to the humans, especially the ones that are foolish enough to enter the woods at night. Bottom's head is transformed into that of an ass, and the lovers' affections become confused, yet the fault lies with mortals for being in the Fairy realm in the first place.

The Sandman's world is not the same. It is ordered, and although it is the domain of the unconscious and the creative, it never crosses into the realm of Delirium, where causation and result can be divorced. Dream often speaks of rules and responsibilities, and since The Dreaming is a part of who the Sandman is, it is subject to his laws. As he tells Rose Walker, a girl threatening his domain, "Reality here conforms to my wishes. It is what I wish it to be, no more, no less. [. . .] I am the Lord of this Realm, and my wishes are paramount" (#16. p 5).

This may be true, but they are governed by a set of laws, more strict than those of Athens, and he takes these rules seriously. As the narrator points out, "of all the Endless[. . .] he is the most conscious of his responsibilities, the most meticulous in their execution" (#21. p. 11). It is his nature to make rules and establish order, and he has done so since time was young. He demands that his subjects follow these rules, as well. When he learns that two of his former servants have severed a child from The Dreaming and are living in his mind, he takes immediate action against them. "They know the law," Dream says, "*My* law. And they have wantonly defied it. [. . .] I am angry, Lucien. And it's my move" (#10. p.24). The punishment is not specified, but the reader can take Dream at his word that his former servants will not enjoy the next five thousand years.

Even outside of his own realm, Dream abides by the rules and honors his responsibilities. He is careful not to overstep his bounds as an immortal being, realizing that his existence depends on the mortals, and he is not to manipulate them. As he tells his younger siblings, humans are not toys to be played with or swept from the game, even though Dream and his family are powerful enough to do so. The rules of conduct must be obeyed, much like the law in Athens. And it is interesting to note, that when Dream does, in an act of fairness and responsibility, break the law, it is the Greek Furies who come after him and bring his punishment.

Dream usually acts out of rational thinking, rather than any feelings of kindness. Time and again, he tells those to whom he is indebted, "I owe you a boon." They did something for him, and in turn he will do something for them. His sense of fairness is the reason he rewards his servants, why he has Shakespeare write *A Midsummer Night's Dream*, and ultimately, the reason he kills his own son. He is one who honors his debts and holds to his responsibilities, and by doing so, he marries within his realm the dualities of place set up in Shakespeare's play. Rationality and creativity happily coexist in The Dreaming.

However, it does not seem that Dream is able to balance rationality and love, which is another major force of *A Midsummer Night's Dream*. Shakespeare's play makes much of the arbitrary nature of love. Titania falls in love with Bottom, Lysander turns from Hermia to Helena to Hermia again, and Demetrius finally returns Helena's affection. Certainly, it is due to the love potion and the tricks of Puck and Oberon, but there is little indication that any of the relationships will turn out any better or worse than another. Helena and Demetrius are as content as Lysander and

Hermia at the end of the play. Love falls where it may. Although it has underlying assertions about love as the basis of marriage, the play can rather simplistically be summed up in Bottom's words that "reason and love keep little company nowadays" (III.i.145). His statement comes just after Titania has fallen surprisingly in love with him, despite his rather donkey-like appearance, and it serves as a comment upon the action in the forest as a whole. Those who are falling in love aren't exactly following logic as a guide to their actions.

In *The Sandman*, as previously noted, the Dreaming is a far more logical place than the wood of Fairies, and yet Bottom's maxim still rings true, although Gaiman inverts the meaning of the words. For Dream, love and rationality hold little company, not because of love's arbitrary nature, but because of Dream's cold rationality. He doesn't show love, and he hides himself in his responsibilities. Hy Bender, the author of *The Sandman Companion*, notes that "The Sandman comes across as someone who is very conscientious, and even self-sacrificing when performing his job; but he's markedly deficient in handling people and relationships" (32).

He is notoriously bad at every relationship he's been in, and according to his servants there have been several. The series chronicles three of his liaisons, none of which ended well, the episode of Nada, possibly the worst. He condemns her to Hell because she hurt his pride, never realizing until his older sister later confronts him, that this, in her words, is a "really shitty thing to do" (#21. p 22). The muse Calliope, to whom Dream was married, describes him as "unable to share any part of himself," and she realizes later he may have never loved her at all. And everyone but Dream knows that his final lover Thessaly is, in the words of critic Mikal Gilmore, "walking talking bad news" (10). He should have known better, but as Gaiman himself points out, "It's part of his big problem. He's useless at relationships." (Bender 115).

He casts off his son Orpheus more heartlessly than he did his lovers. Orpheus, much to his own detriment since he ended up as an eternally living head without a body, had failed to take his father's advice, and Dream walks away, vowing never to see him again. When Dream's brother disappears, he is more concerned about the abandonment of responsibilities than his brother himself. "I have no desire to find my brother," he says. "His whereabouts are unimportant to me" (#44. p 16). He is content to leave him in his decision to abandon the family.

The narrator notes that "Dream accumulates names to himself like others make friends," which is a reflection on his numerous titles, as well as his insular nature. He has more names than friends because, as the narrator continues, "He permits himself few friends"(#21. p 11). Or as his servant-raven Matthew remarks to his family, "Nobody was close to your brother. Not unless you're talking about astronomical distances . . . Y'know—the sun is close to Alpha Centauri . . . He . . . He wasn't very good at close" (#71. p 23).

And as much as he lectures his siblings about treating mortals as their toys, Dream's strict *laissez-faire* attitude and complete lack of caring for humans within his sphere of influence has drastic consequences. He cannot, at the end, look to the mortals and tell them, as Puck can, that if he has offended them, they can pretend it was dream and "all is mended." He is the King of Dreams, and he cannot dismiss his own reality that easily. It also matters little to him whether the injury occurred in the Dreaming or in the waking world. As he tells Auberon and Titania while they watch the production of *A Midsummer Night's Dream*, "Things need not have happened to be true. Tales and dreams are the shadow-truths that will endure when mere facts are dust and ashes, and forgot" (#19 p 21). Whether waking or dreaming, the truth of the matter will be carried forward.

Dream's sister reminds him that responsibility is more than exerting influence and control. "The things we do make echoes," she says. "Our existence deforms the universe. *That's* responsibility" (#64. p 8). In other words, everything that Dream and his family do has repercussions, and they owe the humans, not complete lack of interference, but kindness and mercy. Even realizing the truth in her words, he is unable to change his rule-bound nature, and he does not know how to balance duty and compassion, responsibility and love. He cannot do both, and comes to understand that he must find a way to bring about a new Dream: one that can change, understand, and love. But even that choice is made with cool, unemotional rationality. He understands what is needed and gives the world a final boon out of his sense of duty.

As at the end of Shakespeare's *Midsummer Night's Dream*, the realm of the lover overtakes the realm of the rational. The Fairies dance in the house of Theseus, blessing the lovers and even shaping their futures through their offspring. Rationality cannot keep love forever at bay. Likewise, in *The Sandman* the new Dream displays compassion and tenderness in a way that his predecessor could not, and in his person, love and reason can hold company, as they should.

Mikal Gilmore in his introduction notes that "Neil himself has never disguised the real source for his surreal-existential brand of story-telling: it springs from a deep affection for William Shakespeare's *A Midsummer Night's Dream*, and a desire to translate that play's mix of horror and playfulness into modern forms" (9). Working toward that end, not only has Gaiman translated the elements of Shakespeare's work into a modern fantasy tale, he has offered a new response to the play, in which the course of true love still fails to run smooth, but no longer are mortals the only fools.

Works Cited

Barton, Anne. "The Synthesizing Impulse of A Midsummer Night's Dream." *Modern Critical Interpretations: William Shakespeare's A Midsummer Night's Dream*. Ed. Harold Bloom. New York: Chelsea House, 1987. 7-14.

Belsey, Catherine. "A Midsummer Night's Dream: A Modern Perspective." *A Midsummer Night's Dream*. Ed. Barbara A. Mowat and Paul Werstine. New York: Washington Square 1993. 181-190.

Bender, Hy. *The Sandman Companion*. New York: DC Comics, 1999.

Frye, Northrop. "The Bottomless Dream." *Modern Critical Interpretations: William Shakespeare's A Midsummer Night's Dream*. Ed. Harold Bloom. New York: Chelsea House, 1987. 117-132.

Gaiman, Neil. *The Sandman*. Originally published in single magazine form as The Sandman #1-75. New York: DC Comics, 1988-1997.

Gilmore, Mikal. Introduction. "The Wake." *The Sandman*. New York: DC Comics, 1997. 8-11.

Shakespeare, William. *A Midsummer Night's Dream*. Ed. Barbara A. Mowat and Paul Werstine. New York: Washington Square, 1993.

A KING FORSAKES HIS THRONE: CAMPBELLIAN HERO ICONS IN NEIL GAIMAN'S *SANDMAN*

Peter S. Rawlik, Jr.

In *The Hero with a Thousand Faces*, Joseph Campbell reveals the common patterns that appear to permeate what he calls the universal monomyth of the adventure hero cycle. Neil Gaiman's series of *Sandman* graphic novels not only serves as a finely crafted example of Campbell's traditional hero cycle, but also explores the subtle and more uncommon variations and icons of the myth. The following pages will examine the Sandman saga in relation to the Campbellian hero theories in eight parts: (1) "The Ignoble King"; (2) "The Fallen Man in a Fallen World"; (3) "The Hero Quest"; (4) "The Warrior"; (5)"The Redeemer"; (6) "The Tyrant"; (7) "The Renouncer"; and, (8) "The Reborn."

The parts or stages described above represent a linear movement of the hero through his life. While the majority of the *Sandman* narrative is linear in nature, Gaiman often makes use of flashbacks to act as counterpoints to the current or pending action. While this makes for adept story-telling, it complicates the critical examination of the hero. Therefore it is beneficial to break the nonlinear scenes and vignettes out of the various story arcs and place them in chronological order. Using this technique, the evolution of the focal character of Morpheus through the various stages of his life, death and transformative rebirth can be examined and discussed in a linear manner.

The Ignoble King

Campbell suggests that many heroes may initially exist in a state of ignorance as either a victim such as Sleeping Beauty, or as an ineffectual or doomed leader such as King Minos. This state is an unconscious choice by the potential hero who is either purposely ignoring the possibility of adventure, or awaiting the call for a higher adventure. In either case, the resulting individual can be described as an Ignoble King, a figure of immense power and respect who has adopted an egocentric world view and essentially ignores the plights of those around him. Like Prince Gautama Sakyamuni, who would one day become the Buddha, and in a more contemporary character, Peter Parker who fails to stop a petty criminal, the Ignoble King wields great power but only in his own interest, ignoring the everyday minor tragedies and needs of those around him.

Gaiman establishes Morpheus as the Ignoble King by showing his behavior in various tales and scenes that occur prior to the beginning of his hero quest. In "Tales in the Sand," Morpheus falls in love with a mortal woman named Nada who refuses to become his queen. Spurned, Morpheus exacts revenge by imprisoning Nada in Hell, a sentence that Gaiman has earlier told us, has lasted 10,000 years. "The Song of Orpheus," presents a similar act. Orpheus, the son of Morpheus and Calliope, loses his new bride Eurydice to a tragic accident. Devastated, Orpheus requests that Morpheus ask Hades to return Eurydice from the Underworld. Morpheus calls the notion foolishness and refuses. Orpheus, in a fit of spite, denies his father, saying "I am no longer your son." Later, when Orpheus is dismembered by the Bacchante, leaving only his pleading and immortal head, Morpheus reminds Orpheus of his denial and says "We shall not meet again."

Both "Tales in the Sand" and "The Song of Orpheus," show how Morpheus behaves or rather misbehaves as lover, husband and father. In counterpoint, the next two stories show how Morpheus behaves in his role as king. In "August," Morpheus advises Augustus Caesar how to hide from the gods and plan the fall of the Roman Empire. In contrast, "Ramadan" tells the tale of how Caliph Haroun Al Raschid of Baghdad convinces Morpheus to preserve the splendors of his city forever. Here Morpheus acts both as destroyer and as preserver, not out of his own desires but rather out of the desires of his peers.

Having shown how Morpheus deals with his family and his peers, Gaiman must also establish the Ignoble King in relation to the common man. This is accomplished in the first half of the story "Men of Good Fortune," as well as the stories entitled "Midsummer Night's Dream" and "The Tempest." "Men of Good Fortune" opens with Morpheus and his sister, Death, in a London pub in the year 1389. Also in the pub is Hob Gadling who announces to his friends that he does not intend to die. The amused

Endless, Dream and Death, make the man's absurd claim a reality; and Dream and Hob agree to meet back at the pub in 100 years. In 1489, Morpheus queries Hob about the events in his life and is amused by Hob's desire for continued life. The meeting in 1589 is notable for the introduction of another character, William Shakespeare. Just as Morpheus was able to make Hob Gadling's desire for physical immortality a reality, so too is the Dream King capable of transforming Shakespeare from a minor playwright into the immortal bard.

The introduction of Shakespeare to the storyline sets the stage for the next two appearances of Morpheus. In 1593, Shakespeare delivers the play *A Midsummer Night's Dream* to the Dream King in a story of the same name. Here Morpheus uses Shakespeare to entertain the fairie folk, knowing but disregarding the dangers of mortals interacting with the fey. The results are catastrophic. Shakespeare's son, Hamnet, accepts a gift from Titania, an act that is deftly implied to cause his death at age 11. More terrifying is the release of the hobgoblin, Puck, on the mortal world, an event that will come back to haunt Morpheus.

Morpheus next appears with Shakespeare in 1615 in "The Tempest." In this episode, which is actually the last issue of the series, Morpheus and Shakespeare discuss the motivations behind both the play and Morpheus' desire for it. It is a frank discussion and Morpheus reveals the philosophy that he has adopted for his role as Dream, saying "I am not a man and I do not change. I am the Prince of Stories, but I have no story of my own. Nor shall I ever." This is telling because to this point it has been true. In the vignettes discussed up until this point, Morpheus has been at best a motivating force but has yet to obtain the position of an active hero. Based on his commentary to Shakespeare, he has no intention of assuming such a role. In essence, Morpheus is consciously avoiding any call to adventure; he has chosen to remain the ignoble king.

The remaining events in this stage of his life serve to reinforce his conscious position. There are meetings with Hob Gadling in 1689 and 1789, and a brief interlude with Isaac Newton and Destruction in 1685. These do not serve to motivate Morpheus out of his philosophical rut. In fact, the next two scenes have Morpheus acting as a grand manipulator. First, in "Thermidor," Morpheus cajoles Lady Johanna Constantine into braving the terrors of the French Revolution to rescue the head of Orpheus. Here Morpheus acts as a sort of supernatural M to Lady Constantine's James Bond. It also serves to reinforce the distance between Morpheus and his family. Recall, that Morpheus told his son that he would not see him again. In having Lady Constantine rescue Orpheus, a task Morpheus could easily undertake himself, the Dream King assures that he himself remains true to his word.

If the manipulation of Lady Constantine seems cruel, the events of "Three Septembers and a January" are terrifying. In this tale spanning the years from 1859 to 1880, Morpheus uses the madness of the self-proclaimed Emperor of the United States, Joshua Norton, to teach both Despair and Desire a lesson in human nature. Although the touch of Dream is less harsh than that of his siblings, the lesson here is that at this stage of his being Morpheus can, will and does manipulate the lives of mortals with little regard for their own welfare.

Firmly entrenched in his role as the ignoble king, Morpheus is unprepared for the events of his next meeting with Hob Gadling. The year is 1889, and Hob is firmly convinced that regardless of his lifespan he will remain the same. Furthermore, Hob suggests that Dream's continuing motivation for these meetings is that Morpheus enjoys Hob's company. Morpheus is flustered and moves off in a huff. Hob calls after him, "I'll be here in a hundred years' time. If you're here then too, it'll be because we're friends. No other reason." Thus, Hob has trapped Morpheus in a quandary, if he is to keep the appointment he must change, he must cease being the ignoble king, he must accept a call to adventure.

The Fallen Man in a Fallen World

Before Morpheus can accept a call to adventure, he must first become The Fallen Man in the Fallen World. To quote Campbell directly, "The composite hero of the monomyth is a personage of exceptional gifts. Frequently he is honored by his society, frequently unrecognized or disdained. He and/or the world in which he finds himself suffer from a symbolic deficiency." Thus, before he can accept his call to adventure, Morpheus, like Prince Gautama Sakyamuni or the young King Arthur, must be devoid of both material and spiritual trappings, the people around the Fallen Man must forget what he once was.

Gaiman accomplishes the transformation of Morpheus the Dream King into The Fallen Man in the first issue, "Sleep of the Just." In 1916, the Magus, Roderick Burgess, and his Order of Ancient Mysteries, in an attempt to capture Death, instead capture Dream. Realizing that Dream is still a valuable prisoner, Burgess has Morpheus stripped of all possessions including clothes, and imprisoned in a glass cage inside a magic circle. While the loss of physical possessions should be sufficient to convey a symbolic deficiency, the medium of comics allows for not only a textual description, but also a graphical depiction of Morpheus. Early in his imprisonment, Morpheus is rendered with a high level of detail including well defined ears, pupils, and mouth. Yet by 1988, the details of Morpheus' face are lost in shadows. The face of Dream has faded; becoming a physical symbol for his spiritual deficiency.

The imprisonment also allows for Morpheus to become both the honored man and the unrecognized man simultaneously. Like a prized bird or fish, he is kept in a glass cage, for all members of the Order to marvel at. Unfortunately, the Order, which in 1916 appears to comprise dozens of members as suggested by the multiplicity of blurred faces present at his capture, dwindles over the decades. By 1970, the narration reveals "The young people have drifted away." Throughout his whole imprisonment, the single constant is Alex Burgess, the son of the original Magus, and the individual who worked out that the prisoner in the basement was the King of Dreams. Burgess tries to bargain with and threaten Morpheus with no result. By 1988, Burgess has become a tired and bitter old man who tells Morpheus "You're nothing special. You know that? You're nothing at all. A naked man in a glass box. That's all you are. You're nothing at all." Later in the day, when Morpheus feigns death, only six people come to investigate. The Order has dwindled away to nothing, and even one who helped in the capture has forgotten what Morpheus truly is. In this way Morpheus is both the honored and unknown.

However, it is not enough just to be the Fallen Man; the world itself must be deficient in some manner. In *The Sandman Companion*, Hy Bender suggests that this is accomplished by removing Morpheus from his realm of dream and nightmare and placing him in a common everyday basement. Bender explains, "In a standard hero quest, the hero starts out in ordinary surroundings, and then experiences some kind of shock that sends him into the shadow realm where he does battle with primal forces." Unfortunately, this isn't entirely accurate. The starting world of the potential hero is anything but ordinary; it is fallen, in chaos or out-of-balance. These out-of-balance worlds may be overtly so, such as that in Jim Henson's film *The Dark Crystal* where the shattering of the crystal has also shattered the UrSkek into the Skesis and UrRu. The loss of balance may also be subtle, such as in that of the young Arthur whose land lacks a rightful king. In the case of Morpheus, the world is out of balance exactly because the Dream King has been removed from the world. It has found a new state, one not much different from that with the Dream King, but certain individuals have not been able to adjust. As a result of the imprisonment of Morpheus, individuals across the globe fall victim to a baffling disease referred to as the "sleepy sickness." These individuals, such as Unity Kinkaid, who falls into a perpetual sleep; and Daniel Bustamonte, who walks around unsleeping and undreaming, are the physical manifestation of the deficiency of the Fallen World. Gaiman makes this plain by showing this to be the motivating force behind the creation of the Golden Age hero, the Sandman, "The universe knows something is missing and slowly attempts to replace him. Wesley Dodds' nightmares have stopped since he started going out at night."

With Morpheus firmly established as the Fallen Man in the Fallen World, the stage is set for Morpheus to take up the call to adventure. Typically, the call takes the form of an accident or blunder, Campbell says. Here, that blunder occurs when Alex Burgess' wheelchair crosses the magic circle, giving Morpheus the freedom to escape and begin his transforming hero quest.

The Hero Quest

Transformed by his acceptance of the call to adventure, Morpheus as the hero must first encounter both a protective figure and a threshold guardian before the true adventure can begin. In this case the protective figures for Morpheus manifest themselves as his former servants Cain, Abel, and Lucien. Note, that all three of these supporting characters are, like Morpheus, masters of stories: Lucien is a librarian; Cain was the host of *The House of Mystery*; while Abel was the host of *House of Secrets*. As such, these three, who unlike Morpheus have maintained their positions, are in possession of the tools and secret powers needed to restore Morpheus to his former position. In fact, all three seem to be tacitly aware that Morpheus is not what he once was. Cain and Abel refer to him as "The Prince of Stories," while Lucien simply calls him "My Lord." A careful review of the first two issues of *Sandman* will reveal that only in a medieval grimoire is he identified as the "Kinge of Dreames." This lack of kingly title is acknowledgement that Morpheus is no longer the King of Dreams and must regain this position through his adventure. Like the Three Musketeers to the naive D'Artagnan, the three storytellers reveal the true state of the world to Morpheus and supply him with the tools to aid him in the assumption of his proper position, and with him follows the return of the world to normality.

Moving on, Morpheus proceeds to summon the Hecateae, the three witches who also once were storytellers, hosting *The Witching Hour*. Campbell suggests that the guardians of the threshold are often represented as women ". . . of mysteriously seductive, nostalgic beauty." Accordingly, the three witches continually metamorphosize through their various incarnations as Maiden, Mother and Crone. To convey their position as guardians of the threshold to the regions of the unknown, the graphical representation of the background to the three witches transforms from a open plain of green, to grey blue, and then to purple and black. In contrast, the background color for Morpheus remains white.

While the protective figures served to educate the hero about the current state of the world, the guardians of the threshold serve to instruct on how it may be changed. They are guardians of secret knowledge, like Aughra in *The Dark Crystal*; they reveal the prophecies and the rituals which will return the world to its proper state. They also give warning, reminding the hero that even with his charms and weapons, the tasks will not be easy. Even the knowledge itself is dangerous, just as Yoda warns Luke Skywalker of the dangers of the dark side of the Force, so do the witches cackle, "We haven't helped you! Your troubles are just beginning!" With this admonishment in mind, Morpheus begins his quest by passing through the First Threshold, the Horn Gate, the gate of true dreams, and into the world.

According to theory, the hero now enters a road or labyrinth on which he must survive a series of trials. Like Dorothy in *The Wizard of Oz* or Alice in *Alice in Wonderland*, these trials force the hero to confront his negative traits, often represented by an opposite self, in order to assimilate and harness those traits. In the case of the Sandman, the road-labyrinth is represented first by the motorways of London, then by the ever changing landscape of Hell, and finally by Morpheus' tangential journey through the dreams of unknowing mortals. During these travels, Morpheus does indeed encounter his opposites: John Constantine, a mortal man who battles with his own nightmares; Lucifer, the King forced to share his kingship with both Beelzebub and Azrael; and finally, John Dee, who turns dreams and nightmares into reality using one of Dream's own tools, which were taken from him by Roderick Burgess. This is Morpheus' quest: to regain those tools of office, which will restore him to his full glory.

Yet, in each encounter, Morpheus is presented with situations in which he has the opportunity to render aid or mercy without the need for compensation. Rachel's painful death is diminished by a dream of love; John Constantine's nightmares are dispelled; Scott Free is rescued from his childhood nightmares; and J'onn Jonzz is granted a dream of the City of Focative Mirrors. Even John Dee, whose twisted abuse of the inhabitants of a diner and the world is reminiscent of Morpheus' own behavior as the Ignoble King, is rewarded with a gift of sleep.

The only person who requests a boon from our hero and is denied is Nada, who is imprisoned in Hell. Nada begs for Morpheus' forgiveness which would, in turn, grant her freedom, but Morpheus responds, "It has been ten thousand years Nada. . . . yes. I still love you. But I have not yet forgiven you." This rejection of Nada's plea serves two purposes in the hero quest. First, it serves as an unfulfilled portion of the quest that allows our hero to assume the form of Redeemer, a continuation of the hero storyline in which the hero rectifies past mistakes. Second, and more importantly, it represents Morpheus' rejection of the bride or, more plainly put, his feminine self. In doing so, Morpheus is choosing to reject a particular version of the hero quest, in which the hero finishes his quest, marries and adopts the role of husband and father. This is the common quest of Prince Charming and the unnamed hero of the Rapunzel fairy tale.

The alternative path to the role of husband/father is often represented in messianic tales in which women struggle with their role in the tale. Here, the most common example is that of Christ and Mary Magdalene. By example then, the rejection of Nada, the rejection of the feminine self, places the hero on the path to divinity, the transformation of the hero into a god. Indeed, by the close of his battle with John Dee, Morpheus has regained all of his former glory and he now is able to carry his opponent in the palm of his hand. Morpheus has achieved a state of apotheosis, a glorified ideal in which all is right in the world. "Tonight," Morpheus tells us, "humanity will sleep in peace."

Unfortunately, this is never the end of the story. While the hero has conquered himself and gained the prize that can restore the world, the final task of returning home is often refused or denied. Just as Christ expresses his doubts, so too does Morpheus, "I had been sure that as I had everything back I'd feel good. But inside I felt worse than when I started. I feel like nothing." This instance of self doubt is universal in the hero myth, and can lead to ultimate failure, such as when Orpheus glances back. The hero must realize that he is the hero and overcome his lingering fears to take that last step in restoring the world. Often help or motivation comes from the feminine, usually the bride figure. In this case, recall that Morpheus has rejected the feminine. Thus, where normally the hero would make one last supreme effort to rescue the girl, Morpheus' sister Death must instead initiate the motivation for him to complete his quest, and thereby restore the world.

The final scene of the hero quest is the magic flight. Like Aladdin on his magic carpet, Luke Skywalker in his X-Wing fighter or Bellerophon on Pegasus, the hero must return on wings. In Morpheus' case, the return is symbolic as he conjures grain, throws it into the air and finds himself surrounded by pigeons and "The sound of wings . . ."

The Warrior

The stories presented in *The Doll's House* arc are, as Gaiman writes ". . . about the houses and walls that people build around themselves and each other, for protection, or for imprisonment, or both; and about the tearing down of those walls." Here, the Doll's House is a metaphor for what Campbell calls Holdfast, the keeper of the *status quo*. In the case of Morpheus, who is attempting to restore his kingdom, the *status quo* must be challenged, defeated, and destroyed.

However, Morpheus, as king, can no longer assume the role of hero and battle against the unknown. Instead, Morpheus must assume the role of the warrior, man of war, and make war against known enemies. The known enemies here are represented first by Hector Hall, who in identifying himself as ". . . the Sandman . . ." reveals himself as an usurper of the throne. With Hall are also Brute and Glob, former servants of Morpheus who abandon the palace to create their own kingdom. More terrifying than Brute and Glob is the Corinthian, an eye-eating nightmare who has created an army of serial killers whom he informs, "We are Gladiators, and we are soldiers of fortune, and we are swashbucklers and heroes and kings of the night." Also among the renegade dreams is Fiddler's Green, a dream who was more a place than a person. Morpheus describes him as a vavasour of his own domain. Thus, while Brute and Glob tried to usurp the kingdom of Morpheus; and the Corinthian raised an army, the betrayal of Fiddler's Green is particularly more grievous, as Fiddler's Green was not a servant, but rather a vassal, a representative of Morpheus himself.

Additionally, Morpheus must not only make war against the internal threats of rebellious disobedient dreams; he must also deal with the external threat of the Vortex, Rose Walker, whose existence threatens the Dreaming itself.

Thus, in *The Doll's House*, Morpheus assumes the role of warrior to battle against a pretender to the throne, a usurping staff, an evil knight, and a seceded nobleman. With these symbols defeated, the *status quo* is shattered and the Holdfast defeated. Campbell tells us that traditionally, the defeat of the Holdfast is symbolized by a woman, such as the unnamed heroine present in so many knight-versus-dragon tales. In this case, the woman is Lyta Hall, the wife of Hector Hall, who has been imprisoned in a dream for years during which she has remained six months pregnant. With the destruction of the dream prison, Lyta's pregnancy is free to proceed, but at a price. Just as Paul Atreides took the wife and children of the fremen he killed, so too does Morpheus make his claim, saying ". . . the child you have carried so long in dreams. That child is mine. Take good care of it. One day I will come for it."

While Morpheus has assumed the role of warrior, there is a marked change in his personality. The opening of *The Doll's House* begins with the story of Morpheus imprisoning Nada for refusing to be his queen. This episode can be used to contrast with his treatment of Lyta Hall and Rose Walker. Here is more evidence that Morpheus is no longer the ignoble king. Nowhere is this transformation made more visible than in his meeting with Hob Gadling where Morpheus says, "I have always heard it was impolite to keep one's friends waiting." Consequently, *The Doll's House*, and the story "Men of Good Fortune" in particular, can be seen as a tool to compare and contrast the behavior of Morpheus before and after his hero quest.

The Redeemer

Another role often assumed, following the hero quest, is that of redeemer. In this variation the mission of the antagonist is to refute the acts of the previous incarnations, particularly those carried out by the ignoble king.

The first indication that Morpheus will assume this role is found in the story "Calliope." The muse Calliope, a past lover of Morpheus and the mother of Orpheus, was captured and imprisoned sixty years ago by Erasmus Fry. Fry later trades her to the writer, Richard Madouc. Both men serially rape Calliope to provide inspiration for their literary creations.

In her desperation Calliope pleads for help, and eventually, Morpheus arrives to aid her. Her release is eventually obtained after Morpheus gives the gift of too many ideas to Madouc. Afterwards, Calliope notes that Morpheus is no longer the ignoble king ". . . in the old days you would have left me to rot forever, without turning a hair . . ." Morpheus acknowledges the change saying "I have learned much in recent times . . ."

This episode foreshadows the events in *Season of Mists*, in which Morpheus is reminded of his poor behavior towards Nada and must undertake a journey to Hell to free her from ten thousand years of imprisonment. Here the effort to redeem the sins of the old ignoble king is clear. Unfortunately, where the rescue of Calliope was straightforward, Nada's captor is Lucifer, lord of his own realm, who must therefore be treated as the Dream Lord's peer.

To follow the protocols, such as they are, Morpheus sends Cain as an envoy to announce his visit. Yet when he actually arrives at the gates of Hell he comes ready for war. "... I am here as Dream of the Endless. I wear my helm of office. I am caparisoned formally. I have no choice but to use the main gate. If necessary I am prepared to storm the gateway. To force an entry." Thus, while Morpheus comes in his capacity as a king, he also comes ready to assume the role of warrior.

Once in Hell, Morpheus is shocked to discover that Lucifer has resigned, and that "Hell is over." Morpheus is cautious, fearing a trap. Lucifer, to assuage Morpheus' fears, swears "... I give you my word that while we are within the bounds of Hell, I will do nothing to harm you. There, now take off your helmet . . ." Morpheus removes his helmet, which in theory, symbolizes his shedding of the role of warrior. Yet Morpheus here misinterprets his own symbols. The helmet, as Morpheus told us earlier, is "... my helm of office." In removing his helmet, Morpheus has shed not the role of warrior but rather has removed himself from the role of king. No longer is Morpheus dealing with Lucifer as king to king; Morpheus is the warrior and Lucifer has become the trickster. Morpheus fails to recognize the transformation and even that he is being tricked when Lucifer hands him the key to Hell saying "Well, we are outside the boundaries of Hell . . . This is for you Dream Lord. Take it."

In many ways, the gift of the key to Hell is a traditional riddle-problem in that there is really no satisfactory solution that does not engender other problems. In this case, the problems arrive in droves as ambassadors arrive to discuss Hell with Morpheus. Among the envoys are representatives of: the Norse, the Egyptian, and the Japanese pantheons; the Lords of Order; the Lords of Chaos; and Faerie. Two angels from Heaven and a contingent of demons led by Azazel also arrive. All the parties make offers or threats for the key to Hell. Yet if Morpheus gives the key to one group, he engenders the enmity of the others. In this situation, Morpheus is trapped and cannot resolve the problem. Like a traditional Greek hero, Morpheus requires the assistance of a god, a *deus ex machina*, to resolve the issue. This is essentially what happens when the Creator, speaking through the angel Remiel, announces "Hell is now directly under Heaven's control, and Duma and I will be Heaven's regents in the Underworld."

Thus, the riddle that perplexes Morpheus is removed from his consideration, although the situation is interesting in light of Campbellian theory. Here, in trying to decide what to do with the key to Hell, Morpheus is cast into the position of world-redeemer, who must set forth to restore the world to normality by re-establishing Hell. Yet by acknowledging that he cannot resolve the matter, Morpheus establishes his own theological limitations. Morpheus makes this plain: "I did not create the Hell of Lucifer . . . nor the realm of which it is a shadow. If its creator wishes to take it back, that is its creator's affair, not mine." Here Morpheus abandons the key, finally realizing that the burden of the key was not his to carry. Like Tolkien's elves who refuse to bear the One Ring, Morpheus cannot hold the key to Hell; for the simple fact of the corrupting force embodied in each. Indeed, in the case of the angel Remiel, the corruption is almost instantaneous as he announces "This is . . . wrong. We can not . . . Hell is for the Evil. Hell is for those who have offended against his love. Hell is for . . . I . . . I will rebel. Like Lucifer. I will Protest. This is wrong . . ."

With the world redeemed, Morpheus can once more turn his attention to redeeming himself and rescuing Nada. Nada is held prisoner by the demon Azazel who has actually hidden her inside his own body, along with the demon Choronzon. Once again the riddles of kingly protocol must be endured. Morpheus notes that Nada is as much a guest as any other of those assembled, and thus under his protection. Azazel renounces Morpheus' hospitality and a riddle bargain is struck. If Morpheus can find and release both prisoners, they may all leave; if not, Azazel will feast on all three souls. Morpheus succeeds, but Azazel breaks the bargain and attempts to devour Morpheus. Morpheus, who reminds Azazel that it was foolish to attack Morpheus in his own home, imprisons the demon in a small glass jar. The events cow the remaining envoys, who acknowledge the righteousness of Dream's decision.

The remaining story arc encompasses even more redemptions. The first two are connected as Morpheus helps keep Loki free from the Underworld while also saving the Japanese storm god Susano-o-no-Mikoto whom Loki charmed to take his place. More importantly, Nada accepts Morpheus' apology, and thus the Dream Lord is redeemed. Nada is reincarnated as a newborn baby to live out the life she should have had. On a grander scale,

Lucifer acknowledges that he must respect the Creator and His creation. Finally, the angel Remiel accepts his position as one of the sovereigns of Hell but is changing the very philosophy of Hell announcing, "We will hurt you. And we are not sorry. But we do not punish you. We do it to redeem you. Because afterward you'll be a better person. And because we love you. One day you'll thank us for it."

The Tyrant

Transformed from hero to king, the protagonist must now undertake the everyday tasks of keeping his kingdom running. In this situation, it is inevitable that the king will be forced to make a decision that requires him to place the needs of the kingdom over those of an individual or group. Often this is an opportunity for the king to display wisdom, such as when Solomon ordered the baby cut in two. Other times, when his motives are not plain, the king may appear malevolent. The appearance of malevolence was apparent in the *Dune* series in which first Paul Atreides and then Leto II appeared to grow malevolent, all the time preparing the human race for an unknown danger and vast transformation.

In either case, the king appears to some or all as transformed into the tyrant. Yet, while the term "tyrant" may now have connotations of despotic abuse, the term here is used to simply describe one who wields absolute power. Morpheus has become the tyrant wielding absolute power over the land of Barbie's dreams in *A Game of You*. In this story arc, Morpheus has moved from being the protagonist to being a supporting character, or even the motivating force for the conclusion of Barbie's quest. The fact that Morpheus allows the Cuckoo to complete its transformation and fly away only serves to reinforce his position as tyrant. From the Dream King's point of view, the Cuckoo is following a natural cycle, and the intruders are Barbie and her friends. In his interview with Bender, Gaiman says, "Yes, the gods have their points of view; but in *Sandman*, those have no more validity than the point of view of anyone else, even that of the humblest character." In *A Game of You*, the same can be said of questing heroines (Barbie and her friends) and monsters (the Cuckoo). Who should come to completion is entirely dependent upon your point of view.

Transcendent now in the role of the Tyrant, Morpheus should

be about the continued management of his kingdom. Yet, in the opening scenes of *Brief Lives*, we find Morpheus not the least bit tyrannical or even kingly. Rather Morpheus is morose over the departure of his latest lover. Here is the first hint of what is to come. Recall that, in *Preludes and Nocturnes*, Morpheus rejected Nada's pleas for help and in doing so rejected his feminine side. This conscious decision to reject the feminine, to reject the role of husband, placed Morpheus on the path to divinity, a role in which he has excelled. Yet, by rejecting the feminine during his hero quest, Morpheus cannot expect to be able to accept the feminine in his role as divine tyrant. Thus, in a small way, by looking for love, Morpheus is violating the natural order of the Campbellian hero.

This violation of the hero mythos is a primary theme of *Brief Lives*. Morpheus joins Delirium on a quest to find their missing brother, Destruction. Given Delirium's irrationality, such a quest should be doomed to failure, or at least be a challenge. Yet, with Morpheus joining Delirium, as a subordinate member of the party, the rules of the hero quest are broken. Morpheus has vast supernatural power; there is no need for him to go questing, particularly as the secondary hero. What ensues is chaos. Every individual—mortal, immortal, or god—who could help in the quest is supernaturally attacked or destroyed.

Seeing the damage that he and Delirium have been causing, Dream ends the quest for Destruction, not entirely unaware of the fact that Destruction is exactly what they have been encountering. Here Morpheus is like the demigod Hercules, who, in joining the Argonauts, must be removed from the quest because his very presence leaves no doubt to the outcome. If Morpheus remains part of Delirium's quest, the victory is assured.

Delirium, as irrational as ever, refuses to accept the termination of the quest and, instead of embarking on it alone, once more convinces Dream to help her, this time with all of his attention. The truth of the matter here is that Dream usurps the role of the central hero from Delirium. It is Morpheus who leads Delirium through the labyrinth to ask Destiny for advice. It is also Morpheus who must confront his son Orpheus to gain the secret knowledge of where Destruction is hiding. It is interesting to note here that Destruction is just a short rowboat ride away from Orpheus. This is symbolic in that, given the powers of the Endless, the distance to Destruction's hiding place is unimportant. Once the location is gained, the quest is essentially over.

Note the multiple violations of both the Campbellian hero myth and the rules that Morpheus must abide by. First, as a king, Morpheus has no business questing; like King Arthur he should be using his knights and envoys to carry out such business. The very process of accepting the quest violates his position. Once in the quest, Morpheus again violates the process: instead of seeking out information from unknown sources, he uses known sources, indeed in the case of Orpheus, the source, as his son, is theologically subordinate to Morpheus. Indeed, just in visiting Orpheus, Morpheus has violated his own oath never to see him again. This of course is a preamble to the ultimate violation; Morpheus, in a supreme act of contrition, puts Orpheus to a merciful death. The gravity of this act, of spilling family blood, was foreshadowed both in "Three Septembers and a January," when Desire vows "But, I'll make him spill family blood; I'll bring the Kindly Ones down on his blasted head"; and in the end of *The Doll's House* when Morpheus questions Desire, "Was I to take the life of one of our blood, with all that would entail?" Thus, the stage is set for the ending story arcs and the final transformations of Morpheus.

The Renouncer

Campbell's hero theory suggests that prior to his death, the hero may obtain one more state, one he calls the saint, the ascetic, or the renouncer. The hero who has become the renouncer has reached a state beyond myth and beyond adventure. The hero now moves toward the ultimate mystery: the very paths which had been ignored or rejected previously are now seen as the road to bliss. In essence, the hero must now enter into a new stage of his existence, one that he has previously refused to embrace.

Indeed, *The Kindly Ones* story arc is entirely about the acceptance and exploration of alternative states. In the opening pages the raven, Matthew, inquires of the three beasts that guard the door to the castle, asking them, ". . . Did you do anything before?" Matthew also wonders about the previous ravens and the one called Aristeas of Marmora who became a man again. Morpheus ignores Matthew's question, being focused on his work of recreating the nightmarish Corinthian. "It is rare that I return to a previous theme . . ." He tells Matthew, "The last Corinthian was a fool. This one will not be." Morpheus describes the Corinthian as "the dark mirror of humanity," and this concept is echoed when the faerie Cluracan strays from the proper path and creates his own Nemesis.

While the scenes with Matthew and Cluracan hint at alternative states, others seem to embrace states previously thought only temporary. Lucifer confirms to the angel Remiel that he has indeed abandoned his role as the King of Hell. "Been there, Remiel. Done that." Similarly, Nuala of Faerie, forced by Morpheus to abandon her glamorous appearance while in the dreaming, attends the fairy revels as her true self, telling the Queen, "I gave the matter a certain amount of thought and decided I felt comfortable without, um, glamour." In contrast to Nuala is Hal who in *The Doll's House* was a landlord who worked on stage as a transvestite. In *The Kindly Ones*, Hal has all but abandoned his true persona, embracing instead the role of high profile, anti-lesbian comedienne Vixen LeBitch.

Of course the most startling and important transformation is that of Lyta Hall. Lyta is fanatically devoted to protecting her son, Daniel. This fanaticism has driven Lyta to the edge and she seems ready to lose control at the slightest threat, real or perceived. If anyone needs to explore alternative states, it is Lyta Hall. Admittedly, she tries as she has dinner with a perspective employer, Eric. Eric recaps Lyta's entire life, calling it strange, and setting the stage for a new direction in life as his assistant. While Lyta's life is about to change, it isn't in the way that Eric expects. There's a lovely turn of phrase that becomes prophetic here. When Lyta has a sudden feeling that something is wrong at home, Eric tells her, "Look, you go and phone home from the lobby. If everything's okay, we finish our dinner like civilized people. If there's anything wrong I'll drive you home." Of course, there is something wrong, and Eric does drive Lyta home, implying by contrast that Lyta is no longer civilized. Indeed, the majority of the rest of the story arc details Lyta's descent into madness, and the exploration of all her various roles in life, all of her possible states. Unconsciously, there is a self perception of what is happening to her, made manifest by her former incarnation, the super heroine Fury, who implores Lyta to turn off the path she is on. "You don't have to go through with this. You can open your eyes, climb off this bed, walk out the door, put your life back together again." Lyta rejects that option, smashes the mirror image and makes a final descent into the madness of vengeance to beseech the Kindly Ones, the Furies, to destroy Morpheus.

Lyta Hall's transformation is a dangerous one. Lyta may have joined with the Furies, but she is not their equal. She has set the Furies in motion, and once in motion they cannot be stopped, not even by Lyta. Indeed, in her blind madness, Lyta fails to hear the hints that Morpheus was not responsible for Daniel's death. Furthermore, Lyta fails to understand that the Furies have no motivation for avenging Daniel's death, but rather would seek vengeance for the death of Orpheus. The Furies are simply waiting for someone to give them motivation. Once Lyta sets them in motion they cannot be stopped. The chain of events is set and cannot be broken.

Lyta's transformation is the trigger needed for the core transformation of Morpheus himself. Morpheus, comfortable in his position, tells the Furies, "This is my world, ladies. I am responsible for it. You will neither destroy it nor will you destroy me." This is essentially true. Morpheus as Dream seems completely empowered to recreate everything that the Furies destroy. Just as Morpheus recreated the Corinthian, there is no reason why he cannot recreate the victims of the Furies' wrath. The victims of course are some of the most visible of the dream supporting cast. The griffin on the gate, Mervin Pumpkinhead, Fiddler's Green, even Abel: all are destroyed by the Furies. Albeit temporarily, for as the Furies observe, "None of you are truly dead until Morpheus himself is dead."

The Furies themselves cannot kill Morpheus. "We don't kill. We can't," one aspect tells Lyta Hall. Instead, what the Furies do is destroy everything around their victim, until the victim himself prefers death. There is a parallel here to the fate of the recaptured Loki when Odin says, "He wants you to kill him, Thor. He wants to die. He was lying to you. He tells lies. You know that. His punishment is worse than death. Death would be so easy." This is Morpheus' choice. He may live and remain the Lord of Dreams, but suffer the eternal wrath of the Furies, or he may renounce his position and die on his own terms. Morpheus, no longer the self-centered ignoble king, chooses to sacrifice himself, telling Death, "I have made all the preparations necessary." Death scoffs at

Morpheus, "You've been making them for ages. You just didn't let yourself know that was what you were doing." With that, and a touch of Death's hand, Morpheus is no longer the Lord of Dreams. As the three Fates say, "There. For good or bad. It's done."

The Reborn

After his death, the hero remains as what Campbell calls a "synthesizing image": like King Arthur or Christ, he will arise when needed; or like the Dalai Lama or the pop media heroine, Buffy the Vampire Slayer, he walks among men in another form. In the case of Dream, Morpheus is replaced by what is left of Daniel Hall. The new Dream is not Morpheus but also consistently claims not to be Daniel. The new Dream seems to be cognizant of everything that Morpheus was, but is not him. Despite the fact that the transition has been made, the actual extent of the new Dream's authority is in question.

Cain mistakenly assumes that his contract is with "Your predecessor," while the remade Mervin Pumpkinhead doesn't even acknowledge the change. Fiddler's Green, slain by the Furies, outright refuses to be recreated. "I lived a good life and it ended." He tells the new Dream, "Would you take that away from me?"

Most confused is Eblis O'Shaughnessy, the envoy created by the Endless to gather the cerements needed for Dream's funeral. "So . . . Who died?" he asks Lucien, Cain and Abel. Cain, the keeper of mysteries, wraps the truth in vague hints. "Nobody died. How can you kill an idea? How can you kill the personification of an action?" Eblis is still confused. "Then what died? Who are you mourning?" It is up to Abel to make things plain, to reveal the secret, "A puh-point of view."

Later, a similar conversation takes place between Matthew and Lucien. "Why did it happen? Why did he let it happen?" asks Matthew. Lucien seems to become very introspective and responds, "Let it, Matthew? I think he did little more than let it happen . . . Charitably . . . I think . . . sometimes perhaps, one must change or die. And, in the end, perhaps limits to how much he could let himself change."

It is fitting that it is Cain, Abel, and Lucien who let slip these revelations, for they are the storytellers, and know the secrets of the Kingdom of Dreams. Taken together then, the new Dream is the old Dream remade, changed to allow a new perspective on matters. In the last issue set in the 1600s, Morpheus tells Shakespeare, "I am not a man. And I do not change. . . . I am the Prince of Stories, Will; but I have no story of my own. Nor shall I ever." Yet, we know now this not to be true. Morpheus does have a story, a grand adventure, and by it he is irrevocably changed from the ignoble king through all the forms of the hero and eventually into the tyrant. Unfortunately, the role of tyrant does not sit well with Morpheus. Given his adventures, he can no longer assume the various roles needed to carry out his position as Dream. Morpheus has made too many enemies, too many friends, too many bargains, boons and debts, to continue as needed. He is trapped by his past into acting as he has, but it is a pattern of behavior he can no longer believe in. Thus, Daniel was prepared and assumes the role of Dream.

Daniel is unburdened by the ties that bound Morpheus, and consequently he may administer and defend the Kingdom of Dreams as needed. Yet, this new Dream seems different from the old Dream. In replacing the griffin guardian of the gate, the new Dream declines to recreate the old one, rather he sends to Arimaspia for an honored subject. Likewise, the new Dream spends time with the guardians, something which puzzles the griffin. "Our Lord would not have done as you are doing. In the thousands of years that I served him, he did not touch me." Similarly, the new Dream ponders what to do with Lyta Hall. "I am permitted to take life only to protect the Dreaming; But I may punish as I desire." Yet instead of seeking vengeance, the new Dream kisses her on the forehead and says, "You have my mark on you Lyta Hall. No one shall harm you. Put your life together once again. Go in peace." The new Dream even goes so far as to end the punishments that Morpheus had inflicted previously. This act is represented by both Alexander Burgess and Richard Madouc waking up from their long nightmares. One of the Endless (most likely Death but possibly Destiny) suggests that this is a process of simplifying his position: ". . . I suppose it means all he has to worry about is us." Thus the only obligation the new Dream has is to the Endless, his family.

The Dream King has come full circle. However, by learning from his previous incarnation, the new Dream has bypassed the state of the ignoble king and entered instead into the position of the Fallen Man, honored but unrecognized by his society. This would explain why many of the residents of the Dreaming wonder about his position. Even the new Dream questions his status. "This is very new to me Matthew. This place. This world. I have existed since the beginning of time. This is a true thing. I am older than worlds and suns and gods. But tomorrow I will meet my brother and sisters for the first time. And I am afraid." When the time to meet the Endless finally does come, Matthew takes a moment to remind the new Dream that while he may be Dream of the Endless he need no longer be bound by the past and that the future is his to write. "The King is dead. Long live the King."

BLUE AND PINK: GENDER IN NEIL GAILMAN'S WORK

Mary Borsellino

Neil Gaiman's work is powerful because he has remembered the things most of us forget. The old truths, the ancient stories that are watered down and cleaned up until they become our fairy tales. One of the most important rules of childhood is that the way to kill the monster is to shut your eyes and ignore it, and Gaiman seemingly applies the same principle to the rules and regulations of our society's gender roles, by the cast of his fictions.

"God gives you a body, it's your duty to do well by it. He makes you a boy, you dress in blue, he makes you a girl, you dress in pink."

This quote from chapter six of *A Game of You* represents a way of thinking and a set of attitudes that Gaiman's work breaks down—not through contradiction or subversion, but through simple disregard.

It's not that his girls don't wear pink and his boys don't wear blue, because sometimes they do. It's that it just doesn't mean anything more than that. His characters simply wear the clothes that fit them best. In chapter two of *The High Cost of Living*, the protagonists meet a pregnant woman, Hazel. Her t-shirt is emblazoned with the word "baby" and an arrow pointing down to the lump in her stomach, and a second word, "dyke," has been added with a direction towards the neckline and the wearer's head.

The arrow pointing to the baby is stating the obvious, directing people to see what is apparent. There's no way of knowing on sight, of course, that Hazel is gay, and this second label is a helpful reminder to readers that the only way to know for sure what a person's sexual orientation might be is for it to be stated outright.

The fact that Hazel is a lesbian is already known to readers of Gaiman's earlier graphic novel, *A Game of You*, which reveals one of the most interesting examples of gender roles in Gaiman's work. But to those unfamiliar with that story, coming into *The High Cost of Living* cold, Hazel's t-shirt slyly points out that there's no reason to assume heterosexuality any more than there is to assume homosexuality.

Sexuality is a force of both immense creative possibility and enormous destructive potential wtihin Gaiman's books. The character of Desire him/herself in *The Sandman* series is a person-ification of this, capricious and beautiful, dangerous and lovely. As Death points out in the short community-service message, *Death Talks About Life*, sex can have two consequences: life and death. In *The Kindly Ones*, both of these are seen in the story of Rose Walker and her relationship with the lawyer Jack. She ends up pregnant; he ends up suiciding.

When Desire, in *Season of Mists*, draws butterflies through a candle flame, the image echoes classical depictions of Eros, love. The non-anthropomorphic version of love within the books is equally rooted in mythologic and ancient stories. Femininity is very much an elemental force, most commonly seen in triad: maiden, mother, crone; and masculine energy is equally powerful. The division of genders among the Endless illustrates the dif-ferent traits embodied by men and women. Death is organic, and happens to the body, while Destruction and Destiny are based on human thought and action. Within the mind, Delirium and Despair are physical, chemical states, but it is imagination and thinking that allow us to Dream. Desire falls in both categories.

This separation of mind and body into female and male does not mean, whoever, that Gaiman's books reinforce gender stereo-types. Rather, they do the opposite. Some of his characters are male, and some are female, but they're all *people*. Labels, like Hazel's t-shirt, don't mean a lot.

Salim in *American Gods* is not gay for the sake of being gay, any more than Shadow is straight for the sake of being straight. They are each what they are because the story needs it. In fact, "gay" and "straight" are not really appropriate words to use in the con-text of the Gaiman books. When, in *A Game of You*, Barbie attends Wanda's funeral, her odd behaviour sets off the prejudices of the family there. This is the same Barbie from *The Doll's House*, who was, in Rose's words, "terrifyingly, appallingly normal," whose ultra-straightness was ridiculous. In *A Game of You*, she is still, presumably, heterosexual, but "straight" is a label that doesn't fit her anymore. Barbie, like all the central characters in Gaiman's work, can be seen as queer-identified, a gender orientation that includes hetero-, homo-, and bisexuality, transgender, and any-thing in between.

A Game of You has a diverse cast, and is perhaps the text in Gaiman's catalogue most concerned with questions of gender. "Is identity *that* fragile?" Barbie asks at the end.

No, the rest of the story seems to say, identity is never fragile, but eternally malleable. In both *A Game of You* and *Time of Your Life* (another story starring Hazel and her lover Foxglove), a theme of names is made explicit, but it runs through all of the *Sandman* stories to a greater or lesser degree. Names are like masks, able to be worn and replaced as life changes. Boys can be girls if they want to, even if the Moon doesn't think so.

After all, what does the Moon know? It thinks Foxglove is a virgin. Old definitions don't fit Neil Gaiman's characters. Barbie has blond hair, blue eyes, and a pink dress, but embarks on the sort of quest typically undertaken by male heroes. She compares herself to Bilbo of *The Hobbit,* and finds her clothing inadequate for the task at hand, almost freezing to death.

When Wanda dreams of the Weirdzos, the situation rapidly becomes incomprehensible because there's no easy binary opposition for most of the stuff in Neil Gaiman's head. A thing is never defined simply by what it isn't—Wanda is so much more than simply "not Alvin." In Hy Bender's *The Sandman Companion,* Gaiman says, "I wasn't pursuing an agenda with Hazel and Fox," and the same is true for the other characters in his work. They're not there to make statements, to be poster-children. They're part of the stories, unremarkable in their diversity. And that's the most powerful statement of them all.

GODS AND OTHER MONSTERS:
A *SANDMAN* EXIT INTERVIEW
AND PHILOSOPHICAL OMNIBUS

Robert K. Elder

At the time of this interview was conducted (Aug. 9, 1995—the day Jerry Garcia died, for detail sticklers), Neil Gaiman was finishing his comic book magnum opus *The Sandman*. What started as a snapshot of an author at a particular moment in time became an exit interview, of sorts, for *The Sandman*. It also turned into an in-depth, career-spanning conversation that illuminates Gaiman's view of life, the universe and, well, everything.

The year 1995 was a time of change and career upheaval for Gaiman. His youngest child, Maddy, was not yet a year old and Gaiman, 34, had only moved to the U.S. from England three years previously. He was, in his words, "desperately homesick." Personal and professional transitions (as he moved from comics to novels and screenplays) contributed to Neil's colorfully candid, particularly introspective answers during our marathon conversations.

This previously unpublished interview, conducted mostly in a Greek restaurant in Minneapolis, was meant for a book of author interviews that capsized soon after. As I read it again, 10 years later, I'm still struck by how universal the themes are and how they've manifested in Gaiman's later career. I'm happy this piece has found a worthy home.

Originally, the text was a gargantuan, unwieldy thing but I've condensed into a long-form oral history of sorts. Though it reads fluidly from one topic to the next, I've provided chapter headings for scholars and the impatient. Here, we get Neil in full force—from his hilarious skewering of Hollywood to his insightful thoughts on the nature of good and evil, and their respective personifications in literature. As in all my conversations with Neil over the years, he was exceedingly warm, patient and, if only a little, protective of his secrets. Thanks again to you, Neil, for sharing a few of them.

Q: *What will it be like to be done with* The Sandman?

GAIMAN: I think in some ways that I will feel very, very lonely and odd. And in other ways incredibly liberating. I have to write *Sandman* #73, finish #74 and do #75. Right now I just feel like a marathon runner. That last mile and a half. You've run 24 miles, you can't keep going anymore but you may as well keep going for that last mile and finish the marathon.

Sandman has a story that goes from the beginning of *Sandman* #1 to the end of *Sandman* #75 with of couple of specials and bits and bobs along the way. It's a huge entity. It's about four or five thousand pages of script, two thousand pages of comic. I'm very glad that it's done with in some ways and I'd never want to do it again and I'm terribly pleased that I did it. You're talking about something that's taken up seven, going on eight years of my life. It's probably the single longest thing that I will ever do. Right now I don't plan to start anything I can't finish by teatime.

When I started writing *Sandman*, I wanted to write the comic that would get me to go down to the comic store every week. That was what I wanted to do, that's what I wanted it to be. I was 27—26 actually—when I started writing it and I wanted to write something that did what Alan Moore's *Swamp Thing* had done for me. All of a sudden, I was 23, a working journalist and I was looking forward each month to going down to the comic shop. I found that desperately exciting.

It was what I wanted to do since I was a kid. What I wanted to do was be a writer, and one of the things that I really desperately wanted to write was comics, particularly American comics. And then I sort of gave up on that idea. I was running into work that Alan Moore was doing at the time, particularly on *Swamp Thing*, where he was writing a comic that had every bit as much intellectual power and weight and concentration behind it as the best of mainstream film, short stories, or poetry. I got interested. I had been doing nothing but being a journalist.

[The graphic novel] *Violent Cases* with Dave McKean was really done in order to have something that one could wave at people. The trouble I found then was that when you wave good comics at people—you'd show them *Swamp Thing*, or *The Watchmen*, or *The Dark Knights Returns*, or *Maus*—they'd say, "Well, it's got a swamp monster in it, it's got Batman in it, it's got superheroes in it." It's got little cartoony mice that they didn't get. We showed them *Love and Rockets* and they couldn't get past the fact that it was drawn in the style halfway between *Archie* comics and Jack Kirby. So we set out to do something that could be shown to the mainstream. That was more-or-less a mainstream short story written as well as I could write it, drawn in a more-or-less mainstream illustration style as well as he could draw.

Q: *Looking over the arc of* The Sandman, *what type of story would you classify it in the classical sense? A tragedy? An epic?*

GAIMAN: Clive Barker probably described it best in the introduction to *The Doll's House* where he described it as a giant cake with all sorts of bizarre things in it. It's like when we were kids at school they'd serve us Christmas cake. It's this giant Christmas pudding every year, and hidden in your Christmas pudding would be things like coins and thimbles. You'd have be careful not to break your teeth on them. I think of *The Sandman* as something like that.

What is it? Some of it is very funny, some of it isn't. Some of it is very dry, some of it isn't. It's got short stories, it's got historical stuff in it. It's partly, I suppose, a tragedy. But I'm not sure it ever gets to be a huge hubristic classical tragedy. If any thing, it's a bumbling little tragedy in which the real tragedy is just that people act like people and sometimes lousy things happen. It's a tragedy in the sense that any story is a tragedy if, as explicitly stated in *Sandman* #6, "You keep any story going on long enough, it ends in death." And, as I said at the end of *Season of Mists*: "The secret of happy endings is knowing when to stop."

Q: *I read an interview in which you said that you like working in comics because "comics allow you to do things you can't do with prose."*

GAIMAN: Um-hum.

Q: *Like what?*

GAIMAN: Like . . . let's take a very, very basic and obvious example: *Violent Cases*, first book I ever did. There's a point in there where we have the character of the osteopath. We've drawn him as sort of this old, Albert Einsteiny, rumpled old man. Then you get to the point in the thing where he [the narrator] says, "Now I have to say at this point I no longer remember him as this old, rumpled old man. I now remember him as looking like Humphrey Bogart's sidekick in *The Maltese Falcon*."

From that point on, that's how we draw him. If you said that in a prose work, by that point the reader would have built up a picture in his or her head of that character. And while I can say, "I now remember him looking like something else," it doesn't really do anything. It doesn't have very much effect—whereas if we did that in the theater or in film, it would be a big deal. All of a sudden you've got an actor being played by a different actor. In a comic we just do it, in a quiet sort of page of interruption and then interpolation and then that's how we draw him for the rest of the thing. You've quite cheerfully done something you can't do in prose.

Other things you can do in comics that you can't do in prose is you can make people read every word, which is really quite hard to do in prose. One of the things prose is about is where people are skipping. It's about where they don't read.

I did a story called "Murder Mysteries," which is in *Angels and Visitations*, in which I bury a story in the framing device. It wasn't that hard a story and it wasn't that well buried. If I had done it as a comic, 99 percent of the readers would have got it. As it was, roughly 5 or 10 percent of the readers, most of those from a literary criticism background, actually seemed to get it. I find that very interesting. It wouldn't have been any easier in comics but I would have insured that everybody reading digested every piece of information.

Q: *What are the weaknesses in the comic medium?*

GAIMAN: You can't go and do stuff inside people's heads. Example: Pick a book. Pick a major book that you like that hasn't been made into a film.

Q: *Oh God. Is* Catcher in the Rye *a film?*

GAIMAN: I don't think so—it's a lovely one. How many people have read *Catcher in the Rye* do you think by now?

Q: *A great deal. I don't know . . .*

GAIMAN: A million? A hundred million? Fifty million, whatever. There are fifty million different people . . . there are 50 million different pictures of Holden Caulfield in their heads. Your Holden Caulfield looks nothing like mine. Your Holden Caulfield probably sounds nothing like mine. We've built up [our own images]. The book is a collaborative experience between a reader and a writer.

A comic is not a collaborative experience in the same way because I'm providing the reader with pictures, or somebody is providing the reader with pictures. Everybody knows what the Sandman looks like, an obvious example. In prose, there'd be a million Sandmans wandering around.

Hollywood

Q: *What do you think about comics moving into the mainstream culture? There are certainly a lot more movies. . . I'm even going to see* Crumb *tonight.*

GAIMAN: I'm not sure, in the long run, it's anything more than a distraction. I don't like the strange idea that making a movie in some way legitimizes the comics. And it doesn't. Anytime you let a committee loose on something, you get a dilution of the original idea. I don't see that three blockbuster Batman movies have produced better Batman comics than we had before the blockbuster movies. I think if anything, the last two great Batman comics were *The Dark Knight Returns* and *The Killing Joke*, both of which were extensively ripped off by the first movie.

I don't see anything wrong with films, but it's a different medium. It's not comics. I don't think it applies to or legitimizes comics in any way. It would be like you saying to me: Do I see an upgrade in the regard that the public has for horror novels because they've made films of a lot of Stephen King books? No.

The great thing about comics is that they aren't film. There are a number of things that films can never be, including the good ones done by a lot less people, done cheap. I have a friend who tried to make his own film who is now $40,000 in debt with a bunch of uncut film. He knows that he needs another $65,000 to $100,000 to finish what he's got. I look at that and I think, "Now if you'd done that as a comic, either done it on your own or gone out and found an artist, it would have been cheap." It's a wonderfully, wonderfully, magically cheap medium. What you need are pens and paper.

Q: *You've said that you would not ever consider making* The Sandman *a film, but it was being scripted anyway. As we speak now, in fact. Any progress on that and will you have any control?*

GAIMAN: Oh, of course not. No. The script is finished,

or almost finished. It's being written by Teddy Elliot and Terry Rossio, who did *Aladdin* and various other films [the screen-writing duo went on to pen *Shrek*, *The Mask of Zorro* and *The Pirates of the Caribbean* trilogy—ed.]. They seem terribly nice guys. Their hearts are in the right place and I hope they make me look really good. I hope everyone makes me look good.

But I don't want to get involved. It's like barbecuing your baby, cutting off its little hands and marinating them in soy sauce before you put them on the flames. It's not something sane people should have to do.

I don't want to take the call from Hollywood where they say, [Thick mock-American accent which doubles the volume of his voice] "HEY, Neil baby, sit down. Are you sitting down? O.K. good. We got news for you . . . ya ready? Are you holding on to your seat 'cause you're gonna love this . . . We got ARNIE. That's right! We. Got. ARNIE. Can you see it now? 'Pleasant dreams muthderfucker.' Isn't that great? Hey Neil, what do you think? Neil are you there? Neil? Neil?"

I don't want to have to take that call. I don't want to have to play that game. I'm not interested. I've been cheerfully negative about Hollywood. It's got to the point these days where pretty much on a weekly basis I get phone calls from Hollywoody people. I'm going out to Hollywood in a couple weeks time to actually interview an agent so I have someone out there who can field a lot of this stuff. One of my standard replies is that I will begin initial talks if you can assure that at no point will I have to sit around a large table with a bunch of studio accountants lecturing me on story theory. So far, I've only found one person who was willing to say yes and get that written into the contract—at no point will I have to go to any story meetings. I can just write my script and then do a second draft of the script and they'll either film it or I can go home.

Q: *If you don't want Arnie to play Morpheus, do you have any ideas on who could play the part? Or any of the parts for that matter?*

GAIMAN: I don't know. I think a lot of it is . . . Casting *Sandman* is a wonderful way to spend a dinner. And occasionally your see some terrific *Sandman* casts and occasionally you see some wonderfully strange ones. I've seen some people cast *The Sandman* with the Warner Bros. characters with Bugs as the Sandman.

I would assume that you'd be looking at one of the English people. Given the choice, I'd rather see Daniel Day-Lewis than Johnny Depp, for example. This is Hollywood. I have no idea. We sit and we watch.

Q: *I talked to James O'Barr in 1991, before anything was ever signed on* The Crow *movie. He said, "I'm going to have full creative control. I'm not going to turn him into Batman." Well, that's exactly what happened.*

GAIMAN: You see, he had no creative control and it did turn into Batman. But it's like, well, and is anybody surprised? I find it impossible to imagine that anybody could be surprised. The only way you will get creative control is to do what my friend Richard Curtis did. You sit down. You write a script. When you finish the script and you've got it to your satisfaction, go out and find a director that you want to direct it. And then you find the money and make yourself executive producer and then you make *Four Weddings and a Funeral*. And it's your film, and that's how you do it.

Q: *I think that's becoming more common, especially with Quentin Tarantino, Richard Rodriguez and indie people who go out and make films for next to nothing.*

GAIMAN: But I think the next-to-nothing is an incredibly important part of that because you desperately need the next-to-nothingness. Once you go up to $15-25 million it is desperately important to the studio that everybody in the whole world loves this. So everybody wants to get in there.

The analogy from watching Hollywood, the one time I was out there, is that if you came into Hollywood and you said, "Hey, I've got this thing that I've invented. I'm calling it a pizza. And it is flat, a sort of dough-like substance, and on the top is going to be tomato and cheese. I'm going to heat it up in the oven and sell it off as slices."

And they say, [mock-American executive voice again] "Hey that's great. We *love* your pizza. We applaud your pizza idea. Your pizza idea is amazing, guy. We want pizza. And we've been talking and the most popular magazine in America is the *TV Guide* and we were wondering . . . maybe we could make a pizza more popular if we shredded up the *TV Guide* and put in *on* the pizza as a topping?"

And you say, "Well, I'm not actually sure that that would work . . ."

And the other executive says, "Y'know, it's funny you should mention that because besides putting the *TV Guide* on the pizza . . . What is the most popular item of footwear in America? OK, it's the sneaker. So we get these Nike sneakers and we just dig them deep into the pizza. Everybody is going to love it O.K. It's gonna have the *TV Guide*, it's gonna have Niké footwear in it."

You say, "It's not actually a pizza you're going to eat."

But Hollywood loves doing that. They will take petrol, a four-star gasoline, and they will take a vintage wine and mix it together and give you something that you can neither drink nor put in your car. That's merely the nature of the beast. I'm writing a TV series now for the BBC which I'm enjoying to no end because, basically, I have control except for the budget. So I will cheerfully write millions of very, very expensive things and let them cope with that as they may. It's called *Neverwhere*. It's about a world underneath London. It's about the people in the cracks. It's a magic city story really, magic city fiction.

Celebrity

Q: *What do you think is the biggest misconception about your writing? About you?*

GAIMAN: I honestly don't know. You'd have to ask other people.

Q: *I have. I even spoke with Matt Wagner this morning. He said the biggest misconception was that you own more than one set of clothes: black jeans, black T-shirt, black leather jacket and sunglasses. It's a misconception that he, however, believes.*

GAIMAN: (laughing) I wear them less now than I used to. I used to wear them chiefly for the purpose of anonymity. I'm not very good at being a public figure. I don't like it; I get very uncomfortable with it. I can do it for short periods of time, but then I don't like it intruding in anyway on my private life. I feel awkward when I'm being given V.I.P. treatment for being Neil Gaiman. I feel like, "I'm not really famous, I'm not really important either. God, maybe they'll catch on in minute." When I get that kind of treatment for being me, I feel vaguely fraudulent. I think it's very nice. It's all a distraction and it's all an enormously enjoyable distraction, but it is a distraction and it's one about which I tend to feel I'm some kind of bizarre fraud.

I figured rapidly awhile ago that if I wore the dark glasses and the leather jacket, then people would stop looking at my face and start looking at the dark glasses and leather jacket. And it works. It means that if I take off the dark glasses and leather jacket, I have thirty seconds lead time during which I can get out of a convention or get through a crowded hall.

What else did Matt say were the biggest misconceptions about me? I rather like that I have misconceptions.

Q: *Actually, that's about it. He also said that you are very American, but awfully very fucking British too.*

The Philosophy of the Sandman

Q: *You wrote in* Season of Mists *that Dream casts a human shadow. Is that your shadow?*

GAIMAN: Oh, I don't think so.

Q: *How much does Dream emulate you? How much of him is you?*

GAIMAN: I think you'd probably have to ask my friends that one . . .

Q: *I did.*

GAIMAN: What did they say?

Q: They said, yes, you were a lot alike although the Sandman tends to be a bit more stuffy.

GAIMAN: Yeah, he's a lot more stuffy than I am and . . . he's not very funny. The one time that he laughed in *Sandman*, it was not good news for anyone. Karen [Berger], my editor, says we're very similar. I'm not sure that I believe her. We share certain things. We share dress sense. And we both think that stories are very important. I think that I'm ever so slightly better at human relationships than he is. I think we both go a little bit overboard on the idea of the work. We both tend to define ourselves by our work.

Q: *Whom do you consider yourself closer to, in terms of personality, Hob* [an immortal human who chooses each century to renew his immortality] *or the Sandman?*

GAIMAN: Oh, I'm all of them. That's the problem, there's bits of you . . . I'd hate to think how many characters I've created in *Sandman* by now . . . and there is some of me in all of them. Very few of them are quite definitely other people. Death maybe. And Delirium maybe.

Hob is me. Hob is a line, one of my lines in *Good Omens*, where the demon Crowley is talking about one of the things that had sustained him — the blind, stubborn and rather stupid belief that, after the end of the day, the universe would look after him. I think that that's definitely Hob's belief and that's also mine. I like the idea that death isn't inevitable. It probably is. I know on an intellectual level that everybody else in the whole world is going to die. On the other hand, I could get lucky. I may beat the odds. I know that nobody has so far, or very few people have. It could be me.

Q: *Speaking of which, how much of* The Sandman *is reflective of a personal philosophy?*

GAIMAN: Depends what we're taking about and what philosophies. Most, I suppose, and I'm really not trying to weasel on this, but I think all of it is, but then the question becomes, "What is a metaphor?"

Q: *You wrote about Gnosis. Is that something you believe in?*

GAIMAN: I think in terms of Destruction's big rant at the end of "Brief Lives," which is fundamentally a very Gnostic rant, that everything can be known . . . sure, I'll go along with that.

Q: *But Gnosis is not only that every thing can be known, it's that . . .*

GAIMAN: . . . everything is known. I like to think that. I have no idea whether it's true or not.

Q: *Doesn't that sort of go along with the Platonic idea that nothing can be learned, it can only be remembered because we already hold the knowledge inside ourselves?*

GAIMAN: Or at least the idea that we don't know things in order to make it fun. We don't know things in order to make it interesting, to have a game. I think that's definitely true too. And whether or not I actually believe that or whether or not it is a literary conceit, I have no idea.

Q: *These questions are about the character of Death. She certainly seems to be a foil to all traditional perceptions of Death. She's pretty much the most positive, full of life, and — well — a rather bouncy character in the series. How did she formulate?*

GAIMAN: She was really a reaction to the Sandman. I wanted a character who would be everything the Sandman wasn't. If you know the Sandman is a brooding, Byronic figure all in black and you know that he is Death's younger brother, then you say to yourself, "Jesus, then what is Death going to be like?" You start conjuring up someone a hundred times more Byronic, a hundred times more dressed in black, a hundred times more dangerous.

Q: *You've said that she writes her own dialog.*

GAIMAN: Mostly she does. She and Delirium. Delirium does it too, on the whole. You give them straight lines, then you type what they say. The hard part is thinking up the straight lines.

Q: *Did Death act as you pictured she would, or did she change from her original conception?*

GAIMAN: I thought she was going to be a lot colder. I thought she was going to be a much chillier, ice maiden sort of character. I wanted somebody who was together. I figured death—it's a steady job, you get out and meet people. It's not very easy for the Sandman. He's a very out-of-touch character by definition. He goes off into ivory towers; he has no real friends, no real relationships. She gets to see everybody, on a daily basis. She's out there personally meeting everyone. I really didn't want a brooding Death. I didn't want a Death who agonized over her role in life. I figure that by this point, she'd have gotten used to it. But then she found out she was perky.

Q: *Why is Death female?*

GAIMAN: Death really became female because I wanted to fuck with the innate sexism of language up front. I just loved the idea. Language is sexist. You may fight this or you can get it to work with you. I loved the idea of announcing to the world that the Sandman was Death's younger brother and knowing that no one would say, "Oh, then Death is his older sister."

The letters immediately began to follow in saying, "When are we going to meet the Sandman's older brother Death?" I loved that. And that was really the initial motivating force, just knowing that nobody was going to think about it. I was just playing against reader expectation and also because most literary incarnations of Death had been male. I can only think of one, a Peter S. Beagle short story called "Come Lady Death," in which she was female. That's sort of it.

Q: *One of the writers to your letters column said that they were half in love with the character Death. Are you, yourself, in love with that character?*

GAIMAN: Well, I hold an affection for her but it's very hard to be in love with somebody you know you made up. It's much easier for everyone else. I remember reading an interview once with George Harrison where he was asked about the Beatles. He said, "You have to understand there was only me and three other guys who never heard the Beatles. We had no idea what happened in Beatlemania, we missed it."

I've never read *The Sandman*. I've written it. When I read it, I read it looking for typos. I read going, "I wish they'd put more detail in this panel." Sometimes time goes by and I read and go, "Y'know, this is better than I thought it was."

Demons and Hell, Personal And Otherwise

Q: *I am particularly interested in your concept of Hell, your construction of Hell. Lucifer Morningstar—where did the name come from?*

GAIMAN: The name Lucifer Morningstar is a very old name. Originally it comes from the Bible, I forget the exact quote, but it's something like, "How art thou fallen O Lucifer Son of the Morning." The name Morningstar was of old identified with Lucifer. Interesting to the name Lucifer, it wasn't exclusively the pejorative of demons and so forth until quite later. There was a Pope Lucifer.

Q: *Milton wrote* Paradise Lost *and he didn't even believe in the devil. He wrote "On Christian Doctrine," which underlined this. He didn't believe that evil existed. Do you believe evil exists?*

GAIMAN: Do I believe evil exists? Certainly. Do I believe in a personal devil? No. Do I think it's a dead useful metaphor? Definitely. The other trouble I have is when I start thinking about the devil I wind up wondering, following very convoluted trains of thought. "Season of Mists" just basically came out of one of those trains of thought, which is simply: Can the devil be redeemed? Can the devil quit?—which stemmed from a quote I was told when I was 13 or 14 was from Pierre Teilhard de Chardin.

But it actually turns out to have been from an incredibly swish French pastor named Abbé Mugnier where he says basically that he believed that Hell exists because it is church doctrine that it exists, but he didn't have to believe there's anyone down there.

[Actual quote: In response to the question of whether or not he believed in Hell, the Abbe Arthur Mugnier said, "Yes, because it is a dogma of the church, but I don't believe there is anyone in it."—ed.]

Q: *Teilhaard didn't say that?*

GAIMAN: I found a quote saying something similar to that. If he did say it somewhere he got it from Mugnier.

Q: *Of course, Teilhard was also co-discoverer of the Piltdown Man. So I don't know if that adds or takes away from his credibility.*

GAIMAN: Well, one day I'm going to write my Piltdown Man story. I have three or four really cool and completely contradictory Piltdown Man theories. Piltdown Man *[the purported "missing link" in human evolution]* was actually found about two miles down the road from where I lived in England. I actually went down there and looked at the little plaque. I went down to the solicitors office where Charles Dawson, who found him—or didn't—had his solicitors office.

Q: *What I thought interesting was that through the whole time he was famous, no one noticed that the jaw bone had file marks to fit the skull . . .*

GAIMAN: Well, there are lots and lots of cool Piltdown Man things. My favorite Piltdown Man theory is that it was all real. The most logical case for Piltdown Man is perfectly buildable—that it was real but it was necessary to make it appear a hoax, it actually explains why and how the Piltdown Man disappeared. All the top experts looked at the bones and examined them minutely for years and then they were taken off display during World War II. After World War II, when they were put out on display, everybody noticed they were fake. And you say, "Well, maybe they faked them then? Maybe they took the real ones away." It was only at that point that lots of evidence started popping up. I never figured out why anybody would want to un-fake the Piltdown Man.

Q: *Back to Lucifer . . . In the biblical sense then, why do you think Lucifer fell? There are a couple theories. One is that he wouldn't bow down to Adam, because he loved God too much and it was a conflict of loyalty. Another is that he created free will . . .*

GAIMAN: Any and all of them depending on what I was writing at the time. My favorite one is probably the one I used in "Murder Mysteries." I basically suggest that he was set up by God because he had a part to play in the universe.

Q: *What would be Hell for you?*

GAIMAN: No books, that'd be Hell for pretty much everyone.

Q: *I'm also interested in Crowley, the demon from* Good Omens. *Is the name Crowley a reference to Aleister Crowley?*

GAIMAN: Oh yes. Definitely. Originally, well—in the very first chapter I call him Crawly. He sort of keeps the name Crawly but it becomes Crowley because he thinks it's rather cooler.

Q: *Did you study anything by Aleister Crowley?*

GAIMAN: I've read some Crowley, but he's such an appallingly bad writer, one of these cosmically bad writers. I wind up going, "I don't care what the ideas are, just let him have a decent sentence." Have you ever tried to read his autohagiography? It sets your teeth on edge. Crowley's prose is fingernails going down a blackboard, which I think is a terrible pity. The best Crowley accounts you read are stuff other people wrote about him. The best piece I ever read about Crowley was a piece by Avram Davidson, which I think was published in *Weird Tales.* It was a wonderful little essay about Crowley.

Q: *For years he was considered England's biggest Satanist, or at least biggest occultist. Do you think that this holds any merit, any element of believability?*

GAIMAN: Crowley, as far as I can tell, believed in the basic principle of magic which is, "Say it and it shall be so." So he announced to the world the he was the world's wickedest man, and said that he was the Great Beast and stuff. Seeing that words have a certain amount of power, I think to some extent he was. I also think he was definitely, to some extent, considered in occult circles a bit of a joke. Or a lot of joke. You can go back and read the writings of back then.

Q: *Why do you think Satan is such an attractive character, for authors in particular?*

GAIMAN: I think partly because he's the rebel in all of us . . . It's very hard to write a good God. Who would you rather write about? Who is more interesting? The guy being taken up to a high place and being shown all the cities of the world or the guy who's doing the taking?

Q: *But there's no actual account of Satan in the Bible.*

GAIMAN: Oh no. There isn't. There is a tempting angel. He's there by the New Testament, but he's absent earlier . . . even in *Job* he is listed as the tempting angel. It's explicit in *Job* that it's his job, he's working for God.

Q: *And he sits at the right hand of the Father. He's basically the attorney general.*

GAIMAN: Yeah. Exactly. "Look, here's this bloke, let's fuck up his life." That's basically the plot of *Job*.

Q: *If you believe in evil then, what things are inherently evil?*

GAIMAN: I'm not sure anything is inherently evil. Actions that harm other people are evil. After you've met a couple people of the evil persuasion you go, "Yeah, there is evil and it's something you can choose." To me the biggest riddle and the scariest part of the nature of human evil is that the guards in the concentration camps were just like anybody else and they were just doing their job.

So do I think there is evil? Certainly there is evil. You watch the Jews go into the camps and you go, "There is certainly evil here." The most horrible evil though is very often complacency and the willingness to stand by and let bad things happen.

Q: *Are good and evil temporal then?*

GAIMAN: I'm not even sure they're exclusive. Which I think, on a lot of levels, was what *Good Omens* was about. There's the part in there where they talk about the problem of good and evil. The real problem is that you very often get evil that would turn the stomach of Hell and an act of wonderful goodness that would leave angels rocking on their heels—and you get it all in one person. That's true.

Q: *In* Good Omens *you wrote, "Hell is not as bad as what people do to themselves, what they think up themselves."*

GAIMAN: I think that's definitely true. And I think that's true if you want to take it on a *Season of Mists* level, which is a way of concretizing the metaphor. In *Season of Mists* you have a Hell that is explicitly a place where masochists essentially punish themselves. That's the Hell of *Season of Mists*. You have the Livonian chained to his big stone thing and saying, "I was the most evil man in the world."

Q: *And no one cares anymore.*

GAIMAN: Nobody cares. Nobody even knows where Livonia was anymore. *[Present-day Estonia plus Latvia.—Ed.]*

Q: *In terms of that then, is Hell punishment or redemption?*

GAIMAN: I would like to think it's redemption, but I tend to think it's self-flagellation, rather like the flagellants of the 14th century who go from city to city hitting themselves with boards and smashing themselves with whips. If given a choice, I would like to think it's redemption but then again . . .

I thought it interesting that people accused me in *Season of Mists* of being sacrilegious. I thought, "Well, I don't see what's so sacrilegious about the idea that the devil is redeemable."

Q: *Even in the Koran it says that in the end the devil will be redeemed.*

GAIMAN: Well by definition, one would have thought. Which again, goes back to the idea of Hell being empty.

Q: *You even quoted Shakespeare in* Good Omens, *"Hell is empty and the demons are all here."*

GAIMAN: The actual quote is from *The Tempest*, from the first scene of *The Tempest*.

Gods and Old Testament Poker

Q: *We've talked about your idea of Hell. I'd like to talk about your idea of God. This is a passage from* Good Omens: *"God does not play dice with the universe; He plays an ineffable game of His own devising, which might be compared, from the perspective of any of the other players (i.e. everybody), to being involved in an obscure and complex version of poker in a pitch-dark room, with blank cards, for infinite stakes, where the Dealer won't tell you the rules and who* smiles all the time." *Is that pretty much your view of God?*

GAIMAN: I find that if I'm going to believe in a biblical God, which sometimes I do and sometimes I don't, my main problem with God comes in the very first chapter of *Genesis* where He begins by telling Adam and Eve, "All this garden is yours except for this tree because it is poisonous and will kill you."

The serpent comes along and says, "He's lying. It won't kill you. It will give you the knowledge of good and evil." They taste it. The serpent is correct; it does not kill them. It gives them the knowledge of good and evil. At this point God, you are informed in the Bible, was scared that they would eat of the tree of life and become like gods so he threw them out of the garden. Check your Bible, this is what it actually says.

And you get—hang on, who do you believe here? What kind of behavior is that and is the person that behaves like that necessarily trustworthy? I've never been sure. Did you ever read *Outrageous Tales From the Old Testament*?

Q: *No.*

GAIMAN: It's a book that Knockabout Comics brought out that I wrote a few pieces for, one of which was illustrated by Dave McKean. You may want to see if you can find a copy. There's a story we did from Judges in there.

Basically the entire plot is: There is a prophet who's gone off to curse somebody. So he goes off and curses somebody and God has told him, "You have to go all the way and curse this guy, then go home, and you're not allowed to stop anywhere."

So he's on his way home when another prophet comes out of the city and says, "Come with me and have dinner."

The first prophet says, "God has told me to go straight home and not have dinner at all."

"Ah-ha!" says the other, "but it's O.K. because I received a direct revelation from God and he says that you can come with me for dinner."

So the guy says, "Great! I will come with you for dinner."

Then, they're halfway through dinner, having a very pleasant dinner and suddenly the prophet who had invited the guy to dinner stands up and says, "The word of the Lord is upon me. *You* have disobeyed God by coming to dinner with me. You must go away and you shall not rest in the tomb of your forefathers."

The first prophet, who had so far done everything that God had said except for going to dinner, says, "Well, fair enough." And he goes off home and on the way he gets eaten by a lion and killed. Indeed his bones do not rest with those of his forefathers.

As far as I can see, the only message you get from that, the only biblical interpretation I can take from that, is: Do not listen to anybody who tells you they know what God wants you to do.

Going back to your original question, perhaps a Gnostic revelation may well be the safest.

Jewish Punk: The Formative Years

Q: *In what tradition were you raised?*

GAIMAN: I was brought up Jewish. But I was Jewish and attended High Church of England schools, which is everything you get in Catholic education, without nuns. It was a lovely way of receiving all the religion one ever needed, as an outsider. It was very odd. I was the kid scoring the top marks in religious studies despite the fact that the religious studies would be on the *Book of Matthew* or whatever and I wasn't even a Christian, which was a lovely position to be in. One got everything as an outsider.

Q: *Are you still practicing?*

GAIMAN: I don't know, Judaism is one of those interesting things that you don't—I don't think I've particularly practiced since my bar mitzvah. Then again, I take a certain amount of comfort in the fact if ever anywhere they institute the camps and they want to start sticking Jews in them again, I'd go in and fry. I don't think it's something one particularly stops being because you've stopped practicing.

Q: *You were brought up in Sussex and were a teenager during the '70s. Does that make you a Sex Pistols fan?*

GAIMAN: Oh sure. I was a 15-year-old hoodlum. There are still photos of me with my orange spiky hair and my dog collar 'round my neck. At the time, I believed myself to look deeply menacing. Looking at those photos now, I look at them and I think, "He looks like a choir boy."

Q: *Those are the photos that Mom likes to keep.*

GAIMAN: Exactly. What one took away from punk, as far as I'm concerned, was incredible liberation, the idea that one didn't need anything before one did something. You don't have to go to music college and turn into Yes or Pink Floyd. You want to be in a band? Well look, this is the end of the guitar that you hold and this is the end of the guitar that you *hit*. There's four of you, that should be enough. I can shout loudest, so I'm the singer . . . and you take it from there.

Q: *What do your parents think of you writing comic books?*

GAIMAN: I think these days they're terribly, terribly proud of me. But that's these days. It was a slow process. These days, there are articles on me in British newspapers and their friends ring them up. They're proud.

Q: *Is your family religious?*

GAIMAN: They're a very traditional family but they're not particularly religious . . . my parents are still very Jewish. I have aunts and uncles who are terribly Jewish.

Q: *How did your religious or, at least, your educational background contribute to your writing?*

GAIMAN: I suppose my background in mythology was just loving the stuff and finding it wherever I could, beginning as a kid with finding books with titles like *Norse Myths*. Any books on fairy tales, folk tales, anything like that. That was what I dug up.

I would tend to, if one were listing influences, probably be looking much more at a mob of science fiction and related studies writers that I read when they really do burn into your head. The Samuel R. Delanys, and the Fritz Leibers, and the Roger Zelaznys, the R.A. Laffertys . . . that mob on one hand. Then you've got people like G. K. Chesterton, James Branch Cabell, definitely, and Lord Dunsany, Ernest Bramah, people like that on the other side. Sort of the stylists of Fantasy before there ever was Fantasy, before there was a genre racking. Then you've got the weird ones like Saki (a.k.a. H.H. Munro) and John Collier. When I was growing up, a lot of the fiction I liked was written so long ago that it was historical.

When I was a kid, you would read things that gave you that buzz. There weren't really genre categories in the horrible way there are today. You keep looking for the buzz anyway. You read the complete H.G. Wells short stories and you'd get the buzz from that. It wouldn't occur to you that some of them were horror, some of them were fantasy and most of them were sociological science fiction, but you get the buzz. You'd read Chesterton, and it would be there, whatever it was.

Sexuality

Q: *I was also interested in your use of sexuality, especially with the* Sandman *characters. Is there a reason that a lot of your characters are lesbian or gay?*

GAIMAN: I think it runs about ten percent, which is roughly what it runs in society. It would seem like a fair enough reason.

Q: *I was thinking in terms of literature and especially comics, their appearance is, I would guess, less than one percent.*

GAIMAN: Oh, I'd agree. Which again, you get around and meet comics creators and somewhere between 10 and 20 of these guys are gay or 10 and 5 percent, something like that. I don't know, I was writing the people I know. Trying to write everybody. One does not hold up any kind of an accurate mirror to life when you write or you create fiction. You are by definition lying. But you may as well try and hold up a distorting mirror that gives an illusion of something vaguely approaching reality.

Q: *Is that part of the philosophy that any view of the universe that is not strange is not accurate?*

GAIMAN: Of course. Oh definitely. Yes. And it also goes back to the very basic philosophy that writers are liars. The completely disingenuous answer to why some of these characters are gay is because that was how the character turned up in my head. Why is the Clurican a gay, alcoholic elf lord? That's the Clurican.

Q: *You said that you write people you know. Does this include the people you're friends with, your family? Are they in your books?*

GAIMAN: Not really, but occasionally reflected through an entire sequence of fun house mirrors. Wanda, for example in *A*

Game of You, is none of my transsexual friends. She's not any of the transsexuals I know.

On the other hand, I think Wanda got her genesis from hearing about a person, who is also the flatmate of a guy who has also now died, who was a transsexual who contracted AIDS through the blood transfusion during the operation. The last thing she read before she died was *The Doll's House*. I heard that and it sort of just kept sitting in my head, this sort of poor dead character. I suppose that combined with the fact, figuring there really hadn't been any transsexuals in comics, in literature. Actually, it wasn't that there hadn't been any transsexual characters in literature to that date, but it was that any transsexuals that I had run into in comics had obviously not been written by anybody who knew any transsexuals. They were just sort of beautiful women. You look at *Black Kiss*, the Howard Chaykin thing. And all of a sudden you discover one of the gorgeous women has a dick. And it's just another opportunity to draw another convoluted sexual thing. That has nothing to do with any other transsexuals I'd know, so I thought I'd do one who was. And what is nice the reaction I get, from transsexuals, to that character.

Q: *Do you think that the subject has become less taboo?*

GAIMAN: I don't really think about it. There have been gay characters in *Sandman* since *Sandman* #1. I never particularly expected any flack for it.

Q: *I know you caught some hell from The Concerned Mothers of America for "glorifying homosexuality."*

GAIMAN: And other things. I forget what they were. Oh that was fun. I liked that. It was a whole list of things, some of which didn't make very much sense. It was a very badly written letter. One assumes these people are twits.

I think, as far as I know, the gay characters in *Sandman* were probably the first gay characters in mainstream comics. What I think about that now is just how much has changed in comics in the past seven years.

In Retrospect

Q: *Looking back, and I know you're not completely through with The Sandman, is there anything you would change if you could?*

GAIMAN: In a perfect would, I think I would have taken a couple of years off after *Sandman* #50.

Q: *Why?*

GAIMAN: Because I was tired. I would have just gone out and done a lot more living and had a lot more fun, then come back and do *The Kindly Ones*. There was definitely a point in there where it wasn't a lot of fun. Having said that, I'm really, really enjoying doing *The Wake* and I'm really enjoying the last few stories. I'm really feeling back in my stride, which is nice.

Q: *Are there any artists that particularly captured your vision of your characters?*

GAIMAN: I think all of them did. I think part of the fun of *Sandman* was being this kid in a candy shop, starting out with people like Sam Keith and Mike Dringenberg, moving on to people like Kelly Jones, Charles Vess, Chris Bachalo—you have a wonderful range of artists in there.

Q: *How did G.K. Chesterton come to be the model for the character of Fiddler's Green in* The Sandman?

GAIMAN: I think because Fiddler's Green wanted a role model. He has that line about not being a very good human being, and then he says he wasn't a very good copy of a human being. I like Chesterton, he was so much larger than life and I wanted a character who was larger than life.

Q: *You even dedicated* Good Omens *to Chesterton, [reading the dedication]* "To a man . . ."

GAIMAN: "To a man who knew what was going on."

Q: *What did he know was going on? Where did your philosophies meet?*

GAIMAN: Talking to [*Good Omens* co-author] Terry Pratchett, it became obvious that both of us were frightened at an early age by a Chesterton book called *The Man Who Was Thursday*. And really the plot of *The Man Who Was Thursday* can be summarized into: "God is the devil; everybody who thinks they are working for God may be working for the devil or vice versa. Do not take everything at face value and do not be surprised when all the masks come off."

I think in many ways that was also that plot of *Good Omens* . . .

just the idea of ineffability. The idea that really you don't know what's going on, but it may well work out. It seemed like a very Chestertonian idea, a sort of gentle paradox.

Q: *Looking back on your career so far, and this is not exclusive to your work in comics, what have been your greatest disappointments?*

GAIMAN: The dissolution of Eclipse was definitely one of them, just not getting to finish the story I'd started in *Miracleman #17.*

I've been obscenely blessed with good luck and all that stuff. I can't think of anything that didn't fall through that was probably not for the best. Leaving aside the sort of on-going general disappointment of it being very rarely as good as it was in your head before you did it, there have been very few disappointments.

The biggest one was probably the Duran Duran book. It was one of those cheap and cheerful, cash-in rock biographies that you assemble by listening to each of the records twice, reading all the press clippings, and watching the videos. I remember when I wrote that first book, I was terribly hungry. They paid real money as an advance.

The publisher phoned up and said, "Listen, we were told that you might be willing to write a book for us. Would you like to do Barry Manilow, Def Leopard, or Duran Duran?" Barry Manilow had done many, many albums and there was actually a real book to write but I had *no* desire to write it. And Def Leopard, I had absolutely no desire to write. Duran Duran had only made three albums at the time. I said, "Well, three albums . . . they'll be around a few years."

I wrote the book in a frantic two weeks, handed it over, it came out a couple weeks later, was an immediate best seller. It sold its first print run in about a week. It was just about to go back to press and the company, Proteus Books, went into bankruptcy. I was really rather disappointed by this, I mean, they never went back for a second printing and it meant I never got royalties. All I ever got was the advance. On the other hand, had it been a big success, they were already trying to persuade me to do more books like that and I'm not sure I could have afforded to say no. So, that fact that I wound up getting burned was really good for me. It was sort of like, "OK, I won't do any more books that I don't want to do." That was that.

Q: *I saw Duran Duran on Greg Kinnear's show last week. They sang The Doors' "Crystal Ship." I think they're one of those bands that has a comeback album and then sort of hangs on forever.*

GAIMAN: Yeah, if only so that people know who they are when they ask me when I'm 60, "You really did a Duran Duran book?" I'll finally have gotten the Nobel Prize for literature and they will say, "We give this to Neil Gaiman for everything he's done *except* the Duran Duran book!!" I don't even have a copy. I don't know why I don't have a copy, but I don't.

Impact

Q: *You wrote this in the* Black Orchid *introduction: "I know that some people regard this writing as escapist fiction, but I think that tales of myth and horror are probably the easiest and most effective way to talk about the real world. They are like the lies that tell the truth about our lives."*

GAIMAN: Real life is a great big messy thing. The fantastic gets through the sort of protective cordon one has around one's head. One can go in and change the way people think about things. You spoke about Wanda earlier from *A Game of You*. The letters that we were getting when Wanda came on the scene were all from comic book fanboys going, "Eh, Eh, we don't like this. Eh, quit doing this to us."

By the last issue the same people were writing us saying, "I can't fucking believe this, they cut Wanda's hair before they buried her. That's obscene." It can change people's minds about things. You can get them to encounter things they would never otherwise encounter. And you can talk about true things.

A Game of You is all about the relationships between people and stories. It's about the dreams little boys have versus the dreams little girls have. It's about the fragility of identity. It's all about things that are big clomping elephantine things. But because there's all this weird and wonderful shit going down, they don't seem so clomping and elephantine. They go in through the defenses. They go in underneath the anti-aircraft fire.

Gene Wolfe once said, in a letter quoted in his book *Castle of Days*, and I'm misquoting here, "Good literature should be capable of being read once by an educated reader with enjoyment and reread with increased enjoyment." And that's always what I wanted to build in *The Sandman*—something that could be enjoyed. Something that you read it once and go, "Oh cool, that's the story." And then you go back and read it another time, in context of the graphic novel, and say, "Oh cool, that's how that tied in."

You can start at *Sandman* #1 and go all the way through after that point and see, "Shit, that bastard set that up all the way back there and I didn't realize it!" You should be able to do that. And then, hopefully, you can go back and read the whole thing again, in light of how it all finishes and what happens, and go, "Oh, O.K. I really did that character a disservice at the time." I want the reading experience to provide more.

Q: *Joseph Campbell said that in order for mythology to have power you must update it for every generation . . .*

GAIMAN: Yes, that's very true. When I created The Endless, I wanted to create a family of mythical beings every bit as cool and interesting as the Greek gods, but of whom the kind of people who were reading *Sandman* would say, "Oh, I know you. I can believe in you."

I realized that I'd probably done that when I got a letter a couple years ago from a reader saying she was going to be 18 in a few weeks' time and she decided it was time to pick a religion. She said she was going backwards and forwards between Buddhism and believing in The Endless, which I thought was rather sweet.

It really is *not* a religion . . . it is an inclusive religious structure. Everything is welcome. Nothing is untrue. All is true. In theory, you think the whole structure would collapse under a neatly eroded suspension of disbelief. But in actual fact, it worked fairly well. I'm still not entirely sure how or why, but it has.

NEIL GAIMAN IN WORDS AND PICTURES

Ben P. Indick

One of the brightest names in horror and fantasy writing today, blurbed almost embarrassingly on the wrappers of his many books by nearly every writer of any repute in the horror and fantasy genre who ever wanted to see his or her name in quasi-critical print, Gaiman has made it big in comics, short fiction, long fiction, novels and screenplays. Does he actually deserve the hoopla? This essay will examine several of his many graphic novel comics and a representative few of his early and most recent novels to see how he handles them.

Pictures

In 1987, Gaiman's graphic books *Violent Cases* and *Outrageous Tales of the Old Testament* brought him initial fame, followed by *Black Orchid*, and then his most successful, the *Sandman* series (1989-1996). The stories appeared initially as individual comic books, but were bound in hardcover later under collective titles. After Gaiman had been given, to the astonishment, and consternation, of many, the 1991 World Fantasy Conference Best Short Story award for "A Midsummer Night's Dream," which was a Sandman comic, there was even some suggestion that the rules should be amended to forbid awards being granted to comic strips. Fortunately, this was not actually done. However, obviously sufficient people thought his graphics were as outstanding as fiction. The young writer was obviously a force in fantasy with which to be reckoned.

Born in 1960, Gaiman was fascinated by fantasy literature and absorbed a sound background, which he would turn to his advantage in his stories, graphic and ordinary fiction. When he turned to the comic field in the 1980s, his work was revolutionary enough to turn the nature of the genre around. Whatever else might be said, it had a serious and often a literary content, without any relationship to previous "comic" strips other than form (and a few sentimental attachments to classics of the comics field). There would be no funny animals, no families, no adventure strips. His ambition was far broader. Using classical legend and sometimes biblical motifs, he intended to examine the soul of man and an existential meaning of life itself. Furthermore, he consciously adopted a cinematographic approach, in angles, close-ups, epic scenes and even interior thought, as he added graphic bursts to emphasize them, plus a crisp clarity of prose. The nature of the story as he conceived and directed it for the artwork was to lead very naturally in time to working in film itself, and his *Neverwhere*, which would appear soon as a novel, had its initial incarnation on BBC-TV in 1996. Currently he is working on full-fledged films.

Despite the immediate success of his graphics, restlessly he refused to be identified with a single style. We shall examine just a few of his books as illustration. *The Doll's House*, "produced" and introduced by Clive Barker, a major Gaiman enthusiast and nearly a mentor, is a collection of interconnected short stories, which range from genuine human feeling to blatant sensationalism. "Sandman" is a generic title covering the entire series. A supra-mundane "family," Destiny, Desire, Delirium, Delight and Death, controls the world of the Sandman. Although they would seem to be of legendary status (and the Norns even make an appearance) they resemble Greek gods and goddesses far less than they do a collection of British punk rockers, spiky hair and torn clothing and skin decorations and bangles. In a poignant prelude, "The Sound of Her Wings," Death is a very pale young woman who does not express any emotions visibly, but is nevertheless internally feeling and caring. She visits humans for their last such visit, although it may be a prior one as well. Once a young man, playing basketball in the street, sees her and tells her hopes he will meet her again. She tells him, mysteriously, that he will, which he cannot appreciate. Shortly thereafter a car fatally hits him. Unaware that he is dead, he is happy to see her, but she takes his arm, and guides him to a crowd standing around a car. "There's something you maybe oughta see," she tells him. Dramatically proper, the sequence stops here. A mother leaves her baby to get it a bottle. Death comes first. She picks up and holds the baby. It speaks, knowing her. "But . . . is that all there is? Is that all I get?" it asks, helplessly, poignantly. "Yes," she replies, unemotionally, but still holding it. "I'm afraid so," she adds. The mother returns to her child and sees it lying there in its crib, still. She screams in anguish. An old Jewish violinist, weak and dying, sees Death approach him. First he begs. "No! Not yet . . . please?" Then, realizing it is the end, does what he has rarely done, recites the *Sh'ma*, a Hebrew prayer affirming the oneness of God.

"The Doll's House" itself follows, one of his most finished in the series and worthy of close examination as revealing his style and interests. A young woman, Rose Walker, has flown from America to England with her mother to the home of a rich woman, whom they do not know, but who has asked them to come and has even paid their travel expenses. She tells them she is, unknown to them, mother and grandmother, respectively, to each, and wants to make amends. They will be rich. There is also, they learn, another child, a brother to Rose, Jed, younger than she. The story follows Rose back to America, searching for Jed, often in fantastical circumstances, sometimes merely extraordinarily dreamed sequences. In her rooming house, she becomes friendly with a very heavy older British man, known only as "Gil" or "Gilbert." If the reader is aware of Gaiman's tastes in authors, or even of how the author actually looked, he knows this man represents one of his favorites, G(ilbert) K. Chesterton. Like adding icing to the cake, Gaiman adds the propensity of Chesterton to get involved in vague religious exegesis, although Rose usually curbs this. Nevertheless, he is a self-appointed protector for Rose, until, ultimately, after he has aided her for the final time, Gilbert must leave, as Dream, here for Death's task, approaches her. Reality abruptly intervenes in Gaiman's and the Sandman's world. Gilbert apologizes "for not being a very good human being, not even a very good copy of a human, perhaps I should say."

In another instance of his love for classic fantasy, this time in the graphic comic form, Gaiman constructs a loving if sardonic pastiche of Winsor McKay's brilliant early twentieth century comic, "Little Nemo in Slumberland." Each Sunday episode of Little Nemo, generally acknowledged as the most beautiful comic strip ever created, ended, after a dream in gorgeous *art nouveau* coloring and wild imagination, plus superb art of bodies in space, with the earthbound clunk in the final panel of Nemo falling out of bed, and some drab statement about eating the wrong thing at dinner. Gaiman's version, interpolated into the action of the book only several times, is entitled "In the Land of Marvelous Dreams," and artist Dave McKean has aptly captured the essence of McKay, all the royal presences Nemo generally encountered, but dolled up this time as comic book superheroes, and the final waking up, unfortunately for his Nemo-surrogate, transmogrified into a gruesome moment of horror. Thus, his mother, hearing him clunking out of bed, rather than McKay's simple scold, tells him, to emphasize the horror of the dream Gaiman has given Rose, as Nemo lies on his blanket, "Shut up you little bastard, or I'll really give you something to scream about!" Worse, in a second dream, curious, he frees a few gerbils, who immediately multiply, genuine McKay manner, to a horde, but of rats, not gerbils, and they gnaw at his face.

Part Four, "Men of Good Fortune," is a fine bird's-eye view of much of British literary history, and includes fleeting glimpses of Chaucer, Marlowe, Jonson, Shakespeare and more, moving beyond the past to Restoration, Victorian and Edwardian, including an encounter with Jack the Ripper, right into modern times, when Mrs. Thatcher comes in for a comment, all via a man who never died, although at the end Death joins him in a crowded pub. The daring of the concept is only matched by the ability to pull it off, although the story promptly returns to the travails of Rose, for soon she will face a murderous pedophilic rapist.

Rose must endure many adventures, often repulsive or horror-laden, with killers and fantastic fiends, but finally, her grandmother, who has died, appears, as a young woman now, and is able to save her in a beautiful garden scene, and even have her brother returned. The trauma of the events, however, has been so heavy on her that Rose buries herself from society, until at last she is able to face a return to full life.

A brief summary captures neither the beauty that is here, nor, it must be added, the portentous weight of much of the dialogue, overloaded with symbolic baggage. Simplicity and subtlety are not part of the Sandman, or, perhaps, the comic milieu in general. It remains a literal medium, where a picture *must* tell a thousand words. The book remains, nevertheless, a triumph for the author and the genre, for its ambitions and for what it achieves.

Season of Mists followed, in size and format similar to its predecessor, but with less emphasis on the cinematographic style, and more a return to normal comic book pattern of panels on a page. There are no deliberate McKay "Little Nemo" pastiche scenes, except in the opening scene, Episode 0 (*sic*), and the Prologue, when Destiny calls the family of gods together, they meet in such splendid baroque halls as Nemo walked (or climbed). For such potent entities, they remain, visibly at least, British punk rockers, except for Death, goaded by Destiny, who walks somberly about in a hooded and floor-length monk's robe and carries an enormous book, into dressing "appropriately." Death does indeed dress in an attractive and modest closed-neck black dress with full skirt and high heeled boots, a not unattractive Death at all. Pages of textual words, imprinted over or alongside pastel colored artwork follow, as the qualities of each one are described, but this is an interruption of the graphic flow and invites skipping over, no less so for the shallow and pretentious gravity of those words.

This will, in some measure, persist throughout until the end when the value of Hell itself is the subject, but there are scenes that are fine exceptions. A delightful sidelight scene in Episode One, which precedes Chapter 1 and contrasts nicely by its wit to the blather of a traditionally bat-winged Lucifer and his staff of demons running around conscious of their power, and offers humor to the literary loves of the author. The illustration portrays a library in a branch of Hell, modest in itself, but, in one scene of McKay-designed proportions quite beautiful, with a robed and bookish Lucien in charge. He is discoursing about his collection with a friendly raven (who says "Nevermore" when Poe is mentioned). This library is more than just books. It contains the novels their authors *never wrote*, or never finished, except in dreams. On the top shelf one may see and dream of the marvels within such non-existent titles as "The Return of Edwin Drood" by Charles Dickens, "The Dark God's Darlings" by Lord Dunsany, "Poictesme Babylon" by James Branch Cabell, "The Lost Road" by J.R. R. Tolkien, and among more, "The Man Who Was October" by G. K. Chesterton.

Thereafter the weight of words and crowded, busy art is only relieved occasionally and by brief but sparkling moments such as "the Silver City" which exists out of Time and Space as we know them, or Episode 4, when Charles Rowland "concludes his education" by gaining exacting revenge on his tormentors, and decides then and there with his friend Edwin that he has had enough, although still a boy, of school and it is time for life. They stride on out.

The Sandman series continued, but in 1995, the ever-adventurous Gaiman wrote a graphic variation, *The Tragical Comedy or Comical Tragedy of Mr. Punch*. This is a larger sized volume, and the art is a mixture of photographs (sometimes featuring clay sculptures), hand-drawn illustrations, as well as a mixture of the two. The typeface script is not in block letters but is hand-written, as though for autobiography. The counterpoint to the expressed memories is the invariable violence and mayhem of the well-known pair of British village hand-puppet characters Punch and Judy, here drawn and sometimes sculptured traditionally. The drawings of the young protagonist as the narrator remembers himself (as from an old photograph) are mostly unvarying. His face is seen in sharply chiseled features at ¾ frontal, which leaves little room for any variety of expression. He is unnamed, but describes each of his older relations by name, once in a little piece of artwork he had drawn, as he says he remembers best in minia-ture and the art depicts a vague picture of his head, with an old photo of two children, with, presumably, parents behind them, superimposed over it. He recalls a stay with his grandparents. His grandfather, Arthur, eventually had gone mad, but first he had owned a small arcade, with a Punch and Judy show, and his grandson associates him with Punch, who usually acts in a manic manner. Arthur sometimes argues with a Mr. Swatchell, a man who occasionally works for him, and once tells the narrator about the earlier life his grandfather had lived.

"I had heard," he writes, thinking of his boyhood, that nowa-days, considering the violence common to Punch and Judy, "they had sweetened the show," but it is untrue. Going to a churchyard presentation of the violent old classic, he soon discovers Punch is his irascible nasty self. He pleads his innocence to the audience of children, who all condemn him, after which he throws a baby puppet out the window and fights with his wife. A policeman puppet appears, to the laughter of the audience, except, he re-members, for himself, as a boy, when he became ill and fled the tent, hearing "Mister Punch's shrill inhuman voice as he beat the policeman to death."

He remembers the attraction of his grandfather's arcade, a treat gratis to the customers, of a mermaid in a tank, combing her hair and singing. Someone tells him snidely that her suit will soon fit no longer, but he is too young to know about pregnancy. He learns about "bottlers," who pass the hat for money after the performance, and also laugh to encourage the audience's laughter, but his dreams are filled with nightmares induced by the puppets. He recalls staying with his grandmother, and his parents calling, to tell him he will shortly have a baby brother or sister, but does not care when the baby is born whichever sex it is. He wonders whether his father will throw the baby out of the window. In time he overhears a fight at the arcade between several men and a woman, behind a screen. The woman comes running out, crying, holding her stomach. He recognizes the mermaid. In time, his grandfather, mad, has to be hospitalized, where he dies. As his parents drive him home, past the sea, he thinks he sees a woman swimming in the stormy Channel, and that she has waved at him, but the cold wind makes his eyes sting and he blinks. When he looks again, she is gone. As the story ends, an adult now, he has visited the Punch and Judy show in the local church. He enters, and talks to the man in charge, and thinks he sees hunched in a corner Mr. Swatchell. He could not, of course have been there, but the "professor" in charge, for all Punch puppeteers are called "professor," is friendly. He shows the narrator a gadget used to make the voice of Punch, a little contraption of cotton, tin and tape. It is called a "swatchell." The professor offers him a mask of Punch to try on, but he cannot and draws away. He cannot put it on. A bottler approaches him. "For the showman, sir?" she asks. He leaves the courtyard, shivering, although the weather is warm, to go on with his life. The book's final artwork is a crumpled Punch lying, as though finally dead, on the stage, in a profusion of coins.

The story is a non-sentimentalized, stark memory, with no overt fantasy nor overstatement, a picture of the innocent child's mind in the dark, enigmatic world of the adult. It is brilliantly illustrated, with some attention to effect as might be achieved by cinema, and simply narrated. The mercurial Gaiman offers a view of one of the many directions he will take.

Words

In 1990 Gaiman, already known for his comics, which were appearing in individual episodes, and collected later in book form, collaborated with Terry Pratchett, author of the irreverent *Discworld* novels, on *Good Omens: The Nice and Accurate Prophe-*

cies of Agnes Nutter, Witch. The book begins, appropriately, "In the Beginning," which is probably the last logical thing in the madcap novel. It is concerned with a prophecy made in the seventeenth century by Agnes about the imminence of Armageddon, which she said would come on a Saturday. The book introduces its biblical and other characters, saunters eleven years forward and then goes on a daily countdown, from Wednesday through that final presumably tumultuous Saturday. Except it is not all that tumultuous and, as it generally does, Sunday follows. The difficulty with the prediction was, typically for Mrs. Nutter, that her prophecies could not be understood until "after the thing had happened." However, enough unbelievable things happened so that the broad title of Sunday is subtitled "The first day of the rest of their lives."

The book actually emerges as a manic Monty Python ride through a wacky, often hilarious biblically inspired world. It includes a rebirth of Satan in the apparent guise of that baby Rosemary bore, along with hopeless demons whose understanding was so limited they would have missed such sure-fire tortures as "Welsh-language television. Or value-added tax. Or Manchester." They were "fourteenth-century minds, the lot of them. Spending years picking away at one soul. With five million people in the world, you couldn't pick the buggers off one by one any more; you had to spread your effort."

On the other hand, the Chattering Order of Saint Beryl represents virtue. In a sober footnote, Saint Beryl Articulatus is reputed to have been martyred in the middle fifth century. Betrothed against her will, she prayed for a miracle such as a beard, and laid by a small razor. Instead she was granted by the Lord the miraculous ability to chatter continually about whatever was on her mind, however inconsequential, without pause for breath or food. One version of her tragic death is that she was strangled by her husband, still virginal and still chattering. However, another version held that he bought himself a set of earplugs and that she died in bed with him, at the age of 62.

An interesting counterpart is Sister Mary Loquacious, a devout Satanist. She adores His baby, but is disappointed when she sees no "teensy-weensy little hoofkins. Or a widdle tail." Worse yet, no horns. Still, she counts his "little teensy-toesies," happily reassured he is indeed the Antichrist. Anything can happen as the evil forces, that is, the authors, for whom nothing is sacred, assemble, even a pie in the face, although the British refer to it as a "cream cake." Whichever, it lands fully in the face of Aziraphale, a demon. The book goes on and on, with a lot, an awful lot, of talk, but really, these demons are ultimately quite harmless. They couldn't lick a lollypop. The book, incidentally, is dedicated to the memory of the great fantasist, G. K. Chesterton, "a man who knew what was going on." Chesterton would be a major character in a Sandman novel, *The Doll's House.*

Gaiman collaborated after this lark with artists for his graphic novels, but for his novels dependent on words, he would be his own master. In 1997, *Neverwhere,* his debut solo novel, appeared, a *tour de force* on a not unfamiliar theme. Here we find a sub-culture that worships rats, fondles poisonous centipedes of extraordinary length, offers gory visions of individuals such as the heroine's brother floating bloodily and very dead in a pool, lives lived in sewers known and unknown to man, and much more. No, it is not Clive Barker. It just seems that way, and scarce wonder. Barker himself can be very inventive and revels in the omission of logic from his equations. There is actually a certain hectic and unexpected fun in this trick. Plus, the addition of bits of gruesome horror popping up like chocolate chips in a luscious chocolate cake. Indeed, Barker's effusive approval in culinary terms is quoted on the dust jacket: "Gaiman is a star. He con-structs stories like some demented cook might make a wedding cake, building layer upon layer, including all kinds of sweet and sour in the mix." The taste of "sweet and sour" adds an element of mystery to the "wedding cake" for the reader, and the result may not be unappealing.

What the novel indisputably is, however, is a portrait of an ordinary little man, indeed a veritable textbook case and defini-tion of the genre. He is Richard Mayhew by name, a meek ex-ample of what was once referred to, in a much milder comic strip than those Gaiman successfully turned out for years prior to this novel as "The Timid Soul," in the brilliant single panel drawn for newspapers for years by H. T. Webster, usually featuring the appropriately named Caspar Milquetoast. Uncomplainingly and patiently pushed around by his boss, his fellow employees and his overbearing fiancée (wife in Caspar's case), giving in to all with-out a murmur, he persists in his anonymous compliance to an unfair Fate. Unlike Mr. Milquetoast, who never alters his ways, by chance Richard Mayhew stumbles into an unfamiliar, fantastic world where, eventually, he establishes his manhood. Along the way, Mayhew is conducted by a characteristically gorgeous black woman (in distinction to the Keyes-eyed waif Door, his usual companion) from the sub-culture in which he has found himself, to a block party at Harrods, London's major department store. It is not quite the familiar Harrods, for it is accoutered with sales items this culture seeks, "from dreams to useless piles of shit."

Interestingly, one of Richard Mayhew's Milquetoastian predecessors, who successfully established the genre for countless successors, was Hector Owen, Thorne Smith's meek hero in his classic comedy, *Rain in the Doorway*, who also stepped into a department store doorway 70 years ago, to escape the rain, and found a department store such as Macy's or Lord and Taylor never dreamed of. The wildly fantastic hidden culture Richard Mayhew discovered when he helped what appeared to be a young woman crumpled and bleeding on a sidewalk (Door), and took her to his apartment to bandage her, beggars by any odds except merit, however, the humorous and by today's standard mildly erotic doings of Smith's fantastical other world. Mr. Owen engages in very high and champagne-flavored life of the Art Deco era, and Mayhew unexpectedly echoes that era, at the staid British Museum, which he visits with Door to steal a valuable supernatural item that the curators were possibly unaware they possessed. As Mayhew looks at the broad steps leading up to the museum, he thinks that he is "going to go home. Everything is going to be normal again. Boring again." Then he decides those steps "were made to be danced down by Fred Astaire and Ginger Rogers." Impromptu and caught up by the magic of the moment, and the newly gained sense of living in an unpredictable life, he does a soft shoe version of Astaire, even doffing his imaginary top hat to the giggling Door.

A pair of inventions by Gaiman give the book much of its sparkle, one being a pair of seemingly unconquerable villains, very formal in conversation to one another and to each of their victims, in the best of British dramatic and even Music Hall style, and these are Mr. Croup and Mr. Vandomar, who commit unspeakably nasty acts while engaging in the lightest and even most courteous of vocal banter. Villains, after all, do make the literary pie interesting, and these are champions. It is nearly a tragedy to see them falling, one after the other, without losing their dignity, into a bottomless void. The other is an unlikely heroic figure, haughty and serenely confident in his royal and royally bedraggled garments, as well as lacking an initial capital, the marquis de Carabas. Not only can he be relied upon in moments of hazard, but, at the conclusion, when Richard, unhappy back in the mundane world he has abandoned, outlines a door upon a brick wall, the marquis appears there, irritated at Richard's unseeing hesitation. "Well," he asks, "are you coming?" and "they walk off together, leaving nothing behind them, not even the doorway."

Mr. Owen had one impediment Mr. Mayhew lacked: he had a wife, not a mere socially conscious, status-driven girlfriend; but in neither case is the woman a hindrance. Ultimately each is shucked. Owen's Lulu, thinking he had died, had remarried, much to Owen's delight now, for he has a more than adequate replacement; and Jessica, the socially-conscious woman who had harried his life, has abandoned him (while retaining the engagement ring). While Richard does not go off into normal life bearing a new woman on his manly arm, one who has brought light, excitement and danger into his life, as does Hector, Richard does discover the return route to the hidden world he had ruefully thought he had abandoned, when the marquis appears at the doorway he had sketched. It is not too much to hope that the Lady Door, a contraction for Doreen, will be there and very likely waiting for him. Why should a man seventy years his senior get all the breaks?

A year later, Gaiman, after his own manner, ready if not anxious to prove he could produce something quite unexpected of a creator already famous for uniquely different graphic stories and a weird and occasionally horrific novel, published a follow-up novel differing completely from *Neverwhere*. This was *Stardust*, for the inspiration of which he thanks many classic fantasy writers, whom he enumerates as Hope Mirrlees, Lord Dunsany, James Branch Cabell and C. S. Lewis, for "showing me that fairy stories were for adults too." He is unfair to himself. *Stardust*, with only a few reader tsk-tsks and mutterings of "Oh! that irrepressible Gaiman!" for occasional naughtiness, is equally delightful and actually intended for young people who love and understand a breath of romance, fantasy and beauty. His novel may even inspire some of them to investigate those predecessors, and see how Gaiman's writing is indebted to or differs from those prede-cessors.

The story is simple enough, commencing in the dull and com-monplace backwoods English village of Wall, at some time in the past, a long-ago past. There is actually a wall, high and gray, of "hewn granite," but what makes it unique is a six-foot wide opening, unfenced, with what appears to be merely a pleasant wooded area stretching off into the distance beyond it, but never-theless forbidden in access to anyone. Each day and night as well two villagers stand guard to be certain it is not trespassed, from either direction, and it never is. With the exception of every ninth year, when a great Fair is held, indeed, a Faerie Market, and pos-sibly at this time some unusual individuals may appear from the world beyond the wall. Young Dunstan Thorn, fresh from guard duty at the breach, encounters a "tall gentleman in a black hat" who needs a room for the night. Dunstan generously offers him his own, and will sleep in the shed, and the tall man, accepting, tells Dunstan that he will meet his "heart's desire" the next day.

It is charming, if typical stuff of fantasy until the next day, when Dunstan buys a pretty glass bell, perhaps as a gift for his Daisy Hempstock, from a beautiful girl at a faery stand, a girl with the furry ears of a cat but haunting violet eyes, and who wears a fine silver chain binding her to the stand. She sighs when he inquires about the chain, and says she cannot be free of it until there are two Mondays in a week and the Moon loses a sister. However, if he will return that evening, "when the moon goes down," she says, coquettishly, she will show him other things. Dunstan returns, fascinated by her, and perhaps in love. He does return and hoots like an owl, as she had instructed him. She appears. "What do you want from life?" she asks. "I don't know," he says, "you, I guess."

They kiss and embrace, and make passionate love. Afterward, she straightens herself and says, "Now get along with you," and kisses him "with lips that tasted of crushed blackberries," and then she leaves. The next day the Fair is over and the fields beyond the wall are empty. Dunstan finally marries his Daisy, but nine months later a basket is found at the breach, having been pushed through, and within it, a little baby boy, and, on a note pinned to his blanket is a name, Tristran Thorn. The story will be his.

Years have passed and Tristran is a young man, and adores

Victoria Forester, an attractive young village woman who had not seemed to be aware of his existence, but one night they speak, and he tells her he would like to marry her. A star falls in the evening sky above and, laughing, she promises him "anything you desire" if he can recover the star and bring it to her. It had fallen beyond the wall, and, the next day, Tristran, carrying the glass bell his father had never forgotten and had given him now for his journey, passes "beyond the fields we know" through the space and into Faerie. The expression is, of course, from the respectful Gaiman's acknowledged master, Lord Dunsany in his masterpiece, *The King of Elfland's Daughter* and Gaiman will use it several times, just as he uses some of the stylistic mannerisms of Cabell, although he will not match the literary elegance and brilliance of a Dunsany or a Cabell. Not yet, anyway, but he is young, although, perhaps, too much in a hurry with other productions. For that matter, several times he uses the subtitle of a Tolkien masterpiece for children, "there and back again," although his story is not in the adventurous mode of the great master.

Tristran will have many adventures and will meet many interesting, or humorous or even dangerous individuals in the land of Faery, and he will never be other than his own sweet and unassuming self. He will encounter witches and warlocks, a unicorn, a goblin-sized man and a witch who, changing him into a dormouse, appears to have become a giant. He will sit atop clouds and ride sky ships, which capture lightning bolts in metal cans and take port on harbor-trees. He will meet, as had his father, the beautiful violet-eyed lady with the furry ears of a cat, and will know she is his true mother. When, finally, he returns to Wall, and sees another Faery Market being readied, he feels more in common with the Faerie folk than with "the pallid folk of Wall in their worsted jackets and their hobnailed boots." To tell all of his adventures is to deprive the reader of a charming, gentle, whimsical fantasy, as unexpected in Gaiman's oeuvre as it is welcome. Exception, however, must be made for Yvaine, who is nothing less than the falling star he has sought to bring back to Wall for Victoria. But as she sleeps beneath a sky "filled with the twinkling of a thousand stars, the star-woman glittered too, as if she had been brushed by the Milky Way." She will be his love, and he will have to satisfy Victoria, break the spell that has enchained his mother, and save the star from crossing the breach in the wall, which, should she do so, she will become a stone meteorite, lost forever. *Stardust* is a magical confection, worthy of a place near the great fantasies.

Having moved from his native Britain to the United States in 1992[2], Gaiman has made himself entirely at home, and his most recent novel demonstrates a comprehensive travelogue of the primarily small-town America with the virtuosity of a seasoned tourist guide. In *American Gods*,[3] Shadow, his hero, traverses the continent like a Humbert Humbert, without a precocious snot of a little girl but with a larger-than-life, cigar-chomping, ingratiating, brilliant, colloquial and finally treacherous one-eyed man who twists reality as the ordinary man might know it into shapes more to his needs. This is a novel of myths and reality, and the planes across which they intersect. Every religion has myth at its core, and in time the truth is impossible to ascertain with certainty. We read in linguistic and historical journals and then in newspapers that no Israelite ever lived in ancient Egypt, that no hard evidence has ever been found for the positive existence of Jesus Christ or Buddha. Even in literature the same uncertainty persists: did an individual named Homer ever exist to tell those stories? Was "the man from Stratford" really the author of Shakespeare's plays? Mythology, however, has its own power of becoming real. America, in Gaiman's view, has become the repository for the gods of the world, and is simultaneously creating new gods, new mythologies. His laconic, physically strong but passive protagonist, Shadow, encounters many of them, from goblins and leprechauns to "all-powerful" world movers, and the long novel flows around him and his experiences.

Shadow is paroled after serving three years out of a sentenced ten in prison, for a crime he had not committed but which he had served to spare Laura, his loving but unfaithful wife. He will always love even after he discovers she had died in an automobile accident with a lover on whom she was practicing what was once

---

2   Gaiman is quoted on his Internet website as saying he always wanted to live in an "Addams Family type of house." He found it near Minneapolis, Minn., where he lives with his wife and three children.

3   *American Gods*, William Morrow, New York, 2001

considered an unnatural act. She had been a travel agent and had obtained air travel accommodations for him. He uses them despite knowing she has just died, and on the plane ends up through seat confusion sitting in first class next to a large, jovial, and amazingly knowledgeable man. What is amazing about his knowledge is that he knows all about Shadow and likely was responsible for the seating difficulties that caused Shadow to end up in the seat next to him. "Why don't you call me Wednesday?" he tells Shadow, "Mister Wednesday. Although given the weather, it might as well be Thursday, eh?" he adds, as Gaiman once again offers obeisance to his beloved G. K. Chesterton.[4] Wednesday, who has one glass eye, offers him a job, which will entail lots of traveling, and even more blind obedience, without explanations, but the pay is good and Shadow has nothing else. He is, after all, only going to a funeral, although he will discover Laura never remains entirely dead.

Shadow rarely expresses his own desires thereafter, simply observes and rarely acts, at least until the climax, but had he wanted to do small-city, backwater town Americana sightseeing, he will have his full, from Wisconsin, to Illinois, Las Vegas, Mount Rushmore, Georgia and elsewhere through the South. Although Wednesday never offers him background information, Shadow comes to realize the enterprise on which they are so pre-occupied is concerned with nothing less than the survival of ancient gods who have come in past times from all over the world to America. Primarily they consist of the Norse gods, who had arrived here before Leif the Fortunate (Erickson) "rediscovered that land, which he would call Vineland," coming as silent baggage with earlier explorers, and when Leif came, "Tyr, one-handed, and gray Odin gallows-god, and Thor of the thunders" were here, waiting. Readers who recall their Norse mythology will recall Wotan, or Odin, had, like Wednesday, only one eye. Shadow, although he had whiled away hours in his cell with Herodotus, on classical history, had not had time to read up on northern gods. He catches on quickly, however.

---

4   Wednesday even quotes Chesterton: "There," he says, about a dull waitress, "is one who 'does not have the faith and will not have the fun.' Chesterton."

After A.D. 813 other gods came to the new land, from different traditions. Cousin Jack, a Cornishman, comes early in colonial times of Virginia to see Essie Tregowan, the widow Richardson, her children grown and gone, her husband dead, and the stranger is dressed all in green. "It was you," he says sadly, not unkindly, "that brought me here, you and a few folks like you, into this land with no time for magic and no place for piskies and such folk, and they go off hand in hand, leaving her aged body behind. More exotic gods come. Compé Anansi, or "Mr. Nancy," whom Shadow meets in a strange arcade, "an old black man with a pencil moustache, in his check sports jacket and his lemon-yellow gloves," and Mama-ji, from India who appears to be just an old woman, "her dark face pinched with age and disapproval," but another glance might see her as a "huge, naked woman with skin as black as a leather jacket, and lips and tongue the bright red of arterial blood. Around her neck were skulls, and her many hands held knives, and swords, and severed heads." From Egypt, "a crane-like man with gold-rimmed spectacles," accompanied by a black dog with a long-snout, who can talk, sarcastically at that. It is the jackal god, who, together with Mr. Ibis, runs a funeral parlor as *Ibis and Jacquel,* appropriately, in Cairo[5]—Illinois. Jacquel complains to Shadow that business is bad and their savings are dwindling. The gods are very much down to earth, and their conversation can be very ungodlike. Of other migrant Egyptian gods, they warn Shadow "Horus is crazy. Really bugfuck crazy, spends all his time as a hawk, eats roadkill, what kind of life is that? We arrived and America just didn't care that we'd arrived."

Wednesday, however, quibbles about Johnny Appleseed, who was much less than his legend, "If the truth isn't big enough, you print the legend. The country needs its legends. And even the legends don't believe it anymore." Shadow remonstrates. "But you see it." Wednesday snaps, "I'm a has-been. Who the fuck cares about me?" Shadow is not finished. "You're a god," he points out. Wednesday slumps. "So?" he asks. Shadow is stubborn. "It's a good thing to be a god." Wednesday's closing comment is "Is it?"

5   For the uninitiated, Gaiman spells it out phonetically as pronounced by the locals, "Kay-ro."

That is the problem. Thirteen hundred years after they had started coming, they have lost much of their power. Quite transmogrified now from their legendary appearance and powers, they have become "down-at-heel" in appearance as he describes them, making do against new gods such as, first, the railroads, then the automobiles, later the shopping centers, credit cards and ATM machines, all venerated and worshipped. Thor, disillusioned entirely, Shadow is told, had laid down his hammer one day in 1932 and put a pistol into his mouth, and blown his brains out. However, Wednesday is uninterested in allegory; a rival group is trying to create a god-destroying war of extermination, and Shadow's function is to help him in the final combat. Wednesday will apparently be murdered at truce talks with the shadowy enemy, but events work out in unexpected ways for Shadow, whose last major travel is to Reykjavik in Iceland, where he learns about the ways of gods. He decides "he had had enough of gods and their ways to last him several lifetimes" and what he will do is keep moving.

In this most ambitious of his works, Gaiman demonstrates a remarkable grasp of figures of legend, and chooses to present them as less than all-powerful, possessed of a dazzlingly accurate if profane speech pattern, entirely adapted to the milieu in which they live but still fascinating. Death is only another phase of life, and like Shadow, a master prestidigitator in the manipulation of coins, Gainem is a master magician himself. The future is inexplicable, even when it has become the present. The book is like none other of his or of any other writer, and provokes laughter frequently and tears occasionally. Ultimately, it is mystifying.

In 2002 Gaiman did a one-step from *Stardust*, his novel for a young adult as well as adult audience, and issued a short novel for children of "Ages 8 and up." *Coraline* is the eponymous heroine of a fantasy in which the dauntless young heroine opens an unused door in her home and finds it faces a brick wall. She uncovers a passage through the wall and enters a neighboring house. To her surprise, it is a skewed mirror version of her own home, complete even to parents who look the same as her own, call her "darling" and are otherwise appropriately affectionate and do not want her to leave. Nevertheless, Coraline has forebodings. They turn out all too true. Love is not here. She has many adventures, some genuinely frightening, before she finally is able to return to her own proper home. Along the way, she and the author have fun with frequent mispronunciation of her name as the more familiar "Caroline," the only touch of humor in a dark tale. Despite its obvious relationship to Lewis Carroll's immortal heroine and her adventures in a mirror world, the subtext here, whether or not intended by the author, is a potent comment on the situation of today's child in an age of divorce, pulled between two homes and two arrangements of parents. Possibly for this reason, Gaiman does not attempt to catch the wonder as well as the inspired nonsense and the loveliness of its poetry of *Alice Through the Looking Glass*, although he does indeed capture the ugly horror of W. F. Harvey's short horror story "The Beast With Five Fingers" at the climax with a crawling hand in pursuit of the heroine.

This is a writer who has earned the kudos which has showered down on him, and his readers await his next novel impatiently, aware it will present yet another aspect of this amazingly multi-dimensional writer. *Prodigious* would appear to be the most descriptive term.

Pictures

The Sandman / The Doll's House, © 1990 DC Comics, New York, previously published in single magazine form as *Sandman* 8-16, © 1989, 1990, Introduction by Clive Barker.

The Sandman / Season of Mists, © 1992 DC Comics, New York, previously published in single magazines as *Sandman* 21-28, 1990, 1991, Introduction by Harlan Ellison.

The Tragical Comedy or Comical Tragedy of Mr. Punch, © 1995, Vertigo/DC Comics, New York.

Words

Good Omens, Neil Gaiman and Terry Pratchett, Workman Publishing, New York, 1990.

Neverwhere, Neil Gaiman, Avon Books, New York, 1997.

Stardust, Neil Gaiman, Avon Books, Inc., New York, 1999.

PAY ATTENTION: THERE MAY OR MAY NOT BE A MAN BEHIND THE CURTAIN: AN ANALYSIS OF NEIL GAIMAN & DAVE McKEAN'S *VIOLENT CASES*

JaNell Golden

Violent Cases, a graphic novel by Neil Gaiman and Dave McKean, is the story of a memory of a young child. The story, told in a first person adult perspective, is of a seemingly chance series of interactions with Al Capone's osteopath, leading up to the osteopath's inevitable death for deserting Capone after Capone's arrest for tax evasion. Gaiman, through his dialogue and Dave McKean's artwork, has teasingly presented himself as the person telling this story. The very first panel is of Gaiman, himself, lighting a cigarette, preparing to speak. "I" appears three times in the dialogue before even the ambiguous "we" appears. There is no definition of who the "we" mentioned is, although the implication is that "we" are sitting down for an intimate chat of some sort. The child pictured is Gaiman himself, as a child; the father, Gaiman's father. Through the blending of reality, cultural memory, and history, Gaiman's and McKean's story-telling skills turn an otherwise simple childhood memory into an edgy, disturbing enigma.

Gaiman and McKean make good use of psychological technique throughout *Violent Cases.* One recurring motif is the repetition of stars. Gaiman and McKean play with the multiple meanings of the symbolism of stars throughout the book. People routinely put stars next to the information that they most want you to pay attention to; stars can also be representative of guidance, and revelation. Here the stars are also used to link incidents and characters in a linear fashion as well, as if to say "and here is where my father and the hitmen act in a similar manner."

A magician, who appears throughout the book repeatedly, wears a costume that is covered in moons and stars; beyond the usual representation of mystical, celestial knowledge they seem to spread maliciously over the panels far beyond the edges of the mage's robe, often obfuscating the other objects in the scenes. The star also appears in the osteopath's glasses as he tells the child that he will see once more before he, the osteopath, "goes"; he has realized that his reckoning for deserting Capone has almost arrived. "I said I'd see you before I went, didn't I?" asks the osteopath near the end, handing the child a drink that, blurry in the osteopath's hand, comes into sharp focus, revealing a neatly crescent-shaped peel pierced by a star-topped stirring stick.

As the mage comes into this scene, having pulled off his robe, stars seem to spill out onto the scene, hovering; later they drift off the mage's tie as he closes the curtains between the party that the child is attending and the bar from which the osteopath is guided by baseball-bat-wielding men with star-like eyes and, in one case, ". . . a diamond glinting in a front tooth." The diamond not only glints as if seen through a star filter but is followed in the next panel by a repeated image of an extraordinarily bright star, seen by the Gaiman character at age sixteen. As he says earlier in the story, recounting seeing this unusual star in the night sky where everything was "illuminated by a freezing white light," "there are those bits of one's memory that simply do not work—or do not work in relationship to the rest of it, anyway." This seems to indicate some sort of epiphany, a sudden realization of what really happened to the osteopath; that "there was nothing about (his) star in the news the next day, and (he) never met anyone else who has experienced a similar phenomenon" reinforces the deliberate use of this powerful symbol of enlightenment. It was a very personal vision, singular to him; a sudden interpretation of events from a more adult knowledge.

The tone of the story, claustrophobic and often jarring, is set from the very first page: the panels seem to wander vaguely over inanimate objects, focusing briefly on a bottle, the detail of a hat rack, the blurry slices of human form, stopping momentarily on a cramped headshot of a young Gaiman; bits and pieces of what may be another person appear. Finally, at the very bottom of the page, a claustrophobic shot of his father; the parts of his father's profile seem only there to outline a void centered in the panel. There is, in fact, a series of completely black panels immediately previous to the appearance of the father, broken up only by a

hand, or part of a sleeve, against solid black, as if it were too difficult to see the whole person, or the whole situation; or rather, as if
it were too difficult to understand the whole, and so, slices are
focused on. When we finally see the father, it is from an angle that
renders him huge, distorted: a symbol rather than a person.

These are visual clues to which we subconsciously respond,
and the sort of pop psychology with which most of us are familiar.
Gaiman's readers, and fans of graphic novels in general, are
almost certainly conversant in the theories of symbolism and
meaning. The very format of the graphic novel necessitates an
almost formalized use of symbolism: the condensed story-telling
style requires the use of text and visuals that are layered and rich in
meaning. Gaiman and McKean are wonderfully apt at this, and
obviously enjoy seeding the story with mazes of references that
intertwine within the story and pull in iconography from outside
the actual storyline that carries its own historical and cultural significance.

One especially elegant use of visual cues is that of the movie
poster. What is, on one level, simply a rectangle of paper, an
advertisement, is in actuality a trigger to layers of cultural memory, a point in time, with a story of its own. A scene near the end of
Violent Cases, set in a hotel bar, has a series of old movie posters
that seem, at times, to be firmly attached to the bar wall, perhaps
representing reality; or drifting mid-air, edited in later as the
memory is reviewed from an adult's perspective. The titles are
sometimes obvious foreshadowing: *The Man Who Knew Too Much*
is squarely fixed on the wall behind the osteopath as he finishes
what he knows to be his final drink; *They Died With Their Boots On*
dominates the next panel behind the hitman who speaks of attempts to contact the osteopath, who has obviously been resisting
his inevitable fate for decades. Other posters in this scene seem to
drift askew, hugely out of proportion, as if superimposed on the
child's memory by the adult's subconscious. One telling example
is the poster for *The Public Enemy,* larger and more dominant than
the characters in the frame, looming overhead; a poster for *Mon
Oncle* is in the background, receded. A symbol of the osteopath's
doom overlays, literally, a symbol of the relationship between the
osteopath and the child; the "big picture" eclipses the child's
small world. There is, throughout the story, a sense of the child
being aware that there is a big picture that he doesn't understand.

Gaiman enhances this feeling of there being a "big picture" based in reality by scenes of his family life that parallel Mob life. His questions are routinely evaded by the adults in his life. "What did the gangsters do?" he asks his grandmother; "Feh, and you should ask such questions!" she replies, before bribing him out of his curiosity with cookies. It is, literally, bribery for silence.

As an adult he asks his father what the osteopath looked like. In response to his question he gets a contradictory, defensive answer from his father: the osteopath is described as Polish, but also a Red Indian Chief; his nose described, dehumanizingly, as an eagle's beak. "There," the father says with finality, "is that the time?" leaving the protagonist, as he points out, unsatisfied. You see a small hand, presumably belonging to one of Gaiman's children, aiming a toy gun from behind the sofa. The reader is left with the feeling that the father, and possibly the family around him, is involved in the osteopath's disappearance.

This feeling is reinforced by the series of children's parties that the child goes to throughout the story. The magician who performs at these parties, the child says, "made things come out of his mouth" and "there were loud bangs," foreshadowing the revelation of the mage as the coordinator of the osteopath's long-avoided fate. He complains to the osteopath, horrified, that the children at these parties are not his friends, but children of his parents' friends. It is as if his friends are chosen for him; that his contacts with other people are tightly controlled by his family. The intimation of the child's family's involvement is strengthened by the fact that it is the father who takes the child to the osteopath, knowing his history with Al Capone. It is almost as if the osteopath is being tested, to see if he'd talk after all these years, or being set up to form a relationship that will leave him off-guard. There is a feeling of the child being used in ways that he does not, and cannot, understand. Perhaps the child himself is being tested for discretion.

One gets the feeling that the osteopath is obliquely telling the child of his own possible future. He lowers his voice asking, regarding an ongoing children's party, "What are they doing?" Behind him hangs a poster for the movie *Things To Come*. At the answer "party games," he signals for another drink against a poster for *No Way Out* and tells the child about Al Capone's "party games." The juxtaposition of scenes of the ongoing children's party with scenes from one of Al Capone's more violent parties is disturbingly apt: the children are playing musical chairs, a child being put out of the game at each turn; Capone is playing, too, each turn permanently removing a player from the game.

For me, the most disturbing point in the story is that, while listening to the osteopath's description of Capone beating in the heads of his cohorts, each in turn, the child, in his head, "(sees) a party . . . green rabbit-shaped jellies and fairy cakes on a crisp white checked tablecloth. A bat hitting. Blood and brains spatter grey and red on the white. Al helps himself to some jelly." Later the child ". . . (thinks) of the other children. Their heads bloody caved-in lumps. I felt fine about it. I felt happy." The child feels empathy for Capone, sees a reasonableness to erasing, violently, peers who are of no use to him. As the osteopath is describing the "almost a hundred thousand dollars worth of flowers" sent by Capone to the funerals of the men he'd murdered at one of his "parties," the page so fills with roses and dahlias that they flow into the vase at the very edge of a scene in the present: the on-going children's party in the next room. The game of musical chairs has ended; the child notices that the last two children are too busy squabbling to see that "the last chair sat empty, un-claimed." He could, if he wished, simply take it. The tendency of this child to focus on objects, rather than people, has taken a new possible meaning: rather than being a desire to focus on what is understandable and safe, such as an inanimate object, we see the possibility of a burgeoning sociopath. His earlier disdain for the children's fights over worthless trinkets seems now to be a sub-conscious realization that he is above all that, not because he dis-dains the cheap toys, but rather because he's not willing to fight over them. Perhaps he is willing to simply take them by whatever means.

At first reading, *Violent Cases* is a small story, almost a vignette from Gaiman's personal mythology; in the end, however, it is a fascinating mix of reality, cultural references, and personal myth-ology that may or may not lead to a true deeper meaning. What is unsaid, or implied, creates a much darker, convoluted picture of Gaiman's fictionalized childhood. Teasing hints imply that the adults in Gaiman's world were involved in some sort of dangerous game. There are intimations of Gaiman, as a child, being prepared to join the game; a question lingers about the position of the adult

Gaiman telling the story. Is it being told, as seems on the surface, as a simple reminiscence, or as a player in the game, bit of chatting up before making the hit? Is he telling his story before his own end, having played the game, and lost? Why would his parents knowingly expose him to such potential violence? The questions left unanswered are more interesting than the story itself; this artistry, of seducing his audience with snippets of personal mythology blended into allusive details, is one of Gaiman's strengths as a storyteller. He has created a literary illusion: an anamorphosis of a very different story that is left untold, reminiscent of the picture of two lovers kissing that, on further viewing, reveals itself as a picture of a vase. Here, there may or may not be a vase; there may be an iguana, a tree, a street scene of Paris, or nothing more than a hazy childhood memory.

As Gaiman himself has said, regarding *Violent Cases*, "That's the problem with using anything in real life in fiction. Fiction eats the real life memories."

AN AUTOPSY OF STORYTELLING: METAFICTION AND NEIL GAIMAN

Chris Dowd

Why is it that Neil Gaiman frequently tells stories about telling stories? His fictional worlds are populated by writers, film directors, puppet masters, actors, oral storytellers, and even a king of stories who rules a realm of fictions, fables, and dreams. Some of these storytellers seem compelled by tradition, others by boredom, and others by profit. In *The Sandman*, Morpheus tells stories because it is his function, Cain & Abel because it is their obligation, and the patrons of the World's End Inn because they have nothing else better to do. In the short story "Murder Mysteries," a fallen angel trades a story about paradise for a cigarette and expresses a sentiment that many of Gaiman's storytellers seem to believe:

> "Mm. You want to hear a story? True story? Stories always used to be good payment. These days . . ."—he shrugged— ". . . not so much."

Even more than all of the storytellers, audiences figure prominently in Gaiman's works. In one of the most popular stories from *The Sandman*, the king and queen of Faerie witness a new play by Shakespeare. In another, a young girl listens to her grandfather's unbelievable tale of werewolves, magic, and love. Two of the early graphic novels by Gaiman and Dave McKean (*Mr. Punch* and *Violent Cases*) prominently feature a child who is an audience to a potentially malevolent adult performer. In all of these tales, Gaiman's focus on the audience emphasizes the function of a story more than the content of the story. His interest is clearly to discover how stories work.

Gaiman holds up a mirror to the storytelling process. His stories allow us to see the relationship between the audience and the storyteller in a new way. The audiences within Gaiman's stories tell us (Gaiman's audience) what our role is in the storytelling process. They instruct us how we should behave. They tell us when to laugh and cheer, when to cry, when to ask questions, and when to remain silent. Similarly, the storytellers that figure prominently in these texts give us an indication as to how Gaiman conceives of his own role in the process. Surprisingly, he repeatedly downplays and undermines the authority of authors and suggests we should be more careful about trusting our storytellers. Instead, Gaiman's stories consistently point to the audience as being responsible for a story's success or failure. The audience is shown to be the real source of narrative energy and capable of the greatest imaginative work, but only when they fulfill their responsibilities to a storytelling event.

Metafiction is self-aware fiction. Metafictional stories purposely draw attention to the artifice of storytelling itself. There is a wink-wink, nudge-nudge effect in metafiction as the characters let *you* know that *they* know that they are just fictional characters. Metafiction almost always involves a transgression of narrative boundaries, which can happen in many different ways. Shakespeare was fond of using plays-within-plays to achieve this effect, and did so in *Hamlet*, *A Midsummer Night's Dream*, and *The Taming of the Shrew*. Irish novelist Flann O'Brien similarly uses the structure of novels-within-novels in his comedic masterpiece *At Swim-Two-Birds* in order to intentionally disorient readers and keep them from knowing which characters are real and which are imaginary. Kurt Vonnegut transgresses narrative boundaries in several of his works. Reality and fiction collide and characters meet their creator face-to-face in *Slaughterhouse Five*, *Breakfast of Champions*, and *Timequake*. Even many popular movies—*Ferris Bueller's Day Off*, *Blazing Saddles*, and *Fight Club* to name a few— utilize metafictional techniques for comic effects. In these films, a character breaks the "fourth wall" and speaks directly to the audience, lifting the audience out of their voyeuristic fantasy and making them co-conspirators in the on-screen antics.

Yet, Gaiman uses the tools of metafiction for something entirely different. He is not simply looking for a quick laugh or clever plot device. For Gaiman, metafiction is a surgical tool. He throws slabs of mythology, fairy tale, and horror onto the autopsy table and cuts into them like a mad scientist, turning them inside out to see how they are built. And then he beckons us closer to have a look at the carcass and shows us something we could never have seen otherwise.

Stories Within Stories

Gaiman's stories remind me of watching Penn & Teller perform. When the two magicians are on stage, they admit that they are deceiving you. They tell you that everything you see is an illusion or sleight-of-hand trick. They will even sometimes show you exactly how a trick is performed; I recall seeing Penn cut Teller in half once, but the whole trick was done using a transparent plastic box! Nonetheless, at the end of a Penn & Teller show the audience is amazed and drawn even further into their magic. Gaiman constantly shows us his own smoke and mirrors. He takes us backstage to see characters putting on their make-up and costumes. He shows us that his sets are just painted cardboard mock-ups. He never allows us to simply take a story at face value. He achieves this by nesting one story inside of another story.

A young boy encounters a dramatic and frightening example of a story-within-a-story in the graphic novel *Mr. Punch*. The child protagonist witnesses his first Punch & Judy puppet show and is initially horrified by the sadistic Mr. Punch. The puppet routinely kills every other character on stage and speaks with a "shrill inhuman voice." Nonetheless, the show excites the boy and draws him in. Eventually, the boy meets the Punch & Judy professor and is invited to meet the cast of the puppet show. He is literally allowed behind the scenery of the show and is given tangible evidence that it is not real. He learns which of the various characters are stick puppets and which are hand puppets. The professor offers personal insights regarding several of the show's characters and describes how the various puppets have evolved over time. The boy even tries one of the puppets on:

> I slid the puppet onto my left hand; and it came to life. I'm not talking about anything fantastical here. You can try it yourself— find a hand-puppet, slide it on your arm, flex your hand, move your fingers. And somehow, in the cold space between one moment and the next, the puppet becomes alive.

The boy's playful explorations demystify the monsters that terrified him only a few pages earlier. He begins to accept that there is a very human man responsible for the magic of the puppet show. Yet, the boy is not allowed to see Mr. Punch—the one character he needs to make sure is just a lifeless puppet—nor will the professor reveal the secret of Punch's inhuman voice. It isn't until years later, when the boy has grown into a man, that he learns the secret of Punch's voice: a simple device made of cotton, tin, and tape inserted into the mouth. A salesman offers him the chance to try on one of the many Punch puppets available, but he is unable to bring himself to do so and muses: "I almost put it on. It would have whispered its secrets to me, explained my childhood, explained my life." The magic isn't gone just because he knows how it works. Knowing the secret of Punch's voice changes nothing. Mr. Punch is still a horrifying and real figure for him.

In one of Gaiman's other early graphic novels, *Violent Cases*, a young boy once again encounters an older storyteller, this time an osteopath who once treated mobster Al Capone. The stories of gangsters and the violent world of Chicago fascinate the child. The osteopath knows how to tell a compelling tale. Interestingly though, he refuses to tell the stories people usually want to hear about Al Capone—stories about "him and the girls, or about bootlegging hooch, or like the time he got the tax bill." Instead, the osteopath tells detailed, violent tales than no other storyteller could ever recount. He tells stories about a homemade electric chair, gangster parties, and a funeral with a silver coffin and five thousand dollars worth of flowers. These stories deglamorize Al Capone and show the gangster as brutal and impulsive. The boy protagonist of *Violent Cases* knows he is privy to an utterly unique storytelling experience. Just as in *Mr. Punch*, the boy is at once attracted to and repulsed by what he hears. The story-within-a-story is another world, an alien world filled with violence and mayhem, that the boy can observe safely from the real world. *Violent Cases*, again like *Mr. Punch*, allows us to see the boy as a grown-up, this time as the narrator who is telling us the story. Just as the osteopath enthralled the little boy with his stories, the narrator now works the same magic on us.

Gaiman also used stories-within-stories frequently throughout *The Sandman*. Issue #11 ("Moving In") featured a comic-book-within-a-comic-book. Issue #18 ("Dream of a Thousand Cats") told the story of a cat telling a story. Issue #19 ("A Midsummer Night's Dream") features a play within the comic (and technically, there is a play within the play within the comic). Sometimes the metafiction becomes deeply layered in *The Sandman*, as if a mirror is being held up to another mirror. In Issue #39

("Soft Places"), Rustichello tells a story to a young Marco Polo that was originally told to Rustichello by Marco Polo's future self. Yet, if Rustichello first heard the story from Marco Polo, and Marco Polo first heard it from Rustichello, where did the story really originate? The most convoluted of all of the stories-within-stories is certainly in the *World's End* story arc. When it's his turn to tell a tale, Petrefax relates a story about Master Hermas telling a story about Mistress Veltas telling the story of her adventure in the catacombs beneath the Necropolis Litharge. At the end of *World's End* we realize there's yet another layer—all of the stories we just read (including Petrefax's convoluted tale) were actually being told by Brant to a bartender in a pub. These stories-within-stories force us to question the fictional nature of our own reality. Just as soon as we figure out where the story ends and reality begins, we learn of another layer. It is easy to get lost in these stories and not be able to recall who the real storyteller is and who the real audience is—which is the intended effect.

Gaiman further utilizes stories-within-stories to allow fiction and reality to collide. By allowing the real and the fictional to mix, the audience is forced to question the commonly held belief that there is actually a difference between the two. In Gaiman's stories, fictional characters often enter the real world, or real world people enter fictional worlds. In *Mr. Punch*, the boy is first traumatized by the puppet show when Punch throws the baby off the fictional world of the puppet stage and out into the real world. As the boy describes it:

> And Punch picked up the baby and threw it out of the window. Not really. He didn't throw it out of the window. He threw it off the stage. It tumbled down from the stage onto the beach—and lay there, silent and bleeding.

Is it the violence that actually upsets the boy, or the idea that a fictional world was invading his real world? The exact opposite scenario occurs in *The Last Temptation*, a graphic novel based upon Alice Cooper's concept album of the same name. In *The Last Temptation*, Steven—a real world boy—is coerced into entering the fictional world of the Showman. Once Steven enters this world (ironically called the "Theater of the Real"), the Showman attempts to recruit him into the permanent cast of the show.

Several of Gaiman's early novels also deal with real people

entering fictional or mythological worlds. The hero of *Neverwhere* winds up stranded in London Below, a place where monsters, angels, knights, and creatures he assumed were fictional actually exist. Tristan, the young hero of *Stardust*, makes his own journey into the strange world of faeries. In *American Gods*, Shadow goes on a cross-country trek and comes to realize that there are myths and legends living in the real world. The novel climaxes with Shadow literally reliving the mythical story of Odin. At this point, he has not only traveled into a mythical world, but also become a myth himself.

Sometimes in Gaiman's stories, the issue isn't crossing from a real world into a fictional world; rather, it's telling the difference between the two. Gaiman makes us question our notions about the nature of our own world. If stories are simply reflections of the real world, and we can see all the strings and levers that make the story work, doesn't it make sense that those strings and levers are here in the real world as well? Gaiman demonstrates that the boundaries between art and life, truth and fiction, and dream and reality are not static. The lines blur and overlap. The hobgoblin Puck notices this as he watches a literal reflection of his life in Shakespeare's play in *The Sandman* #19—"It never happened, yet it is still true."

The overlap between reality and imagination can be quite traumatic. The young protagonist of *Mr. Punch* witnesses a disturbing mixture of fiction and truth. Although he was frightened of the violence of the puppet show, he at least believed it to be confined to the fictional world of the puppet stage. When he witnesses the brutal beating of a pregnant woman later in the story, it is virtually identical to the violence of the puppet show. The confrontation between the woman and three men unfolds very much like the encounter between Punch and Judy. The boy says, "I was scared. No. That's the wrong word. I wasn't scared. I was troubled." It wasn't the violence that was troubling the boy, nor was it the fact that his grandfather was one of the three men he was spying on. The boy was troubled when he realized that the violence of the puppet show also existed in the real world and that there were real world people capable of the same acts that made Mr. Punch such a horrible fictional character. Ultimately, he is troubled that there is no difference between his world and the puppet stage.

A similar confusion of reality and fiction is found in "The

Wedding Present," an ingenious story from *Smoke and Mirrors*. We are told about a story that is given as a gift to a couple on their wedding day. The couple read the story several times throughout their marriage, and it changes each time. Similar to the portrait in Oscar Wilde's *A Picture of Dorian Gray*, the story in "The Wedding Present" details all of the horrible and evil things that the couple never actually experience themselves. However, the wife in the "The Wedding Present" is unsure which marriage is real—the one she's experienced or the one she has read about. Gaiman delights in moments like this throughout all of his works. When the audience isn't sure what is truth or fiction, real or dream, his job is done.

The Storyteller

More than one English teacher has claimed that Shakespeare still lives through his words. Certainly all of us have also heard that the pen is mightier than the sword. Gaiman's stories suggest that this isn't quite the case. Gaiman seems intent in many of his stories to disprove some commonly held beliefs about authors and to strip them of some of the authority they possess. He rips away many of the romantic notions most of us have about writers and leaves us to stare at the unglamorous truth. Repeatedly he shows us that the power of storytellers is illusory and warns us against believing in that power too passionately. Doing so leads to disappointment, tragedy, and death.

In *The Last Temptation*, the Showman tells Steven that if he joins the Theater of the Real, "Nothing can hurt you ever again. You'll never grow old." Essentially, Steven is offered immortality in exchange for becoming a performer. The premise of this story rests upon the notion that storytellers have a supernatural power that can be bestowed upon others. Steven smartly rejects the Showman, knowing that such power comes with an enormous price. "So let me see if I've got this straight," he says, "I never have to grow old by . . . never having anything to grow old for?" Unlike Faust who traded his soul for the ability to perform parlor tricks, Steven refuses to trade his potential future for the flashy, but hollow, power that is offered to him. He recognizes that the power is fake, that it is all just smoke and mirrors.

Unfortunately, many of Gaiman's other characters don't

make the same choice as Steven. Many of the antagonists of *The Sandman* obsess over the idea that the power is real and can be stolen from storytellers. The graphic novel series begins with Roderick Burgess imprisoning Morpheus, the ultimate storyteller, in his quest to gain supernatural power and immortality. Richard Madoc seeks something similar when he imprisons a muse in *The Sandman* #17 ("Calliope"). Tragically, Hector Hall is the only one to enjoy the benefits of fictional power when he is incorporated into a fictional world in *The Doll's House* story arc. Having died in the real world, Hector finds immortality and superhuman power in the mind of a child storyteller. Yet, Gaiman doesn't allow anyone—even the noble, but naïve Hector Hall—to benefit from the power and immortality they think storytellers can provide. The Theater of the Real is destroyed, Hector Hall and Roderick Burgess both die, Richard Madoc loses his mind, and even Dream of the Endless, the all powerful king of stories, is destroyed in the end.

Gaiman makes it explicitly clear that we should not trust storytellers. It isn't a matter of storytellers being unsavory people, although some of the ones in Gaiman's works surely are. The real reason we shouldn't trust storytellers is that they are untrustworthy by nature. In the earlier mentioned *The Sandman* #17, Erasmus Fry tells Calliope, "Writers are liars." Gaiman reinforces and draws attention to this quote by making it the epigraph to the *Dream Country* collection. The idea is also restated in *The Sandman* #38 ("The Hunt") when the grandfather says, "You shouldn't trust the storyteller, only the story." It is an idea that echoes throughout *The Sandman* mythos and into Gaiman's other works. In the introduction to *Smoke and Mirrors*, Gaiman tells us that mirrors can also be liars. This is the point where Gaiman's use of metafiction breaks with tradition and moves in a truly unique direction. Other storytellers have held up mirrors to their audiences and told them "this is who you are." Gaiman holds up a mirror and admits that both he and the mirror are liars. He acknowledges both the powers and the limits of authorship. As a result, Gaiman's audience is forced to accept responsibility for their part in the storytelling event.

The Audience

In Gaiman's stories, the focal point is almost always the audience. Audiences are shown to be more powerful than authors, and even more powerful than the Endless. Dream says to Desire, "We of the endless are the servants of the living—we are not their masters . . . and we do not manipulate them. If anything, they manipulate us. We are their toys." Audiences manipulate the stories the way that humans manipulate the Endless. Each individual personalizes the story and makes it relevant to his or her own experience. The audience controls the story or, borrowing from Puck, they "amend" it to their liking. Ultimately, the audience embodies the real engine of the storytelling experience.

A wonderful example of this dynamic can be found in the short story "The Goldfish Pool and Other Stories." In it, an author travels to Hollywood and stays in the hotel where John Belushi died. Everyone that the author meets in Hollywood tells a different version of Belushi's death, specifically changing who else was in the room when the actor had a drug overdose. He hears it was Robin Williams and Robert DeNiro, Meryl Streep and Dustin Hoffman, George Lucas and Steven Spielberg, and Bette Midler and Linda Ronstadt. Every person that tells him the story changes it—amends it—to suit their own whims and desires. Even the author, as a joke, comes up with his own version of the Belushi story: "John Belushi had kicked the bucket in company with Julie Andrews and Miss Piggy the Muppet."

The author protagonist of "The Goldfish Pool and Other Stories" is the quintessential Gaiman storyteller. He is emasculated, powerless, and not the real controller of stories. His only value to the audience is his function as an author, which gives the audience the illusion that the story ideas magically originate from his head, rather than from the audience themselves. Throughout "The Goldfish Pool and Other Stories," the author meets with Hollywood executives to develop his novel *Sons of Man* into a feature film. The novel is a supernatural thriller revolving around the children of Charles Manson "realizing their terrifying destiny." However, the various studio execs and producers (as an audience) are unhappy with the story and make radical changes to it to suit their own needs. They remove the Charles Manson element entirely from the story, change the title to *When We Were Badd*, and suggest that the story should be about a serial killer who possesses young boys through a video game. As the audience, they have more power over the story than the author does. The author is understandably disturbed by the mutilation of his original idea. When he questions them about plot elements in the "new" story, one producer responds, "You're the writer, sweetheart. You want us to do all your work for you?"

John Dee (a.k.a. Dr. Destiny) helps demonstrate a more extreme version of the power of the audience in *The Sandman* #6 ("24 Hours"). Dee, a recent escapee from Arkham Asylum for the Criminally Insane, enters a diner and, at first, unobtrusively observes the various diners and wait staff. He becomes the audience for the simple domestic stories unfolding around him. However, Dee grows bored and starts to manipulate the various people in the diner with his dream stone. Lovers and strangers are forced to become actors in violent and twisted versions of their own lives. Dee changes the stories into something that makes him happy, something that reflects his nature. The stories change in order to meet the needs of the audience—unfortunately in this instance, the audience is a homicidal psychopath.

A large congregation of cats are told that they can change their stories into something that will make them happy, something that reflects their own nature, in *The Sandman* #18 ("A Dream of a Thousand Cats"). One cat tells the congregation a story about how the world was once ruled by cats. Humans were their prey and playthings. However, the cat-world changed when one human began to preach that "Dreams shape the world." When enough humans believed this, reality changed and cats became the playthings of humans. The cat telling the story argues that cats could change the world back if they could all dream the same dream, but few in the congregation believe. Dreamers and audiences both think of themselves in passive roles. They believe they have no influence on the outcome of a story, when the truth is that the audience controls the shape of the story just as the dreamer controls the shape of the dream.

Audiences in Gaiman's stories often transform into storytellers themselves. In *The Sandman* #19 ("Tales in the Sand"), two tribesmen stop in the middle of the desert to participate in an ancient storytelling tradition. It is the final part of a ritual that the younger tribesman needs to complete in order to become a man.

The elder tribesman tells the story of Dream's tragic relationship with Nada. The younger tribesman is the audience, but after hearing the story, he is transformed into a storyteller himself. One day he will bring a young tribesman out into the desert and tell him the same story, continuing the cycle of boys becoming men and audiences becoming storytellers. The coming-of-age process is explicitly equated with the process of a listener maturing into a storyteller, suggesting that both are a natural progression.

We see another way for an audience to transform into storytellers in the *World's End* arc of *The Sandman*. A diverse group of travelers find refuge from a storm at an inn. They gather around and pass the time by telling each other stories. It is a situation reminiscent of Chaucer's *The Canterbury Tales*. Each individual takes a turn telling a story, and everyone is given the chance to be both speaker and listener. In both *The Canterbury Tales* and in *World's End*, the audience is forced into this storytelling method because they need to amuse themselves and there are no "official" storytellers (authors, playwrights, bards, etc.) present. There is a vacuum left by the absence of a storyteller, so each member of the audience takes a turn filling the vacuum. The vacuum in *World's End* is made even more prominent by the absence of Morpheus. The ultimate storyteller is gone from the world, and the burden of storytelling must fall on others until the storm is past. Morpheus' absence in *World's End* is keenly felt; he appears rarely in this story arc and is not the central figure in any of the stories. Yet, even without him, the stories continue, proving that the audience is perfectly capable of coming up with stories all on their own.

Perhaps the most succinct examination of the importance of the audience is represented in one of Gaiman's earliest works, *Signal to Noise*. Just as *World's End* tells the story of an audience without a storyteller, *Signal to Noise* tells the story of a storyteller without an audience. A dying filmmaker writes and directs his final movie inside of his mind. No one will ever see the film—there is no audience. This story explores whether an author can exist in a vacuum. Is it even possible for a storytelling experience to occur if there is no audience? The filmmaker is reminiscent of the old man in Samuel Beckett's *Krapp's Last Tape*. He tries to serve as his own audience, filling both the role of speaker and listener at the same time. Changing roles worked for the audience in *World's End* because they did so one at a time. There were enough people to fill both roles simultaneously. It doesn't work for the dying filmmaker. He cannot be both storyteller and audience no matter how hard he tries. At the end of *Signal to Noise*, he commits his story to paper so that it can finally have a real audience. It is not an attempt at immortality; he has already accepted his own death and realizes he will be dead before anyone actually reads the screenplay. By committing the story to paper he attempts to achieve communion with an audience and acknowledges that storytelling itself is an imaginative project that requires an intimate union between author and audience. Without the audience, a storyteller's mirror has nothing to reflect.

Neil Gaiman fulfills his function as an author by standing on a stage and holding a large mirror that reflects our dreams and nightmares back at us for our amusement. Using metafiction, he cuts open these reflected images to show us the insides—so we can see how they are put together. Like all metafictionists, he performs this operation partly out of a sheer joy for story structure. But he also does it to show us something truly unique that we could not see without a skilled storymaster to point out to us. When he pulls us in to look at the carcass of a story, he is able to show us how each of us built our own dreams.

TAPDANCING ON THE SHOULDERS OF GIANTS: GAIMAN'S *STARDUST* AND ITS ANTECEDENTS

Darrell Schweitzer

Like most fantasy writers of his generation, Neil Gaiman is very likely a child of the Ballantine Adult Fantasy Series. Certainly he has spoken very highly of it. This line of paperback books, all sporting a distinctive "Unicorn's Head" emblem, lasted only about five years, from 1969 until early in 1974, but it marks the beginning of modern fantasy as a commercial genre. Before the beginning, there were fantasy novels, of course, but only as isolated, eccentric volumes. Fantasy as such had certainly never been taught in schools or noted by mainstream critics, and so publishers and readers were largely groping in the dark when *The Lord of the Rings* sold so extraordinarily well that the word went out, "Find another trilogy." Editor Lin Carter found more than that, making a deliberate attempt, though the series and through its companion volume *Imaginary Worlds* (1973), to establish a canon of fantasy, putting Tolkien in a context that progresses from the most ancient literatures, through William Morris and Lord Dunsany, up to Fritz Leiber and Katherine Kurtz.

As Carter later admitted, the books sold as a function of how much they resembled Tolkien, which enabled later editors (notably Lester del Rey) to isolate the active ingredient and produce the still on-going plethora of multi-volume "fantasy-product," analogous to "cheese-product" and as readily distinguishable from the real thing. But the more immediate and beneficial effect was that the books provided a marvelous education for the next generation of fantasy writers, and an example of what could be done beyond the level of McTrilogies.

Gaiman's second novel, *Stardust* (1999), not to mention the DC Comics version from which it was derived, has two clear antecedents, both found in the Ballantine series, Lord Dunsany's *The King of Elfland's Daughter* (1924) and Hope Mirrlees's *Lud-in-the-Mist* (1927). That Gaiman has read both of these works is beyond question. He wrote an introduction to a Ballantine reprint of the Dunsany in 1999 and an *F&SF* "Curiosities" column about the Mirrlees the same year. But these books came to everyone's attention through the Ballantine series. Likewise it is surely no coincidence that James Branch Cabell is Gaiman's favorite writer. Cabell, who was critically fashionable in the 1920s, had been thoroughly flushed out of academia and the mainstream by the 1970s, but featured prominently in the Ballantine Adult Fantasy Series. Now you can find lots of little Cabell jokes and references in *Sandman.*

Indeed, of the contemporary, younger fantasy writers, Gaiman is one of the most widely-read and appreciative of the classics of fantasy. His work is a fertile ground for influence-tracing critics. It is almost harder to discover what he *hasn't* read. But much more interesting is an examination of how he has transmuted the materials he has borrowed. Or, to mix metaphors, a writer can't merely stand on the shoulders of giants. He has to do something interesting while he's up there. A little tap-dance, maybe. Gaiman does at least that.

The King of Elfland's Daughter is a lush romance, containing some of the most resoundingly poetic prose in the English language. Who can possibly forget the wasteland, "that to cross would weary the comet," or how, when the questing hero turns his back, "Elfland came racing back, as the tide over flat sand"?

The story tells how the people of Erl, bored with their humdrum existence, come before their feudal ruler to ask to be governed in the future by a magic lord. The location of Erl itself is significant, not found on any map, but possibly adjoining one, right at the edge of human experience and "the fields we know," near the "Elfin boundary" which is made of twilight. Sometimes, from Erl, one can hear the horns of Elfland blowing. But the lord does more than that. He sends his only son, Alveric, armed with a sword forged by a witch from a lightning bolt, across that boundary on a mission "to wed the King of Elfland's Daughter," whether parental permission is forthcoming or not.

Off goes Alveric in properly heroic fashion, smiting Elfin knights with his lightning-sword and otherwise introducing chaos and change into what otherwise was a timeless, perfectly static realm. Once he has carried off the daughter, Lirazel, to Erl, he notices that "her crown of ice had melted away."

But Dunsany is not content to let things end happily ever after, or at least not yet. As, S.T. Joshi has notably pointed out, Dunsany's approach is quite modern, notably derived from Nietzsche, and given to ironic distancing effects. So Lirazel and Alveric are wed. They have a son, Orion, half-elvish and magical, but showing to great promise as a future lord. Orion becomes an obsessive hunter, slaughtering unicorns throughout the rest of the book. Lirazel, meanwhile, pines for Elfland; and her father the King, distraught that his daughter is now subject to Time and mortality, writes a rune, which is delivered to Lirazel by a comic troll. As soon as she read it, she wafts away on the breeze with the autumn leaves, back to Elfland. But Alveric actually loves her, and now sets off on a hopeless quest to regain her, hopeless because the Elf King can feel the thunderbolt iron when it draws near, and withdraw his boundaries from it. Eventually Alveric is left wandering through wastelands in the company of lunatics, while the folk of Erl begin to complain of the excessive magic which seems to be leaking over the border. At last, Lirazel pleads with her father and he expends the last of his great runes to make Elfland flow over and absorb Erl, presumably preserving it in stasis for eternity. Except for a Christian friar, who is left with a little patch of Earth on which to dwell, the people are Erl are removed from human experience and human history altogether. In a sense they have gained what they both wished for and feared. Magic has washed over Erl and drowned it.

Gaiman observes of *The King of Elfland's Daughter*, that it is "a book about magic; about the perils of inviting magic into your life; about the magic that can be found in the mundane world, and the distant, fearful, changeless magic of Elfland. . . . it is not a comfortable, reassuring, by-the-numbers fantasy novel, like most books with elves and princes and unicorns . . . this is the real thing. It's a rich red wine, which may come as a shock if all one has experienced so far as been cola."[6]

Gaiman has reportedly been quoted as saying *Lud-in-the-Mist*

---

6   Neil Gaiman. Introduction to *The King of Elfland's Daughter*, in *Adventures in the Dream Trade*. Boston: NESFA Press, 2001.

is the best fantasy novel of the Twentieth Century. Certainly he thinks highly of it, having written in that "Curiosities" column that it is "a golden miracle of a book, adult, in the best sense, and, as the best fantasy should be, far from reassuring."[7]

Dorimare, the setting of *Lud-in-the-Mist*, like Dunsany's Erl, is beyond the edge of the map, bounded, we are told, on the western side by the Debatable Hills, beyond which lies Fairyland. Had Mirrlees read Dunsany? Yes, certainly. A phrase like "the Debatable Hills" could have come right out of *The Book of Wonder*. But like any good writer of any sort, when standing on the shoulders of a giant, she did more than just *stand there*.

In Mirrlees's version, the common people don't yearn for magic. They fear it. They had it once, but a revolution drove the lecherous, cruel, yet decidedly magical Duke Aubrey from his throne, into Fairyland, and a rule of enforced mundanity follows. Fairyland is not mentioned. Magic is clearly equated with obscenity, and the fairy fruit which comes floating down one of the rivers out of the Debatable Hills is strictly forbidden. Yet decorum cannot be maintained. An underground, criminal trade in fairy fruit flourishes. More and more of Dorimere's young people, and even some of its most respectable citizens, have partaken of it. Young girls are behaving improperly. Vile old Duke Aubrey appears in visions. Eventually the hero, Mayor Nathaniel Chanticleer, must cope with the fact that his own son has not only tasted the fruit, but, as many addicts do, run off to Fairyland, from which there is allegedly no return. In the course of his investigations, Chanticleer Sr. breaks up a fruit smuggling ring and solves an old murder in the process, but finally he has no choice but to follow his son's path.

If this had first been published in the '60s, it would have been taken as an "obvious" allegory about youth culture, the generation gap, and psychedelic drugs, but Mirrlees is more subtle than that. Certainly the meaning of her Fairyland is a lot deeper, less simplistic. As in the folklore from which her novel, somewhat more directly than Dunsany's, is derived, Elfland or Fairyland is a place neither in Heaven or Hell (perhaps between them) but nevertheless clearly associated with death and the hereafter. Persons

---

7   "Curiosities: *Lud-in-the-Mist.*" *ibid*. p. 78.

abducted into Elfland pass, as Thomas the Rhymer did in the Scottish ballad, beyond the world, riding for forty days and forty nights in "red blood to the knee," or else under hills, or, like King Orfeo in the Child ballad of that name[8] or the 14th century Middle English romance from which the ballad probably derives, they discover that the way into the other realm is through a "long gray stone," overtly suggestive of a grave. Orfeo is of course a medieval version of the classical Greek Orpheus, probably some monk's bookish concoction which escaped into the public consciousness and not the other way around. Hades has become Fairyland, but is still a scary place.

When Nathan Chanticleer returns, astonishingly, from Fairyland, the dead return with him. Apparitions fill the streets of Dorimere. But nevertheless, as Gaiman notes with approval, this is "a book about reconciliation—the balancing and twining of the mundane and the miraculous. We need both, after all."[9] A compromise is worked out between Dorimere and Faerie, and fairy fruit (which widens the imagination) becomes an acceptable commodity after all.

Isn't this a perfect summation of much of Gaiman's work? So much of what he writes about concerns people crossing boundaries between the everyday and some fantastic realm. In *Neverwhere* it is an alternative London that exists right alongside (or underneath) the familiar city.

In *Stardust* Fairyland exists right beyond the gap in the wall, in the town of Wall, which may be found in rural, Victorian England, sort of. Go in one direction, and you will come to familiar places and eventually reach London. But if you go in another, you leave the Earth as we know it.

This again is a concept derived from Dunsany. In many of Dunsany's early stories characters are able to pass from the familiar London, to more remote places, until they come to that last row of houses in a country village, from the back windows (or out the back door) of which one can see Fairyland or the Edge of the World, the lands Beyond the Fields We Know.

8   In James Francis Child's *English and Scottish Ballads*, #19.

9   Gaiman. *Ibid*. P. 78.

But in Wall, far more so than in Erl or in Dorimere, intercourse with the Beyond is regulated. The one gap in the wall is zealously guarded. This duty is a coming-of-age ritual for young men. Every nine years on May Day, however, there is a fair in the fields beyond the wall, and human and fairy folk mingle. Sometimes they do more than that, because after Dunstan Thorn goes through, there is discovered some months later at the gap a basket containing a baby and a note saying the child's name is Tristran Thorn.

Tristran, unaware of his origins, grows up in Wall, does guard duty, but then, to impress a girl he thinks he loves, promises to fetch a falling star for her, a star he has seen fall into Fairyland. Off he goes, with his father's help. A perilous quest follows. There are strange dislocations of time and space, transformations, secrets revealed, villains overcome, all before Tristran finally embraces the Fairy side of his nature and the beautiful princess who is the fallen star, at least on the Fairy side of the wall. (Fortunately he does not take her to the mundane side, where she would be, irretrievably, a dead lump of iron.)

We see here the same conclusion as in *The King of Elfland's Daughter* and *Lud-in-the-Mist*. Fairyland and the "real" world are reconciled as the hero accepts and even celebrates his magical side. He crosses over into Faerie and stays there until his death. (Being half-Fairy, he is long-lived, but ultimately mortal. Death "whispered her secret" in his ear, we are told, the female Death suggesting the one from the Sandman mythos.)

It's a beautiful story, beautifully written, but what exactly did Gaiman accomplish, standing on the shoulders of giants? To some extent he's domesticated Fairyland, or at least given us an insider's view. Alveric only glimpses Elfland as an outsider, an invader. Nathan Chanticleer's adventures there are not related. We see him vanish over the border, then return, surrounded by ghosts. But Gaiman takes us every step of the way along Tristran Thorn's journey. Tristran is entering a strange country for the first time, but there is a sense of recognition, even belonging, because he is, after all, half-native. This is the essential thematic difference. One hesitates to say "allegorical," because, as Gaiman knows, as Dunsany, Mirrlees, C.S. Lewis, Tolkien, and so many others before him knew, a fairy tale is not the same thing as an allegory.

The strangeness for Tristran Thorn, which is Dream or Imagination, is not something which comes from afar. It is something of which he is already a part. All he has to do accept it, a bit more willingly than Nathan Chanticleer did. When he returns to the town of Wall he finds that Victoria (her name is not a coincidence), the girl for whom he made the extravagant promise, doesn't really approve of him or care for him and is set to marry somebody else. Meanwhile Tristran has to acknowledge that he actually loves the princess, even as Alveric realized he loved Lirazel and recognized her as more than a prize he'd captured at the point of a magic sword. Much more so than the Dunsany or Mirrlees novels, *Stardust* is a coming-of-age story. In Fairyland, Tristran Thorn chases after a falling star and retrieves himself.

What happens in the end? Balance is achieved, the very sort of balance Gaiman finds so admirable in *Lud-in-the-Mist*. The dreaming nature and the rational nature are in harmony. Tristran discovers, as Nathan Chanticleer did, that there is nothing wrong with the former. It is part of us too. Maybe we are very close to the borderland of allegory here, but not quite there. Gaiman veers back from something that cut-and-dried. He tapdances gracefully and pleasingly on the shoulders of Dunsany and Mirrlees. The result is more than just hommage. This is a creative variant of the familiar story, told in a distinct, somewhat more down-home voice. The magical becomes almost familiar, without losing its magic.

Gaiman celebrates the imagination. That is what his work is about, what gives it much of its energy and a certain joy.

Works cited

Dunsany, Lord. *The King of Elfland's Daughter.* New York and London, G.P. Putnam's Sons, 1924; New York: Ballantine/Del Rey 1969, 1999.

Gaiman, Neil. *Stardust.* New York: Spike/Avon Books, 1999.

Mirrlees, Hope. *Lud-in-the-Mist.* New York: Alfred A. Knopf, 1927; New York: Ballantine/Del Rey, 1970, 1977; Millennium Books, 2000.

THE OLD SWITCHEROO: A STUDY IN NEIL GAIMAN'S USE OF CHARACTER REVERSAL

Jason Erik Lundberg

There's an unwritten rule in fiction that says characters have to develop, to change. It can be as subtle as Tom Iremonger in Robert Cremins's *A Sort of Homecoming* accepting who he is, for better or worse, by proclaiming "Yes, I'm Tomás Iremonger." It can be as drastic as Yagharek in China Miéville's *Perdido Street Station* ripping the feathers from his body and choosing to adapt to his new wingless life by walking into New Crobuzon a man. But Neil Gaiman goes one step further in his fiction: his characters sometimes change so drastically that they become someone else.

Gaiman is a writer who loves to play with his readers' expectations, often with sleight-of-hand subtlety or misdirection. It's what makes his fiction so enjoyable to read; you never quite know where you will be taken, like attending a Penn-and-Teller show. The story may be going one way, then abruptly spin 180 degrees without even missing a beat. But the changes are never jarring; they happen exactly as they should, as if they were there the whole time, like that coin behind your ear.

This article examines four of Gaiman's short stories—"Troll Bridge," "Other People," "Foreign Parts," and "Harlequin Valentine"—and his use of the character reversal in each one.

In "Troll Bridge," Jack starts off as a rambunctious seven-year-old, eager to shed his shoes and the other trappings of the school year and anxious to explore. One day, he discovers a path through the wood near his house and decides to follow it. It travels in a straight line, while the landscape around him changes as he walks, almost as if by magic. After a while, he comes to the bridge, and after he trip-traps over it, the troll who lives underneath comes out and bluntly states that he's going to eat Jack's life. Thinking quickly, Jack explains that

> You don't want to eat my life. Not yet. I—I'm only seven. I haven't lived at all yet. There are books I haven't read yet. I've never been on an aeroplane. I can't whistle yet—not really. Why

don't you let me go? When I'm older and bigger and more of a meal I'll come back to you.[10]

The troll ponders this for a moment, then agrees. Jack runs home to the relative safety of his family.

Flash-forward to Jack at fifteen. He has just discovered punk rock and revels in this discovery with his best friend Louise, with whom he is madly in love. After one night of listening to the Stranglers on Louise's record player, she decides to walk him back to his house, a ten-minute stroll away. They get there and talk in the driveway, then he offers to escort her back to *her* house. After getting there, they decide to just keep on walking, and they find a path that rolls through the wood. They take the path down to an old brick bridge, and he starts to kiss her. But then she freezes, and the troll appears. They've taken the same path Jack took as a child, and love-stricken as he was, he didn't even realize it.

The troll again threatens to eat Jack's life and is glad to find out Jack has learned to whistle, since the troll never could. Jack again pleads for his life, stating that he's never even had sex yet or gone to America. In a desperate move, he offers Louise up to the troll to take his place, but the troll declines on the basis that she is an innocent, implying that Jack somehow is not. But the troll again reluctantly agrees to wait and disappears, Louise unfreezes, and Jack walks her home.

Flash-forward again to Jack at around thirty, now married (though not to Louise) and with a toddler. He lives in a house that was once a railway station and works at a major record company in London; consequently, he has to keep a flat there in order to hear the various bands who don't even start playing until midnight. This affords him the opportunity to cheat on his wife if he wants to, which he does. One winter's day, after getting back from a trip to New York, he finds the house cold and empty, a letter from his wife on the table explaining all the reasons she left, principal among them the fact that he never really loved her.

10   Neil Gaiman, "Troll Bridge," *Angels and Visitations: A Miscellany* (Minneapolis: DreamHaven Books, 1993) 32. First published in *Snow White, Blood Red*, ed. Ellen Datlow and Terri Windling (New York: Morrow/AvoNova, 1993).

Despondent and unsure of what to do next, he goes outside for a walk. He finds an unfamiliar path through the wood and takes it.

He soon comes to the troll bridge and realizes he has taken the same path as before, only approached from the other side. He nears the bridge and calls out for the troll, and after several moments of silence, he collapses into a sobbing heap, the combined hurt from all his lost chances flooding out in a torrent. He realizes he ruined any chance with Louise when he offered her up to the troll, though she never knew it; he ruined his chance at a normal life with a wife and a child by sleeping with other women; and he ruined his chance at a relationship with the troll, albeit a strange and perverse one, by constantly evading the troll's advances. But then the troll appears, touches his face, and quietly says, "Fol rol de ol rol." The troll trembles lightly, seeming tentative that the moment of truth is finally here, perhaps scared that thirty-odd years will be too much to eat. But Jack tells him it's okay, it's what he wants. So the troll gently lowers him to the ground like a lover—on top of a used condom, no less—and eats Jack's life with his big strong teeth.

What we don't realize until the very end of the story is that by "eating" Jack's life, the troll steals it from him, and the two end up switching bodies. The troll stands up in Jack's body and, after some parting words, walks back down the path through the wood, whistling away. Jack, who has now become the troll under the bridge, has resigned himself to his fate, never wishing to interact with humanity again, observing from under his bridge but never coming out.

"Other People" is a short-short story about a man's descent into Hell. The man arrives with his expensive clothes and arrogant attitude in a long grey room. Along the walls are 211 implements of torture; a demon stands at the far end. The man, who we can only assume was a high-powered businessman in life, who probably broke a few rules and lived more than a little dishonestly to deserve his fate, approaches the demon. The demon, who is deeply scarred, flayed, and missing its ears and its genitalia, takes down from the wall a cat-o'-nine-tails made of frayed wire and beats the businessman with it. The demon explains that time is fluid in this place, implying that the businessman will not be leaving anytime soon.

"In time," the demon tells him, "you will remember even this moment with fondness."[11]

The demon eventually uses all two hundred and eleven torture devices on the businessman, each one worse than the last, until the businessman is a shivering, gibbering wreck. The scars that have been left on his body are deep and painful and indelible. He hurts more than he has ever been hurt before.

But now, the torture really begins.

The demon lays naked every lie the businessman ever told, everything he ever regretted, every hurt he ever inflicted on another. He draws each piece out of the businessman, displaying them for the man to see. This part is very similar to a section near the end of *American Gods*, where Shadow is met by the dark Egyptian god Anubis:

> All of the things that Shadow had done in his life of which he was not proud, all the things he wished he had done otherwise or left undone, came at him then in a swirling storm of guilt and regret and shame, and he had nowhere to hide from them. He was as naked and as open as a corpse on a table, and dark Anubis the jackal god was his prosecutor and his persecutor.[12]

What Anubis does to Shadow, the demon does to the businessman, stripping him raw with his own life. It goes on for a hundred years, or perhaps a thousand—for time is fluid here—and when it is over, the businessman realizes the demon was right. The physical torture was far kinder.

Then it begins again, but with the businessman's sense of self-knowledge that wasn't there before, which makes it all the worse. When it's over, the demon says, "Again," and this time the businessman is exposed to the consequences of his actions, what happened to the people he interacted with after they left his presence. He sees all the ways he has affected other people's lives, and it leaves him with even more self-loathing than before.

11   Neil Gaiman, "Other People," *The Magazine of Fantasy & Science Fiction* October/November 2001: 169.

12   Neil Gaiman, *American Gods*, (New York: Morrow, 2001) 376-377.

A thousand years later, he finishes. "Again," the demon says.

This time he experiences his life as he tells it, leaving nothing out, facing everything and everyone he ever hurt. He opens his heart completely. When he finishes, he expects to hear the demon say, "Again," but he is alone. He stands up and looks to the far side of the room, where the only door to the chamber has just opened and closed. A suited figure in expensive and familiar clothes stands there, fear and pride and arrogance in his eyes, and the businessman finally understands. As the suited figure approaches him, the businessman (who now looks an awful lot like a demon) tells the new arrival, "Time is fluid here."

In this instance, the switch isn't between two separate characters, as they appear to be at the beginning, but between two aspects of the same character. The character of the demon is forever the persecutor, inflicting pain and punishment, where the character of the businessman is forever the victim, punished again and again for his actions in life. But as soon as the victim realizes what his situation is, that not only is he being tortured but he is being tortured by *himself*, the victim becomes the persecutor, and the cyclical process begins again. This is a version of Hell that Gaiman has proposed in some of his other works, including the *Sandman* storyline *Season of Mists*, wherein the fallen angel Lucifer reveals that there is no torture that can be inflicted by others that is any worse than what we inflict upon our own minds and bodies. And though the title is a play on the words of Jean-Paul Sartre—"Hell is other people"—the story seems to imply that hell is also ourselves.

In "Foreign Parts," Simon Powers has somehow contracted a venereal disease, though he hasn't had sex in almost three years. Every time he urinates, it feels as if he's pissing needles, so he goes to the doctor. His doctor refers him to a clinic that specializes in venereal diseases. That night, Simon masturbates, and the pain is so blindingly intense, it's "as if he were ejaculating a pin-cushion."[13] The clinic physician, Dr. Benham, diagnoses Simon with

13   Neil Gaiman, "Foreign Parts," *Angels and Visitations: A Miscellany* (Minneapolis: DreamHaven Books, 1993) 63. First published in *Words Without Pictures*, ed. Stephen Niles (Arcane/

Non-Specific Urethritis, gives him antibiotics, and tells him to make an appointment for the following week.

Simon takes the pills, and the pain and corresponding discharge disappear, but something new is happening. Simon's penis doesn't feel like his own anymore, like it belongs to someone else. He tells this to Dr. Benham, who chalks it up to side effects from the antibiotics or as some kind of psychological reaction to developing NSU, manifesting as a disgust of one's own genitalia. He gives Simon more antibiotics and tells him to come back the following week.

At the next appointment, Simon still has the disease, and on an even more disturbing note, the nonpossessive feeling in his penis has spread throughout the entire lower half of his body. His legs still work and take him where he wants to go, but he has the sneaking suspicion that if they wanted, they could walk off the end of the earth, and he could do nothing except tag along for the ride. Dr. Benham tries to fix the situation the only way he knows how, by changing Simon's medication. Simon walks out of the office on legs that don't belong to him, passing a pretty Australian nurse who he knows is out of his league, and certain that the new drugs will also prove absolutely worthless. He's right.

Later, as Simon lies in bed, unable to move any part of his body now, he feels a ghostly presence moving within him, taking over his body bit by bit. He can feel it brush his cheek, then his eyes cloud over and everything goes dark.

At the next appointment, Dr. Benham is astonished by how much better Simon looks. Free of the disease, he radiates a healthy glow and even looks taller. He is more sure of himself, less frail. In short, Simon seems like a completely new person. When Dr. Benham asks about the other problem, the feeling his body no longer belongs to him, the new Simon smiles and assures the doctor that all of this body belongs to him. Before leaving the office, Simon talks excitedly to the pretty Australian nurse, who makes no attempt to remove his hand from her arm. He wants to see everything, meet everyone, like someone who has just dropped in from outer space or lived

Eclipse: 1990).

through a life-changing disaster, eager to seize life by the reins.

In this instance, the switchover has occurred as a result of theft. Unlike "Troll Bridge," wherein Jack willingly gives up his life to the troll, or "Other People," in which it is presented as a natural process of Hellish punishment, Simon's life is involuntarily stolen from him. He is completely unaware that anything could happen to him until it already has, until it's too late.

Involuntary character theft also occurs in "Harlequin Valentine," which was written for *Strange Attraction*, an anthology of stories based on *Crowded After Hours*, the gigantic kinetic Ferris Wheel created by sculptor Lisa Snellings. This time, Gaiman chooses the character of Harlequin from the stock characters of the *Commedia dell'arte* and retells his story of unrequited love in a contemporary setting.

Harlequin is smitten with Missy, a young woman who, he is convinced, is the latest incarnation of Columbine, his one true love. As a Valentine's Day present, he pins his heart to her door with his favorite hatpin, then vanishes into the shadows to spy on her reaction. Missy opens her door to find the heart, dripping blood in a steady trickle, and instead of screaming or crying or calling 911, she goes into the kitchen and gets a plastic sandwich baggie. She puts the heart in the baggie, sticks the hatpin in her lapel, and wipes off the door with cleaning spray. Still nonchalant, as if this happens every day, she puts on her coat, places the baggie in her pocket, and leaves her apartment.

Missy walks down the road and Harlequin follows behind, sauntering and capering around her, unseen to Missy's eyes. They arrive at a pathologist's office, and Missy displays the heart for a man dissecting a dead body. Harlequin feels a stab of jealousy as the fat man smiles at Missy. "This is The Doctor," Harlequin decides, "for he is too big, too round, too magnificently well-fed to be Pierrot, too unselfconscious to be Pantaloon."[14] Vernon the pathologist examines the baggie and sees the heart for what it is. After asking if she should incinerate it, Missy bids

14   Neil Gaiman, "Harlequin Valentine," *Strange Attraction*, ed. Edward E. Kramer (Centreville: Shadowlands Press, 2000) 58. First published in the 1999 World Horror Convention Program Book.

goodbye to Vernon and heads back out onto the street, back into town.

Harlequin stops Missy on the road after disguising himself as an old beggar woman. He offers to tell her fortune for a little money, then explains to her that Harlequin has given her his heart, but she must find a way to make it beat. He then distracts her and resumes his invisible state. Missy continues down the road to a diner, where she asks for a plate of hash browns and a bottle of ketchup. Harlequin amuses himself by tripping the diner's owner, goosing a waitress, and switching the patrons' plates when they aren't looking. But his heart isn't in it, so to speak; he feels strange. Then he looks at Missy.

She has dumped his heart onto the plate and poured a generous amount of ketchup over it. She slices the heart into bite-sized pieces with a steak knife, then begins to eat it. This has never happened to Harlequin before, and he doesn't know quite how to deal with it. When she finishes, she looks down at Harlequin, whom she can now see, and tells him to meet her outside. On a bench in front of the diner, she plucks the hat from his head and the wand from his hands. The diamonds begin to disappear from his motley, which transforms into the drab and colorless uniform of kitchen help. Missy kisses him full on the lips, then capers down the street and out of sight.

Charlene, the waitress Harlequin goosed earlier, opens the front door of the diner and says that his break is over, that he'd better get back inside. Now in his new life—one that seems as if he has always lived it, one in which he is in love with Charlene—he wrestles with the idea of telling her how he feels, but ends up not saying anything. He returns to the kitchen and scrapes off the plates, then notices one with a liver-colored piece of meat drenched in ketchup. He makes sure no one's looking, then pops the meat into his mouth. A spot of ketchup falls to the sleeve of his jacket and forms a perfect diamond. A bit of his old self infects him then. He smiles, tells Charlene "Happy Valentine's Day," then starts to whistle.

In this modern retelling of the *Commedia dell'arte*, the trickster character of Harlequin is outwitted by the woman he believes to be his one true love. Columbine becomes Harlequin, stealing all his magical abilities, swapping roles typically assigned in the Harlequinade, switching masks and personalities. Missy, through her strength and cunning, two big things that attract Harlequin to her in the first place, is able to outsmart the trickster, leaving him a pathetic mortal, a creature of mute longing. This switch is also interesting because it's so unexpected. Missy eats his heart and therefore eats his life. Fol rol de ol rol.

Gaiman's stories are often about loneliness, identity, and lost chances, the things that make our time on Earth seem more like a drudgery than something to be cherished. And it is often in reflection upon these things that we realize we must fundamentally change ourselves in order to keep living. There's an old expression that says you can't possibly know how someone else feels until you walk a mile in their shoes. Gaiman takes this a step further by saying we can't really even know *ourselves* until we walk in someone else's shoes, until we can see ourselves as we really are, from the outside.

BACKSTAGE

by William Alexander

"Where are we?"

"Behind the scenes," said Wednesday. ". . . I just pulled us out of the audience and now we're walking about backstage."

—*American Gods*

The SAFETY CURTAIN rose, and then the real curtain.

—*Queen of Knives*

Neil Gaiman begins his introduction to *Smoke and Mirrors* (a collection of his own short stories and narrative poems) by introducing smoke, and mirrors (mostly mirrors), and stories, and some of the things stories are good for. Then comes a brief description of setting on the second page: it's snowing outside as he writes the introduction. It's a nice touch, creating a sense of quiet intimacy. We see the writer at work. It's almost as though we're having a private chat in Mr. Gaiman's dressing room before the show begins. As of yet there's no cause for alarm.

A reader of introductions might, at this point, be distracted by the page numbers. They're Arabic numerals, the ordinary numerals found on phones and digital watches. This is unusual, though by no means unheard-of. Introductions are more often numbered with lower-case, italic, Roman numerals, the sort used to count sequels, superbowls and the hours in fancy pocket-watches. Roman numerals on page corners are a sign that the book hasn't actually started yet. Arabic numerals are a sign that it has. Suddenly we don't know whether or not the curtain has gone up. We don't know whether we're chatting with the author backstage or scrambling for our seats, in the dark, with the help of an usher's flashlight. But it's absurd to be disoriented by such a minor detail. We should move on to the next page, and never mind that it's a "3" instead of a "*iii*."

On this page he starts to tell a story. It's called "A Wedding Present." It isn't listed in the table of contents. Its title isn't at the top, next to those odd page numbers. It's a secret. It's a private show for those of us who read introductions, a hidden piece of fiction where we only expected to find facts. Later in the introduction he'll mention that much of "Queen of Knives" and "The Goldfish Pool and Other Stories" (both properly listed in the table of contents) are perfectly true. He does not reveal *which* bits are true. Fact and fiction, like offstage and onstage, have begun to blur. This is fun. It is not necessarily cause for alarm.

By way of introduction to this new and secret story, the author tells us that it was a gift, made up but never written down. I'll clip this whole paragraph below. Watch closely. It all seems innocent enough, but he'll be using smoke and mirrors:

> I once made up a story as a wedding present for some friends. It was about a couple who were given a story as a wedding present. It was not a reassuring story. Having made up the story, I decided that they'd probably prefer a toaster, so I got them a toaster, and to this day have not written the story down. It sits in the back of my head to this day, waiting for someone to be married who would appreciate it.[15]

Note that two contradictory things are both true. One is that he hasn't yet written the story down. It's still in the back of his head, waiting to exist. The other truth is that *Smoke and Mirrors* was published in June of 2001, presumably with its introduction intact. So the story already exists. It is done. It is written. In this innocent-seeming paragraph Gaiman twice uses the phrase "to this day." Which day? The most mundane explanation is that "this day" was the day he wrote the intro, sometime before June '01 (though even this assumes that he wrote the introduction, "Wedding Present" included, in a single day). He's also created the impression that "this day" is whichever day we happen to be reading *Smoke and Mirrors* in, that the text exists in a kind of eternal present.

Gaiman tells us in the next paragraph (which is the very last paragraph before the title "A Wedding Present" appears, and the secret story begins) that he's "writing this introduction in blue-black fountain pen ink in a black-bound notebook, in case you were wondering," thereby increasing the illusion of immediacy. He started out by giving a general sense of setting, showing us the

15   *Smoke and Mirrors*, page 3 (not *iii*).

snow outside his windows, and now the detail-level rises to the very colors of his pen and notebook. He goes on to tell us that he'll cross out this bit of the intro if he doesn't like the story after writing it, "and you'll never know that I stopped writing the introduction to start writing a story instead." We're further backstage now, *and* further onstage, then we've been at any point thus far. The *facts* are that we're reading a printed, published introduction, far removed in time and space from the writing of it. The *fiction* is that we're watching it happen. We're all sharing "this day." We're there for the actual moment of composition, the movement of fountain pen on notebook paper. He may, in fact, have spent days or months writing and editing this story, but we still get to watch it burst forth fully formed. He even adds a sense of danger, threatening to cross it all out if he doesn't like the results. We need to savor the story while it lasts, because at any moment it might all be gone. Texts usually promise to be more permanent than they actually are; this one is pretending to be *less* permanent than it is.

He's about to begin. He points out that there are people who don't read introductions, increasing a sense of intimacy with those of us who do.[16] He points out that some of us out there might be having weddings. He blurs (or deconstructs, if you like) the binary division between fact and fiction, public and private, turning a private gift into a public story while making it seem as though "A Wedding Present" is *still* a private gift, personally offered to each and every member of his reading public (or at least those of us having weddings).

Gaiman is particularly good at blurring binary divisions. It's been argued that Western traditions and thought-patterns are hopelessly caught up in binaries: Man and Woman, Black and White, it's all as different as Night and Day. The stories in *Smoke*

---

16   Gene Wolfe says similar things in his introduction to *Castle of Days*, a book dedicated to Neil Gaiman. That intro also contains a piece of hidden fiction, a gift for people who read introductions.

Gaiman's blog, incidentally, is a perfect example of another private, backstage conversation which is, in fact, shared by five hundred thousand people at any given moment. The blog can be found at www.neilgaiman.com/journal/journal.asp.

and Mirrors consistently point out that 5 A.M. is Day for some and Night for others. "Changes" does the same with the boundary between genders. Magic and the mundane freely mix in "Chivalry," and both are given their proper due. Onstage and offstage blur in "Queen of Knives" with a frightening example of audience participation. "The Last Sandman Story" (which isn't actually the last Sandman story, and isn't in *Smoke and Mirrors*; the tale serves as the intro to Dave McKean's *The Sandman Dustcovers*) is filled with factually-told anecdotes of improbable encounters with characters that Gaiman made up.[17] Boundaries can be crossed. This is liberating. It can be a lot of fun. It can also be very, very scary.

"A Wedding Party" is a story about another story (he does this often). In it Belinda and Gordon are married, and find among their wedding gifts a typed, unsigned manuscript which describes their wedding as it actually happened. But the manuscript continues to describe their marriage, and this description increasingly diverges from the marriage they actually experience. Eventually Belinda must choose between her life outside this story, and her life as depicted inside. It's a horrible choice. She doesn't hesitate. Boundaries can be crossed, and this is a useful thing to remember whenever reading Neil Gaiman.

"A Wedding Party" is, by the way, *my* story. I read it shortly after my own wedding, and took it as a personal gift from a prescient author. Go ahead and read it, though, if you haven't already. I can share.

Bibliography

Gaiman, Neil. *Smoke and Mirrors*. New York: HarperCollins, 2001.
McKean, Dave. *The Sandman Dustcovers*. London: Titan Books, 1997.
Wolfe, Gene. *Castle of Days*. New York: Orb, 1992.

17   There was snow outside when he wrote this introduction, too; he tells us about tossing an affectionate but annoying orange kitten into a snowdrift because it was trying to help him type. Maybe there's always snow outside when he writes introductions.

NO NEED TO CHOOSE:
A MAGNIFICENT ANARCHY OF BELIEF

Bethany Alexander

Faith can be contradictory. One can believe with a whole heart in "absolute honesty and sensible social lies,"[18] at least three aspects of a storm god, a variety of Hells and "that one day White Buffalo Woman is going to come back and kick everyone's ass."[19] There's a fluidity of belief in Neil Gaiman's work, flitting from one cultural tradition to another, and a willingness to embrace all feats of thought. I, for one, find it comforting when the boundaries between various schools of thought, science and make-believe vanish. With no need to choose between the many things that ring true, it seems that the great looming questions of the multiverse become far less stressful.

Gaiman writes in his introduction to the *Smoke and Mirrors* reprint of his short story "When We Went to See the End of the World by Dawnie Morningside, age 11¼," that he and Alan Moore "sat down one day in Northampton and began talking about creating a place that we would want to set stories in. This story is set in that place."[20] So he sends Dawnie and her family to the end of the world on a picnic.

The end of the world, it turns out, includes a hole in the ground and a hole in the sky. From the lower one "pretty people holding sticks and simatars (sic) that burn come up out of it. They have long golden hair. They look like princesses, only fierce. Some of them have wings and some of them dusnt (sic)."[21] These people

---

18   Gaiman, Neil, *American Gods*, Harper Torch, 2001, p. 395.

19   *Ibid.*, p. 334.

20   Gaiman, Neil, *Smoke and Mirrors*, Harper Perennial, 2001, p.29.

21   *Ibid.*, 274.

"just hang there, not doing anything,"[22] as do those coming down from the sky; "the cat-heady man, and the snakes made out of stuff that looks like glitter-jel (sic) like I putted on my hair at Hallowmorn (sic) . . . There were very many of them. As many as stars."[23]

Now for the "Why is that awesome?" feature of my analysis: Dawnie Morningside gives an uninflected account of what she sees, so the contrast between the bizarre images and her lack of reaction gives me the shivers. Of everything on her family's trip the element that she gives the highest word count is the potato salad. Also, "Hallowmorn" is a lovely word, and the way she just keeps singing lah lah lah in spite of her father's complaints. Lah lah lah!

Back down to the ground: Gaiman's portrayal of the end of the world, here, is also a place of unicorns and a fat naked woman who would like to eat little girls, and who says she's too old for wishes. It is a mix of fantasy and oddity where one can encounter a variety of beings, sitting about or hanging in the air—"I asked Daddy why they weren't moving and he said they were moving just very very slowly but I dont (sic) think so."[24] This place is the one Gaiman and Moore devised together, but it is an example of one of Gaiman's recurring motifs; mythologies often blend in his work, cheerily carousing with folktales, history, happy accidents and dreams. If you follow the pattern, you get the sense that there's no need to choose between religion and science, reality and fiction. What might seem jarring or contradictory becomes a harmonious fusion in Gaiman's work.

Throughout the short story "One Life, Furnished in Early Moorcock"—also reprinted in *Smoke and Mirrors*—twelve-year-old Richard Grey totes his books with their weighty fantastical worlds and forms his own system of belief.

". . . when I was twelve, Moorcock's characters were as real to me as anything else in my life and a great deal more real than, well,

22   *Ibid.*, 274.

23   *Ibid.*, 274.

24   *Ibid.*, 274-75.

geography lessons for a start," writes Gaiman in his introduction to the anthology. Richard Grey himself is never without a Moorcock novel, and the nuances of plot, character and infinite possibility occupy the spaces of his mind that might otherwise be applied to class schedules, sports or crowds of friends. He drinks up stories like milk and they help him form his code, his moral center. There's nothing quite so vivid in his life.

". . . the nights belonged to [Richard's] own religion,"[25] "One Life" tells us, referring to the elements he gathered from fiction to form his personal faith. The formation of one's own religion—a deliciously messy, all-inclusive, cross-cultural religion—is an idea that Gaiman returns to often. He sets stories in such unbounded worlds and shows them to us firsthand. In the Sandman collection *Season of Mists*, gods from Norse and Egyptian mythologies, faeries, emissaries of order and chaos, angels and demons, and Shinto's god of storms and the sea, Susano-O no Mikoto, all try to outdo each other in their suit for ownership of the key to Hell.

Richard Grey, "the boy with the book," gives us a window into the mind of a boy who "believed, with no problems or contradictions, in everything." This choice to remove boundaries—to accept what resonates and feels true or interesting without questioning its logic—is a freeing one. Richard Grey is not the only character to subscribe to a "magnificent anarchy of belief;" Sam of Gaiman's novel *American Gods* "can believe anything:"[26]

"I can believe things that are true and I can believe things that aren't true and I can believe things where nobody knows if they're true or not." She includes in her litany "that it's aerodynamically impossible for a bumblebee to fly, that light is a wave and a particle, that there's a cat in a box somewhere who's alive and dead at the same time" along with "a personal god who cares about me and worries and oversees everything I do," and "an impersonal god who set the universe in motion and went off to hang with her girlfriends and doesn't even know that I'm alive." The opposing deities are justifiable here, because Sam believes in whatever works for her, amuses her, or catches her imagination. She's

25   *Ibid.*, 219.

26   Gaiman, Neil, *American Gods*, p. 393.

willing to accept it all—keeping everything intact—sense be damned. In the context of a novel that is about, in part, gods born from human faith in the New World, her speech articulates not only a perfectly acceptable position, but is also the only one capable of encompassing her reality.

Richard Grey extracts from Moorcock's stories, as well as from others, a moral education about honor, loyalty, freedom and evil. What more can one ask from a religion? When he nearly dies partway through One Life, he finds himself in his version of heaven. He enters the stories.

> . . . rivers of dreams and fields of stars, a hawk with a sparrow clutched in its talons flies low above the grass, and here are tiny intricate people waiting for him to fill their heads with life, and thousands of years pass and he is engaged in strange work of great importance and sharp beauty, and he is loved, and he is honored, and then a pull, a sharp tug, and it's . . .[27]

And the older boy who tightened Richard's tie to mock his slovenly appearance loosens it, and he can breathe again—much to his disappointment. He had, after all, been just where he longed to be.

Successful integrations of realism and the fantastic are plentiful in fiction. One of Neil Gaiman's particular strengths is the custom blend of story elements cross-culture, genre, medium and age group. He can lend excitement to the idea of the world ending, because then the partitions will come down, and we'll see what was behind the scenes all along. Whether it's all the beasts and bogies and vengeful angels coming out of a hole in the sky together, a short flight to a ruined temple where we can all be heroes, or just a little man in overalls humphing through his mustache and sweeping off the stage, Gaiman tells us that it's "the best place in the world," and my, what fun we'll have when we go.

In the case of *American Gods'* Sam, whose reality contradicts itself, subscription to a contradictory faith shows insight. Many things that she describes apply to our reality as well, such as "that while all human life is sacred there's nothing wrong with the

27   Gaiman, Neil, *Smoke and Mirrors*, p. 214.

death penalty if you can trust the legal system implicitly, and that no one but a moron would trust the legal system." When it comes down to it, what do we really know for sure? I see the divergent and discrepant belief system as a kind of acceptance that we do not, in the end, know anything. So Death could be an adorable, loving girl with heavy eyeliner and ass-kicking boots, or author Terry Pratchett's cowl-wearing, blue-eyed skeleton with the reverberating caps-lock voice. Since we can't know, it could just as easily be both. There's no need to choose.

Like the mental gymnastics brought on by a Zen koan, belief in everything has the capacity to broaden our minds and—perhaps—bring on enlightenment. Besides, what catches your imagination more: the idea that we all don costumes one autumn evening to blend with the ghoulies who also walk abroad that night, or that we dress up and collect candy door-to-door for no reason?

Why is Halloween awesome? Hags and goblins and were-beasts—the infinite, unfettered possibility of them—exist on a mind-blowing level of fun. Neil Gaiman borrows rituals, deities, tricksters and fairy tales from under every stone, roof or teacup. He dusts them off and picks out the bits he likes, splashes in his own stories, then offers them up to us. And they're fun, and we like them, and they inspire us to believe in everything.

THE THIN LINE BETWEEN

by Marilyn "Mattie" Brahen

One night I dreamt of the solar system, which widened out into the galaxy, which stretched into all of the galaxies swirling in our universe. The universe then formed itself into a rectangular fish tank, its glass walls compactly holding its beige cosmic gases and matter on a table in a cheerful room, and Neil Gaiman's character Death stood above it, lovingly tapping fish food into the tank to feed her pets, Slim and Wandsworth. The image comforted me in a primordial sort of way. Death was taking such good care of our universe (at least until she turns its last light out).

This is the contrast that encompasses all of Gaiman's works, that things are not quite what we believe they are, that one reality masks or morphs into another, realities we are often blind to in our waking world.

"Reality" is mankind's shared and agreed-upon version of our universe. In Neil Gaiman's ten-volume series, *The Sandman*, he defines these multiple realities, the yearnings and fears leading us to them and our biases denying them. Key human characters discover this dualism through events that interconnect. In the opening story, "The Sleep of the Just," we meet Roderick Burgess, a Dark Arts practitioner. Seeking to capture Death, he instead ensnares Dream, Lord Morpheus, who holds The Dreaming intact. Dream escapes 70 years later to finds the Dream World nearly destroyed and mortals emotionally damaged, their sense of reality impaired by their loss of their dreams during his long absense.

Dream is a sibling of The Endless, who are immortal and yet can die. This seems contradictory until you realize that they represent eternal human traits. From eldest to youngest, they are: Destiny, who is blind and yet knows the future of all things; Death, who takes us from life yet genuinely treasures us; Dream, who controls our subconscious in dreams and in stories that we tell; Destruction who, loving life and peace, abandoned his realm because we are capable of destroying ourselves; Desire who, both male and female, revels in tempting humanity and cannot be sated; Despair, who controls those of us who have lost hope and faith; and Delirium, with her multi-colored hair, mismatched eyes of green and blue, and jumbled, helter-skelter madness that hides sudden moments of painful lucidity.

Denizens of both the Dream World and the waking world leap from the pages into your mind, each world essential to the other. And Dream, the ultimate Master Storyteller, strives to heal the Dreaming while being forced to unravel other plots and designs that draw him away from his duty. But we leave *The Sandman* now to look at other works by Gaiman and find their link to the theme of dualism.

In *Neverwhere*, subways are things of darkness, but not necessarily of evil. Darkness can be a refuge from our workaday modern lives, which often blind us to our faults and prejudices. We treat other people as invisible when they do not fit our waking agenda, their needs not our own.

In *Neverwhere*, if you don't "mind the gap" between the train and the platform you step on to enter the train or exit it, you not only might catch your foot in it, you might very well be grasped by something evil below the tracks. Throughout the novel, we see two worlds co-existing: London Above and London Below, but London Above doesn't acknowledge the lot of those below, lost and cast away. A gap indeed; people well-versed in proper reality would rather not be dragged down.

While his upscale fiancée Jessica stalks away in disgust, the hero, Richard Mayhew, aids a seemingly scruffy and homeless girl bleeding on the sidewalk. The girl, whose name is Door, can magically create doors where and when she requires one. Richard, expecting to get Door medical attention and return to his own life, is instead plunged into the dangerous intrigues of London Below, its tunnels and caverns candlelit, those it harbors often more noble than their counterparts in the brightly lit rooms of London Above. Together, Richard and Door strive to find the truth behind the murder of her parents and outwit their killers, who now stalk Door.

Neverwhere's two wonderful villains, Mr. Croup and Mr. Vandemar, echo the demeanor of proper English gentlemen. They are anything but. Rats, despised by humanity, are sentient, can communicate with humans, and are given respect bordering on deference in London Below. The novel bursts with contrasts of what-is-real and what-is-not-supposed-to-be-real,-but-is. An angel of light proves to be the most monstrous villain of all.

Stardust, Gaiman's tribute to Lord Dunsany's *The King of Elfland's Daughter*, deviates from *Neverwhere* in that there is a tacit acknowledgment that Elfland does exist, and that there are passageways between reality and unreality with commerce between them.

Every nine years, the Town of Wall allows its citizens to pass through a gap in a wall that divides it from a meadow beyond the town, a gap carefully guarded at all other times. Those living on the other side of the wall set up a most unusual market fair, and the mortal and elven folk may intermingle, buy and sell, and then part ways.

Young Dunstan Thorn tastes the wares of love with a comely, young, elven woman at the fair, and months later, the sentries at the gap find a baby boy in a basket, his name written on parchment: Tristran Thorn. Tristran grows up in the Town of Wall, but his heritage lies beyond it, and events take him through the gap to Elfland, to adventures and choices that will affect both worlds.

The question of what constitutes reality will be ever with us, and Gaiman makes us ponder it, creating imaginative venues through which we may explore it. *Mr. Punch*, Gaiman's graphic novel, illustrated by Dave McKean, casts a different perspective on Gaiman's thematic concerns. Instead of fantasy transforming fact into a warm and wondrous revelation, fantastical fears coldly confirm life's plodding horrors. A child's summer with a troubled grandfather, a hunchbacked uncle, and a professor of classic Punch and Judy puppet shows, are depicted in a stark, here-and-now world. In the opening, when Punch hurling Judy's baby to the ground, the baby puppet bleeds, but throughout the rest of the tale, events are psychologically but realistically portrayed through the lead character's memories: this is what I saw; this is how I saw it. And how those events color the boy's viewpoint provides contrast between what actually exists and what is perceived to exist in his life.

The story is empathetic, but leaves the reader disquieted. Gaiman, in one passage, describes "the lessons of death" (as told by Punch) as "amusing and delighting both old and young . . ." Children do laugh raucously at violent puppets and cartoons. Is the true revelation of Mr. Punch that a child's rite of passage is facing up to fear, experiencing fright as preparation for life, which can be naughty, nasty and not nice?

Thematic content is more precise in the short story or the poem which, by its nature, requires brevity and compactness in plot, characterization, and motivation. Gaiman has two short story collections, *Smoke and Mirrors* and *Angels & Visitations*. "Chivalry" stands out, reminiscent of the gentler *Twilight Zone* episodes, which Rod Serling used to lead us into, where the dividing line between imagination and reality vanished for a while.

As "Chivalry" begins, a self-reliant widow finds the Holy Grail in a shop of old, second-hand items sold for charity, buys it and takes it home. The next day, Galaad, Lancelot's son, appears out of myth and on her doorstep, attempting to obtain the Grail from her. She eventually lets him trade for it, but not until she's struck a pleasant acquaintanceship with the young man, testing his mettle through mundane tasks requiring patience rather than heroic feats. Not only are the lives of the realistic characters changed for the better; Galaad, returning to the realm of fantasy, has gained much more than the Grail. In the end, reality joins legend and travels on with it while, at the same time, legend and reality say farewell and go their separate ways.

"The Mystery of Father Brown," an essay Gaiman wrote for *100 Great Detectives*, discusses the development of G. K. Chesterton's lackluster yet intriguing detective. Gaiman compares Father Brown stories to the composition of a dream: ". . . their logic is dream logic. The characters from a Father Brown story have little existence before the story starts, none after it has finished: each cast of innocents and malefactors is assembled to make the story work, and for no other reason. The tales are not exercises in deduction, for rarely is the reader presented with a set of clues and logical problems to work through. Instead they are the inspired magic tricks of a master showman, or *trompe l'oeil* paintings in which the application of a little brown suddenly turns an Eastern swami into a private secretary, or a suicide into a murder and back again."[28]

In "The Goldfish Pool and Other Stories," a young author braves the mediocrity of Hollywood producers, meets an old

28   Gaiman, Neil, *Angels & Visitations: A Miscellany*, Minneapolis, Minnesota: DreamHaven Books, 1993.

groundskeeper at his motel and, in an almost delicate style, contrasts the vacuous creative process of film-making with the realistic illusion of the stage magician. "The illusions," the protagonist explains to a woman incapable of understanding him, ". . . make us question the nature of reality."

In *American Gods*, time distorts, the land distorts, America is a show put on for the gods it believes in, and the old gods, whether backstage, onstage, or in the audience, are rarely amused by our irreverence. Shadow, the protagonist, is a drifter with a good soul, willing to trust, to the point of naiveté, folk who are neither good nor trusting or naive. An old man who hires Shadow, named Wednesday, is actually Wotan or Odin, father of the Norse gods, intent on waging a war between the elder, forgotten gods and the newer gods born of American ingenuity, such as money, transportation, entertainment, and computer science. Another character is named Low Key Lyesmith, this given name a perfect pun on writers: subtle crafters of lies that emulate truth.

The coincidence of reality and unreality merges nearly seamlessly into the novel, and Gaiman's fascination with conjuration and magic tricks serves as a bridge between. Shadow loves doing coin tricks. He conjures coins for a small girl and a dog; the dog, actually the god Anubis, tells him that he's no Houdini. Earlier, Mad Sweeney, a tall, drunken leprechaun, tries to teach him to pull coins from thin air and the pot of gold. The symbolism of the coin is its two-sided nature. Mr. Ibis, a god of the Egyptian pantheon, tells Shadow to remember that ". . . life and death are different sides of the same coin. Like the heads and tails of a quarter." And Shadow says: "And if I had a double-headed quarter?" Mr. Ibis says: "You don't." Duality exists, despite our desire to cheat.

Transference, the illusion of shape-shifting, one life lived concurrently, is explored. Horus is alternately a hawk and, for brief occasions, a naked man, uncomfortable in and confused by his human form. A brown cat befriending Shadow is Bast.

Time and space flip from one reality to another. When Shadow and Wednesday pull their car off the roadside, avoiding pursuit, the landscape transforms from day to a nightmare land of slick, volcanic, black rocks and hills. They travel through it and emerge back into our reality near an Indian reservation. At one point, the transition makes Shadow ill, and Wednesday has him sip from a flask of pungent liquid, telling him: "It's not good for the audience to find themselves walking about backstage." In a restaurant near St. Paul, Minnesota, Shadow notices that in the three days they've been on the road, the dates have jumped from the third week in January to the 14th of February. Wednesday explains that they've walked for almost a month: "In the Badlands. Backstage."

Gaiman has the character of Mr. Ibis in *American Gods* describe how we will seek out fictions, other versions of reality, to ease the trauma of tragedy:

> "We draw our lives around these moments of pain, and remain upon our islands, and they cannot hurt us. They are covered by a smooth, safe, nacreous layer to let them slip, pearllike, from our souls without pain.
>
> "Fiction allows us to slide into these other heads, these other places, and look out through other eyes. And then in the tale we stop before we die, or we die vicariously and unharmed, and in the world beyond the tale we turn the page or close the book, and we resume our lives.
>
> "A life that is, like any other, unlike any other."[29]

Neil Gaiman's works abound with dualistic transmutations. Concurrently everything is real and everything is an illusion, and somehow the world is, if not always better for it, at least more meaningful because of that union. In *Coraline*, a young, undersized girl, discovers a hidden passageway in the flat in which she and her parents live. Her parents love her, but most of the time Coraline is left to herself and goes "exploring."

Their flat is one of several in an old house. Her neighbors are the Misses Spink and Forcible, former actresses who now live with their memories and their beloved dogs, and the Crazy Old Man upstairs who is training a mouse circus no one has yet seen. Another flat, long unoccupied, sits on the opposite side of Coraline's, once connected by a door in the drawing room, which is now bricked up. Coraline's mother proves this by taking a key and opening it, showing Coraline the brick wall. But late one night, Coraline slips out of bed to investigate noises, opens the

29   Gaiman, Neil. *American Gods*. New York, NY: HarperCollins/ Morrow, 2001. p.253

door, and finds a sinister passageway to the opposite flat. No longer empty, it is a duplicate of her and her parents' flat, and there she meets her other mother and father, caricatures of her real parents, with black shiny buttons where their eyes should be.

Coraline soon discovers duplicates of Miss Spink and Miss Forcible and the Crazy Old Man as well, also with black buttons for eyes, and realizes she is in danger. The only creatures not duplicated are herself and a black cat, who can talk in the "other world" on the other side of the drawing room door. Luckily, the real Misses Spink and Forcible have given Coraline a protective talisman, a stone with a hole all the way through its middle.

Returning to her real world, Coraline discovers that her real parents have been stolen. She sees them beckoning to her for help through a hall mirror. Coraline realizes that she must return to the other world to rescue her parents. She bravely ventures forth and discovers three other lost souls captured by the other mother.

Certain elements in *Coraline* resemble Lewis Carroll's *Alice in Wonderland* and *Through the Looking Glass*. The black cat haughtily gives her directions and advice. The mirror and drawing room door are both reminiscent of Alice's adventures. But *Coraline* departs from Carroll's work, developing its own fictional duality and theme. The cat develops a cautious bond with Caroline, realizing it also faces danger from the other mother. The mice owned by the Crazy Old Man are transformed to sinister rats in the other world. Coraline's need for attention is paralleled by her learning to accept limits and compromise, while calling forth her creative imagination and courage, a journey of personal development and triumph against the unknown, rather than a satire of society.

Many other works by Gaiman further illustrate his theme of dual reality. In *The Dream Hunters*, a Sandman tale told in melodic prose by Neil Gaiman and richly illustrated by Yoshitaka Amano, Binzuru Harada, a disciple of Buddha who failed to achieve perfection, gives a monk, seeking to cure a dying fox, a strip of paper to present to the King of All Night's Dreaming. The monk, while dreaming, then reads what is written upon the paper: ". . . they described one who shaped, who moulded and formed things from chaos and from nothing, who transmuted things from formlessness and shapelessness into that-which-was-not-real, but without which the real would have no meaning."[30]

In *The Books of Magic*, illustrated by John Bolton, Charles Vess, Scott Hampton, and Paul Johnson, twelve-year-old Timothy Hunter is told that he has the capacity to become one of the world's greatest magicians, and is taken on a quest through the past, present and future of our world and our universe, all the better to choose between a destiny of magic or reality.

While visiting Faerie, he learns from Queen Titania that fantasy worlds do not exist, and yet their reality or lack of it do not matter. All that matters is that they are there and give our world meaning.

In other adventures, meeting other sages and magicians, Timothy is also told that magic has a price. When his heroic journey ends, literally with the end of the universe (and Death is there to collect it, to make sure everything is tidy with nothing cluttering it up), Timothy must choose between the dangerous world of magic and the sane world of reality, to cross the thin line between or to stay safely in the ordinary world. At story's end, he chooses one and the other.

As a reader, an ending in which we can have both worlds has a certain allure. And if we have to choose, the works of Neil Gaiman and of authors like him seem to imply that there is a bit of magic in the mundane, that Elfland can flow into the borders of our own world as they did in Dunsany's classic tale. And no matter how fearsome things may become in Neil Gaiman's universe, I always feel as if the author, unseen, is whispering on the wind, barely within my range of hearing, "All will be revealed in the end. Read on."

30   Gaiman, Neil. *The Dream Hunters*. New York, NY: DC Comics, 1999. p.86

Works Cited:

Gaiman, Neil. *The Dream Hunters*. New York, NY: DC Comics, 1999.

Gaiman, Neil. *The Sandman #1-75*. New York, NY: DC Comics, 1989-1996.

Gaiman, Neil. *Neverwhere*. New York, NY: Avon Books, 1997.

Gaiman, Neil. *Stardust*. New York, NY: Avon Books, 1999.

Gaiman, Neil. *Mr. Punch*. New York, NY: DC Comics/Vertigo, 1995.

Gaiman, Neil. *Smoke and Mirrors: Short Fictions & Illusions*. New York, NY: Avon Books, 1998.

Gaiman, Neil. *Angels & Visitations: A Miscellany*. Minneapolis, Minnesota: DreamHaven Books, 1993.

Gaiman, Neil. *American Gods*. New York, NY: HarperCollins/Morrow, 2001.

Gaiman, Neil. *Coraline*. New York, NY: HarperCollins Children's Books, 2002.

Gaiman, Neil. *The Books of Magic 1-4*. New York, NY: DC Comics, 1990, 1991; Compilation, 1993.

ON THE DEATH
OF MAD KING SWEENY
IRISH LORE AND LITERATURE
IN *AMERICAN GODS*

William Alexander

Mad Sweeny, the crass, bellicose, seven-foot-tall leprechaun, is a minor character in Neil Gaiman's *American Gods*. He walks through only a few of the novel's pages, and sits, frozen and deceased, through just a few more. But a long line of Irish authors haunt Gods alongside Sweeny, and through him we can explore their influence in Gaiman's work. What follows is an account of three such Irishmen—W.B. Yeats, James Joyce, and Flann O'Brian—and of how each one contributed to the life and death of Mad Sweeny.

William Butler Yeats

Yeats and Gaiman have walked a few of the same roads in style and subject matter, whether or not one was whispering in the other's ear at the time. Both have made oral traditions hold still in print, and both have taken bits of old lore, repaired them and made them run again. The Irish poet set out to prove that Irish myth can be every bit as interesting as the more venerated stuff the Greeks had dreamed up, and I imagine Gaiman's garage as being filled with the clutter of legends; a grail here, a rusty sword there, and the man himself underneath what looks to be an old bathtub on two wheels but was once, in fact, the chariot that pulled the sun across the sky. It's still a bit charred from the lightning Zeus clobbered it with. A hand reaches out from underneath, groping around for a wrench . . .

Walk around the chariot to his workbench (you might hand him the wrench along the way). Look for a flash of green next to the pile of old Roman coins, behind the goose. There it is: a statue of a little man, green-clad, red-bearded, frolicking next to a pot of gold. This is Yeats's legacy: the recasting of superstition into a source of Irish pride. No small feat, either; in Yeats's day, the entire field of folklore was hell-bent on debunking superstition.

Ireland herself has calmed down a bit since then; no one dyes the Liffey green on St. Paddy's day. But Americans still love the leprechauns. Frolicking figurines can be found in every Irish gift shop, waiting for American tourists. They are the only *Sidhé* that every American know by name. They are icons of football's Fighting Irish and of colorful marshmallows in breakfast cereal, and they have about as much to do with Ireland as does the shape of a shamrock traced into Guinness foam.

So it is that Sweeny, accent-lacking, Southern Comfort-drinking, Shadow-boxing Sweeny, is more American than Irish when first we meet him. This is, of course, the point. "I've been over here too fucken long" he tells us in Jack's Crocodile Bar, west of Nottamun, about 250 miles from Eagle Point.

Gaiman often provides us with such a concrete sense of location, creating a solid reality in which the fantastic can occur; *American Gods* is a tour of places, people and divinity in the United States, and *Neverwhere* reveals secrets of the London Underground. Yeats, and the old Gaelic bards before him, would have called this *dinnsheanchas*, or "knowledge of the lore of places"[31]; he himself used description of Irish landscape in general, and of the Sligo countryside in particular, to help forge an Irish national identity during a time when no coherent identity existed. Scholars may look back in a hundred years and likewise praise Gaiman for inventing America.

James Joyce

The most obvious parallel between Gaiman and Joyce is that both of them have used the word "wake" with every possible pun intended, and Sweeny's own wake in *American Gods* is among the most brilliant mix of old lore and new prose to be found anywhere. But before Joyce started writing in dream languages that no one else could read, he mixed together myth and literature without the patriotism of Yeats.

James Joyce found both oral tradition and the European novel to be inadequate narrative forms. Epics might be handy for the praising of great deeds, but they bear little relevance to everyday life; it is difficult to consistently pretend that taking out the trash is

31   Kiberd, Declan. *Inventing Ireland*. Vintage, 1996, p. 107.

an act of genuine heroism. Traditional novels, on the other hand, were too rational and realistic to contain Joyce's multi-faceted storytelling. So he wrote a novel about a day, a perfectly ordinary day, but cast in the shape and semblance of Homer's *Odyssey*.

In *Ulysses*, antagonists in a pub brawl observe Leopold Bloom, "amid clouds of angels ascend to the glory of the brightness at an angle of fortyfive degrees over Donohoe's in Little Green Street like a shot off a shovel."[32] In making the hero of his epic novel a pacifist (a political stance which offended more patriotic characters, beginning the aforementioned brawl), Joyce was chiding the previous generation of Irish artists for their blind nationalism and prettifying of heroic violence. Yeats himself played no small part in elevating Cuchulainn, hero of the *Tain* (an ancient Irish epic in which war began over a stolen bull, which makes sense in the context of ancient Irish marriage laws—if the queen had owned just one more bull, her possessions would have exceeded her husband's and she'd rule the royal household accordingly—but even in contrast to the thousand ships launched for one lady it seems like an overreaction), into a mascot for Irish revolution. In mixing his sense of the everyday with Christian and classical imagery, Joyce challenged all of literature to be epic and ordinary, magical and realistic, at precisely the same time.

Gaiman can perform this juggling act with the best of them. Our man Sweeny dies of drink, and cold, and the loss of a bright golden coin; it isn't a question of either/or, a debate over whether to put a magic or a mundane cause of death in the coroner's report. It isn't a question at all. He died of cold, and of a coin.

In *American Gods* (and in Gaiman's work in general—examples from Sandman would be too numerous to count, and please hunt down his short story "Chivalry" sometime), the contradiction between reality and fantasy simply does not exist. This pragmatism has long been a character of the Irish narrative arts; "a Galway woman, when asked by an American anthropologist whether she really believed in the 'little people,' replied with terse sophistication: 'I do not, sir—but they're there anyway.'"[33]

---

32   Joyce, James, *Ulysses*, Penguin, 1992, p. 449.

33   Kiberd, *ibid.*, p. 2

Flann O'Brian

A few men sit together over drinks. One of them tells Sweeny's story, recounting his temper and his madness and his death. The telling is in high epic style, includes staves of ancient verse, and is periodically interrupted by audience members with gossip, or with little poems about beer. The teller is Finn MacCool, hero of old Ireland, and his audience consists of characters invented by a fictional author. The scene takes place in *At Swim-Two-Birds*, a novel by Flann O'Brian (not his real name).

Without the perverse subtlety of Joyce (who delighted in writing puzzles for academics to spend years decoding), O'Brian put into direct contrast the poets of Ireland, old and new. Finn MacCool, shown as an old man unable to process the strangeness of his modern surroundings, recites epic tales as dignified and exalted as they are long-winded and irrelevant. His companions, ordinary joes out for a drink, give Finn polite attention for as long as they can stand, but they all prefer simplistic, rhyming poems about porter. Finn's tragic recital is later summarized by one as a story "about this fellow Sweeny that argued the toss with the clergy and came off second-best at the wind-up . . . The upshot is that your man becomes a bloody bird."[34] The scene simultaneously lambastes the fetishism of Irish revivalists for all things ancient, and berates the unsophisticated Every(Irish)man for his lack of history and literary taste. Classic storytelling flounders in the modern pub.

Sixty years after O'Brian published *Birds*, I had the pleasure of listening to a great many stories in Irish pubs about why no one tells stories in Irish pubs anymore. Reminds me of a tale about a man walking from farm to farm in his travels and looking for a place to spend the night. The price of lodging at the first farm was a story. "I haven't any," said the man, and the door was shut. The price at the second farm was the same. "I don't have any stories," said the man, and the door was likewise shut upon him. At the third farm they asked for a story, and angrily the man told them about the first two farms, and of their lack of hospitality for this same ridiculous

---

34   O'Brien, Flann, *At Swim-Two-Birds*, Penguin, 1960, p. 85.

reason. That was his story, and they let him stay. Stories, like gods, are difficult to kill, and new ones show up all the time.

The narrator and primary storyteller of *At Swim-Two-Birds* considers the relationship between author and character a tyrannical one. In order to avoid exploiting those who populate his own novels, the narrator gives them separate, private lives. Just as O'Brian shows us what his characters do outside their narratives, so too does Gaiman reveals what gods do when they're no longer gods. Most adapt their original duties to new circumstances, like the two Egyptian deities who run a funeral parlor. While Sweeny sits frozen on a slab in their basement, Ibis and Jacquel (who still has a fondness for human hearts, quietly munched during autopsy) join Shadow in the dead god's wake.

From O'Brian's Finn we learn that Sweeny was a King of Dall Araidhe, that he wronged the monk Ronan in a fury and was cursed with madness, and that he flew from tree to tree in Ireland believing himself a bird. From Ibis, who keeps all lives and stories in his notebook, we learn that the verse recited by Finn was sacred long before it became an amusing story about a naked man in a tree. Then "Holy Mother Church herself arrived and every god in Ireland was transformed into a fairy or a saint or a dead King without so much as a by-your-leave."[35] So it was that Mad Sweeny, a god of ancient Ireland, became first a legendary king, and then an American leprechaun, before freezing to death with a bottle of Jameson clutched in his hand.

Thus we have Yeats's leprechauns, the mythic fiction of Joyce, and O'Brian's tragi-comic Sweeny in the verse of old Finn: Irish ingredients for an American character. How much of Sweeny's story was the actual stuff of legend, and how much did O'Brian and Gaiman dream up between them? Doesn't matter. It was the cold and the coin, you see.

35   Gaiman, Neil, *American Gods*, HarperCollins, 2001, p. 177.

CATHARSIS AND THE AMERICAN GOD: NEIL GAIMAN

Baba Singh

According to Aristotle, tragedy purged the emotions. Theater in ancient Greece was a sacred activity, a sacrifice to the gods. Theater was a ritual, a rite; and its followers were rewarded with *catharsis*, physiological, emotional release. Strangely enough for us today, Aristotle placed little trust in the artist for the success of this process.

Cathartic theater was the highest form of art in ancient Greece. Just the price an audience of that time had to pay— throwing themselves into ritual murder, incest, patricide, infanticide, and feeling all the pain of a Medea or an Oedipus—shows you that they must have been getting their money's worth. Or maybe that's just how Aristotle made sense of things. Maybe ancient audiences flocked to the theater ignorant of the fact that they were participating in something that today we would rather go to private therapy for, or, at best, confide in a close friend. After all, what kind of satisfaction could tragedy possibly give?

Identification with all that is negative in life cleans our souls, Aristotle tells us. And identification with the artist behind this virtual negativity obstructs this process. What good would identifying with a playwright do, anyway? He doesn't even get to go on stage.

There are other forms of tragedy besides the dramatic arts, where the author's relationship with an audience isn't mediated by actors, directors and the like; but these are recent evolutions, not pure tragic forms. If modern authors have moved to the higher ground of novels, short stories, etc., these modern forms of art can be understood as securing for the artist more direct access to identification with an audience. Historically, the function of authorship has mutated around the mechanism of identification, and not vice versa. So it's no coincidence that tragedy originated as a sort of worship, and it should be no surprise that we can find parallels of this process in our own narrative-using culture. In this culture, unlike ancient Greece, the artist is king; however, it may be too soon to assume that he is god.

With *American Gods,* Neil Gaiman presents us with the tragedy of forgetting gods. The very passing of time causes this lapse in memory, and this is tragic. But the difference between past and present is not merely the quantity of years between the time a god is worshiped and when he is forgotten (*American Gods'* gods were worshiped anywhere between 14,000 B.C. and the 1700s). A qualitative rift exists between today and a homogenous "past" characterized by belief in non-Christian deities. Gods "die" when their followers cease adoration, and in the present age they are threatened not only by death, but by extinction as well.

Today there has been a qualitative change in the relationship between god and worshiper. Let's just say that, in *American Gods,* the Atlantic Ocean represents this qualitative rift that makes our age so tragic. Gaiman begins his story with the following quote:

> Irish-Americans remember the fairies, Norwegian-Americans the *nisser,* Greek-Americans the *vrykólakas,* but only in relation to events remembered in the Old Country. When I once asked why such demons are not seen in America, my informants giggled confusedly and said "They're scared to pass the ocean, it's too far," . . .

But they *have* crossed over: in the "piskie" dreams of the Irish immigrant Essie Tregowan (77); in the mammoth skull of the nomadic Northern Plains worshipers of *Nunyunnini* (322); in bloody Viking sacrifice to the god Odin (53). History has led them all to the other side of this fearful ocean, to this very dangerous place called America. Like an inverted *Exodus,* these gods led to the promised land *by* their worshipers live hand to mouth driving cabs, collecting retirement, even prostituting themselves in the land of the faithless. Gaiman wants to communicate to Americans something about our country that we, as natives, may not even realize. As he tells us through Mr. Ibis, the Egyptian god turned undertaker: the "important thing to understand about American history . . . is that it is fictional, a charcoal-sketched simplicity for the children, or the easily bored" (73). Americans delight in historical amnesia, then. If Gaiman's gods had ended up anywhere else, they would not be in danger of being forgotten.

Yet the America Gaiman presents to us is not godless, even if it is faithless: we have gods of technology, of the digital age, of radiation, of cancer (386). But these mutant deities never win Gaiman's sympathy like the gods of the Old World do, whose continued existence in this quantitative, digitized world he questions. Gaiman's sympathy drifts rather to these old gods' personal qualities, their idiosyncrasies, their vanity, their flaws. Wednesday (Odin), who presents himself to the hero Shadow Moon as a charismatic yet untrustworthy con artist/employer, charms everyone in the end. Shadow develops empathy for him and all the old, outdated gods, mourning the assassinated Wednesday despite his flaws: he misses Wednesday's "confidence, his attitude. His conviction" (319). Gaiman's gods of the new digital age lack something that the old gods have: character, personality, individuality. How can qualities like these manifest all their imperfect perfection in an age of quantity, measurement, and precision? Gaiman's America is not so much a godless country, as a country where gods cannot survive for much longer.

But the past is always with us, even as something we are glad to have forgotten. If these gods of the Old (pre-Christian) World are to be missed when they are gone even if they are not entirely to be trusted when they're here, then our attitude as readers toward Gaiman's pantheon of holy has-beens is like nostalgia for a dubious past without which our present would never have been possible. So, as Americans, we shouldn't be too surprised when Gaiman shows us that our kitsch is our divinity.

Nostalgia provides a kitsch-laden backdrop for the action of *American Gods*. As Wednesday tells Shadow: "In other countries, over the years, people recognized places of power . . . in the USA, people still get the call, or some of them, and they feel themselves being called to from the transcendent void, and they respond to it by building a model out of beer bottles somewhere they've never visited" (92). Holy places are places of tourist worship: museums of 1950s-era relics, a "sad little park" in the center of the country (333). The new god Media speaks to Shadow through reruns of *I Love Lucy* (136). America is a land whose culture revels in the lowest forms of art, which is enough to make anyone suspicious of art's function. However, the tourists and native folk of *American Gods* are ignorant of the holiness of the places they visit. Paying blind homage to shrines like The House on the Rock, where relics of Americana collect more dust than ticket money, Americans reduce art to the useless display of a good luck charm.

For its aesthetic appeal, kitsch relies less on the qualitites of objects in themselves than on our feelings of ambiguity toward them: kitsch pleases *and* offends. But objects like The House on the Rock are still art, and should not be disdained just because their repulsion is part of their attraction. If Gaiman uses kitsch as a backdrop to *American Gods*, it is to show us that the ambivalence he fictionalizes between the Old Gods and their worshipers has a real counterpart in the American's relationship to art.

Ambivalent or not, in Gaiman's America, worship is still a pastime. Some gods, in fact, will do anything to get it:

> "Honey, while you're giving it to me, while you're pushing that big hard thing inside of me, will you worship me?"
> "Will I what?"
> She is rocking back and forth on him: the engorged head of his penis is being rubbed against the wet lips of her vulva.
> "Will you call me goddess? Will you pray to me? Will you worship me with your body?"
> He smiles. Is that all she wants? (23).

When we read about a "john" who worships Sheba the prostitute (22-25), a pagan who doesn't know who the goddess Easter is (243), or a police chief named Chad Mulligan who obeys the Kobold that holds his small town captive down to the final command for his own suicide (448), we see worship in *American Gods* as unconscious, ignorant, or forced. Although forgetful, human minds are the battlefield for gods' survival, human participation in these gods' desires need not be voluntary. Voluntary or not, this worship is a prize and sustenance to gods so worshiped. They will fight, cheat, scam to get it. It feeds their physical bodies and rectifies their decrepitude. Worship, in Gaiman's America, is a process of active maintenance, coercion, even extortion; it is in itself an object of contention.

Maybe this state of affairs Gaiman describes is just a reflection of the logic of belief: gods are immortal, but only live through the mortal minds that worship them. And so the vanity that fuels his gods' desire for worshipers can only be satisfied by making time stand still. Gaiman's two opposed groups of deities—those of the Old World and those of the New—represent the only two ways to do this, one freezing the present into an eternal past, the other rushing to be the first to make the future into the present. While the gods of the new age keep pace "with a changing world" for fear that "their time would already be over"(419), the gods of old, like the Slavic Czernobog and his sisters, waste away in apartments that smell like "overboiled cabbage and cat box and unfiltered foreign cigarettes" (60). As the goddess Media tells Shadow, time itself is what people sacrifice these days in their worship (136).

Whether represented by the forced, nostalgic stasis of the Kobold's city of Lakeside, or Wednesday's constant bodily renewal by virgins, or by the "fat kid" who consigns Odin "to the Dumpster of history while people like me ride our limos down the superhighway of tomorrow" (42), the aspiration to immortality on either side of Gaiman's pantheon is doomed to failure. No god can have jurisdiction over eternity, over "the hearts and minds of people" (352). What is at stake in the holy war Gaiman orchestrates toward the climax of *American Gods* is recognition, and recognition only happens in the present, otherwise it's just another monument.

To ensure the moment of recognition of their immortality, these vain gods will go so far as to create their own Armageddon, even at a place like Tennessee's Rock City. But the clash between worship in the old way and worship in the new way is only a sleight-of-hand for Gaiman, as this divine face-off trumps the two-man con game between Odin and his partner Loki, god of chaos and bloodshed. In the midst of the "storm" in *American Gods*, the gods' devotion to godhood itself fuels their vain struggle for recognition.

Our hero Shadow enters this staged Armageddon armed with the wisdom of native America. Shadow takes his cues from the Buffalo Man, who educates him through his dreams about a very different type of worship. The spirit of the land that the native Americans revere without sacrifice or churches pervades an eternal present that needs neither monument nor recognition. Shadow saunters onto the Rock City battlefield indifferent to the deadlines the battling gods fear they wont keep. And just as these gods have taken up arms to defend godhood itself, Shadow finds an ultimate conviction in his actions by reflecting on the nature of belief:

> "People believe, thought Shadow. It's what people do. They believe. And then they will not take responsibility for their beliefs; they conjure things, and do not trust the conjurations. People populate the darkness; with ghosts, with gods, with elec-

trons, with tales. People imagine, and people believe: and it is that belief, that rock-solid belief, that makes things happen" (418).

Belief, worship, is an object in itself: the terminal concern of the pantheon of gods Gaiman has assembled in his story, to be won at any expense. Belief becomes worship only when it condenses around an object; and that object becomes deified by the bare fact of belief.

American Gods is arguably Gaiman's best received work, and its appeal resembles that of his other work in that it portrays our world in contrast to a much older one. The reverence Gaiman expresses for world mythologies and their deities finds its place among everyday details that, so juxtaposed, define it. When we read about Anubis' feather ("We had it made special. You had to be pretty damn evil to tip the scales on that baby"), or about Czernobog in a VW bus (161; 330), we feel the clash of worlds characteristic of Gaiman's writing. This mixture of the familiar and the other-worldly, brinking on drama and humor simultaneously, satisfies the fan of any genre that asks "what if?" and serves the imagination of its readers with the no-strings attached fantasy it craves, anticipates, and even reveres. Gaiman's formula has great appeal at this point in history, when legions of dead beliefs allow art's audience to reflect upon not only the belief system of their culture, but also upon the notion of belief itself.

After his decades-long achievements in comics, prose and poetry, Gaiman has become somewhat of a god himself, to a public he frequently rewards with references in his texts only they can understand. Alongside references to gods and mythology, *American Gods* references Gaiman's own universe. The number 23, Gaiman's recurrent magic numeral, appears as the date on which Shadow bets the "klunker" containing another of the Kobold's child victims will fall into the icy water of Lakeside (433). Delirium, a character from Gaiman's *Sandman* comic, possibly appears as a hungry San Francisco beatnik girl (240). Some of the action in *American Gods* seems to serve no other purpose than to support Gaiman's own mythology. The fan-named "forgotten god" (220-24), present in the narrative as a digression at best, nonetheless keeps fans guessing on several Internet chat rooms a year after the book's publication (where more than one astute follower thinks he is Jesus).

Many of the settings in *American Gods* follow the path of Gaiman's 1999 U.S. tour, which provided material for Shadow's cross-country journeys. Gaiman's on-line journal closed the circuit between author and audience before the book's publication, creating the "pull demand" necessary to any good marketing venture.

Certainly the relationship between an artist and his public figures in the success of art today. Especially in America, artistic success means *both* aesthetic and commercial success. Can these two factors ever be separated, so long as the desire of publishers is, for their very livelihood, to "give readers what they want"? But with Gaiman's story, one wonders if this relationship isn't so much a part of the story as to merge the two factors completely. As the narrative of *American Gods* progresses, with the tried and true mystery of the protagonist's paternity foregrounding resolutions of his adult relationships (*à la* Oedipus), the reader is left wondering which concern—aesthetic or commercial—more dominantly guides the book's progress.

It's not surprising that *American Gods* shows us the ins and outs of magic tricks: its entire structure is that of misdirection. Plumbing the depths of the spiritual underworld, investigating children's disappearances in the small town of Lakeside, Shadow Moon maintains a detective-like posture. And just as Shadow is at his most confident in the narrative when pulling off coin tricks, Gaiman is at his most skillful when misdirecting the attention of his readers. *American Gods* anticipates its audience's anticipations of Gaiman's style so thoroughly that a reader outside Gaiman's fandom will be easily confused as to the book's meaning. The story is a sort of two-man con game itself: on many pages we have two Gaimans, the one who writes and the one who is written about. Are we reading the thought of a meticulous mythographer who has plenty to say about the America we call home? Or are we simply reading *about* him?

From these observations, some might hesitate to call Gaiman's novel art. They might say that the story has no great artistic meaning. While this objection is no doubt well-founded, it ultimately rests on the assumption that meaning has anything to do with artistic effect. It is this assumption that writers like Gaiman must help us overcome, if we are to understand anything about the true function of art. Whatever your idea of "high art" is now, and whatever it has been for others in history, there has been no historical change in the fact that the relation of art to the emotional lives of its audience depends on identification for any effect whatsoever. Only those who are unsatisfied with the idea that our emotional satisfaction has nothing to do with this thing called meaning will look for aesthetic criteria in ideas of beauty or taste.

Aristotle, of course, believed in drama's beauty; but he did so by forgetting its origin as ritual. Like today's fans, ancient audiences flocked to plays they had already seen, already knew, and commonly used as cultural reference. In the *Poetics*, Aristotle places a quite novel emphasis for his time on the creativity of the author. Yet he downplays identification with characters of a narrative to the benefit of plot, which he calls "the soul of tragedy." These two ideas do not conflict in his thought only because Aristotle lacked the foresight to see that audiences would eventually desire identification with authors who create characters resembling themselves.

It would be difficult to maintain that identification with an artist is the terminal point of artistic effect today. Today readers identify with authors who write about getting in touch with themselves: a reality that masquerades as fiction. In today's imploding relationship between author and audience, meaning is becoming secondary to self-reference—that is, reference to the relationship itself. While some would explain this situation by questioning the artistic status of a text like Gaiman's, and locating "true" art elsewhere (according to "timeless" aesthetic values), we should rather recognize that art's true function—to participate in the emotional lives of its audience—has little to do with meaning, beauty or truth.

If there is an audience today for *American Gods*, it is because people believe in artists instead of gods; and also because, in this age of information, the best emotional release is the release of disbelief. As Gaiman incorporates identification with himself as an artist into the very work he produces, he crosses the line that Aristotle used to separate the artist from artistic effect in such a way as to forcibly supplement meaning with biographical detail. In other words, meaning in this modern fictional text is *conditional* upon identification with the author. Such a relationship between artist and audience Aristotle could not have forseen; for it relies on identification with the artist as a necessary precondition for artistic effect.

If authorship has historically developed around the function of identification, then meaning has been the illusion by which this development is denied by all those who actively direct it. Its disguise today is, strangely enough, belief. Believability is crucial to today's narrative fiction, especially in America, where editors will often demand real depictions of a character's culinary and alimentary experiences in the course of a narrative to make a story "realistic"(and *American Gods* is a prime example of this). Such are the current trends in American fiction writing, ironic in itself: as if fiction were only effective when it most closely resembled the non-fictional.

As one sees in the most extreme adoration of fandom, dedicated audiences sustain the idea "this is fiction" by examining a work's fictional feasibility: the way in which it most truthfully distorts reality. It's not enough that Captain Kirk should pilot a starship: without the schematics of the ship's design, *Star Trek* just doesn't seem real enough. Two thousand years after Aristotle, it seems the only true catharsis is belief in something we already recognize as fiction.

Today narrative creates identity *de facto* from the experience of symbolism itself. Can we imagine in ancient Greece two people who, having never met before, form a club only of those who have read certain works? No, because every Greek would already be in the club.

If the experience of narrative creates its own world, it is by refusing its more ancient, communal function. Today we can see audiences continuing the experience of an author's narrative in their personalities, clothing, speech and attitudes. The difference between this activity and the activity of ancient audiences is that narrative provided temporary identifications in the past that purged emotions by their difference from everyday life; and today these identifications have become everyday life itself. Authors like Gaiman are so savvy to this fact that they anticipate these identifications in the content of their work, maintaining them with stories suited to no other purpose.

American Gods evidences a crucial shift in our knowledge of poetics, toward recognition of the true function of narrative in human life. As capitalism drains the last illusions of beauty from traditional aesthetic sensibility, turning readers into narrative addicts, authors like Gaiman hypocritically support the inverse relationship between profit and artistic message that every artist in our society is taught to envy and ignore. Gaiman is a successful puppeteer of figures of ancient mythology. However, a puppet's lips don't mean that anyone is actually speaking to us—that is, conveying meaning. After all, the satisfaction of the puppeteer is not the pleasure of delivering a message, but the pure pleasure of ventriloquism. Likewise, today some audiences are perfectly content—that is to say, satisfied—with merely being an audience—that is to say, being duped—just so long as they are allowed to see and admire the hands of the puppeteer.

The modern, genre-reading audience's needs do not follow Aristotle's simple model of *catharsis* because identification has itself become an object of desire that satisfies just as well when experienced as when witnessed. Suitably enough, it is this audience who is today, more than in Aristotle's time, likely to have at some point taken up the pen and tried their hand at being an artist; in other words, an increasingly literate audience. As such, today's artists face a challenge unknown in earlier times—an audience of potential competitors—and writers like Gaiman have sought refuge from this challenge by becoming both the subject and subject matter of artistic expression.

Maybe with *American Gods* the presence of some overall message on life and the spiritual is less important than the mere fact that the gods have been made to speak. Meaning seldom satisfies anyway, and art must satisfy, else it will be censored (as the comic writer knows far too well). Gaiman has stood for artistic freedom throughout his career; but *American Gods* makes this freedom look like a luxury rather than a right. His text is very telling, especially today, in an age that reveres art in an ever more ambivalent way, and treats the artist as a god to be revered or silenced at the whim of the social will.

So why is *American Gods*, artistically, about nothing? Who knows—these days, maybe even gods have to do what is necessary to get by. In the land of the faithless, all gods are subject to doubt and all adoration must be earned. Once earned, this admiration must be sustained as well; and this may be the hardest task of them all. For today's artists, self-reference seems the surest shelter; yet who knows how long artistic message will serve as blood sacrifice to feed the spirit of artistic image? Maybe we'll all end up perfectly satisfied by this new *catharsis* that purges the body of its emotions by first purging art of its meaning. Or perhaps, in the land of the faithless, time will pick the bones of even the greatest of gods.

THE FRAME AND THE FLASHBACK: ANALYZING NEIL GAIMAN'S STORY "MURDER MYSTERIES"

Marilyn "Mattie" Brahen

In his introduction to *About Writing*, Samuel R. Delany discusses narrative framing around a story's flashback, and the importance of *realistic* flashbacks, ones that are not just *flashes*, but tell ". . . a specific past event with another person, who is stabilizing your attention with questions and comments . . ." He further states: "Fiction is an intellectually imaginative act committed on the materials of memory that tries for the form of history."

In his story "Murder Mysteries," Neil Gaiman demonstrates such a framing technique around a flashback. As he begins his tale, the narrator reminisces about a weather-related stopover in Los Angeles in December ten years earlier that interrupted his flight back home to England:

> "Memory is the great deceiver. Perhaps there are some individuals whose memories act like tape recordings, daily records of their lives complete in every detail, but I am not one of them. My memory is a patchwork of occurrences, of discontinuous events roughly sewn together: the parts I remember, I remember precisely, whilst other sections seem to have vanished completely." (141)

He contacts an old girlfriend who arranges to bring him out to her L.A. home. Due to bad timing on her body's part, she pleases him almost mechanically through oral sex only. Afterwards, quietly and proudly showing off her little daughter sleeping in her bedroom, she speaks of love, drives the narrator (who never names himself, a device that works well for the frame) back to the place he is staying, and leaves him. He walks a short distance, sitting on a bench, smoking a cigarette.

A shabby man approaches and asks to buy a cigarette from him. When the narrator insists on giving him one instead, the man insists on repaying him, if not with cash, then with a story. A *true* story. The narrator finally agrees, and the man begins the inner flashback story of "Murder Mysteries," his memory as an angel in the Silver City:

> "First thing I remember was the Word. And the Word was God. Sometimes when I get *really* down, I remember the sound of the Word in my head, shaping me, forming me, giving me life." (144)

Note the analogy to the writing of fiction, of a story, the allotting of structure to it and, within that structure, the arrangement of what Samuel R. Delany calls a "false memory"—not for the character; for, after all, he is telling a *true* story, but the "false memory" of the author as he *contrives* to create the character's flashback and the "false memory" of the reader accepting the flashback, if well done, as gospel, as *realistically* portrayed. Such is the relationship between character, author and reader which Gaiman sets up so well in "Murder Mysteries."

The not-yet-fallen angel Lucifer names the new angel Raguel and calls him "The Vengeance of the Lord," his function. Lucifer then informs Raguel that he must investigate a "wrong thing," the murder of another angel. In the Silver City, surrounded on its outskirts by the Darkness, all angels work on the Creation. This angel, Carasel, his body and wings broken and bloody on the silver sidewalk, was murdered *before* he fell from the spiraled towers, as he worked with his partner, the angel Saraquael, on the most contradictory attribute of creation: Death.

At spaced intervals, some short, some longer, Gaiman returns us, the readers, to the story's frame, out of Raguel's point of view and back into the narrator's. The narrator questions this shabby stranger who tells the flashback story. Raguel patiently explains that he's translating the tale as much as he can, putting it in a form his listener, the narrator, can comprehend:

> ". . . Otherwise, I couldn't tell the story at all. You want to hear it?"
> "Yes." I didn't care if it was true or not; it was a story I needed to hear all the way through to the end. (151)

In posing this question and receiving the correct answer from the narrator, Raguel (and Gaiman) fulfill what Delany says must be achieved if a flashback is to be realistic and effective: it must, within the construct of the story, have causal and developmental logic that makes the listener/reader *want* to find out what happens next.

Delany also suggests that when frame and flashback don't promote this logic, story will fail, and the reader will not care what happens next. But Gaiman's Raguel deftly controls his audience, thus gaining the narrator's enthusiasm and continuing his tale intriguingly in flashback.

As Raguel interviews Saraquael, working on the yet-unnamed universe in the Hall of Being in the highest of the mezzanine galleries, he, like one of the two senior designer angels, Phanuel, believes that Carasel killed himself to experience the concept of Death in all its aspects:

> "And the *patterns*. Carasel had the notion that what we do here in the Hall of Being creates patterns. That there are structures and shapes appropriate to beings and events that, once begun, must continue until they reach their end. For us, perhaps, as well as for them. Conceivably he felt this was one of his patterns." (152)

Dying to understand Death's pattern is a bit too much to ask of any creator, but the empathetic knowledge of a pattern helps a writer to fashion a story as closely as we can to its true or believable beginning, middle and end, its logical pattern.

Saraquael tells Raguel that Zephkiel, the other senior designer, is the real thinker of the two and mentions that he has seen, in the window of his gallery, Lucifer flying near the Darkness beyond the Silver City. Raguel seeks out Lucifer in a park beside a river, and asks what Lucifer was doing when he came upon Phanuel discovering the body of Carasel. Lucifer replies that he was walking on the edge of the City, trying to think and understand. Raguel then tells Lucifer that Carasel didn't kill himself, for if he had, there would be no need for Raguel.

Raguel then visits Zephkiel, who never leaves his cluttered cell, which is filled with books, scrolls, papers and even pictures. It is the function of Zephkiel, who has no wings, to resolve problems. Zephkiel tells him that he did not kill Carasel, and that it is not his function to tell Raguel who *did*. The discovery and the vengeance are Raguel's functions. Instead Raguel asks if he knows what Lucifer was doing right before Carasel's body was found.

The old angel guesses that Lucifer was walking in the dark.

Raguel then asks about *Love*. While Raguel briefly says that Zephkiel tells him, he doesn't disclose Zephkiel's answer to either narrator or reader. Raguel then returns to where Carasel's body had been. Everything has been cleared. Raguel marks where it had fallen and ascends straight up into the air to the Hall of Being and enters the gallery. He finds Saraquael still working and orders him to go to Zephkiel, then goes to Phanuel and orders him to also meet him at Zephkiel's cell. Lastly, he tells Lucifer that he has found Carasel's murderer and Lucifer must accompany him to Zephkiel's cell.

At this point, a new paragraph opens with: "I looked at my watch: it was almost three." (Page 158) The angel's point of view is abruptly cut off, and we know we are back in the narrator's point of view, who shivers in the cold breeze, prompting the man claiming to be Raguel to ask if he is okay. The narrator confirms that he is both fine and fascinated, and the Raguel character delves back into his flashback.

In Zephkiel's cell, Raguel gets Lucifer to admit to walking in the Dark and hearing voices which promise, question, whisper and plead to him, but Lucifer insists that he is only testing himself and not bargaining with the Dark.

Raguel then confronts Phanuel for taking the credit for Carasel's work, including his work on Love. Saraquael states that Love was his and Carasel's project, but they kept quiet because Phanuel promised them even bigger projects and then assigned them to Death.

Raguel finally gets Saraquael to admit to killing Carasel after they became (asexually) lovers, sneaking time to be alone, exploring the physical and emotional aspects of love. Saraquael had fallen intensely in love with Carasel and had killed him, throwing his body from the gallery, when their project was changed to Death and Carasel lost interest both in Love and in Saraquael.

Raguel, becoming his function, Vengeance, embraces Saraquael in fiery passion, consuming him in flames; then, turning to the others, warns them not to stray from their own appointed paths. Phanuel, terrified, bows out, but Lucifer, in tears, stares at where Saraquael had been and declares Raguel's vengeance unjust, concluding that the very will of God may be unjust and the Darkness may speak the truth. When he leaves, Zephkiel tells

Raguel he has performed his function well and should return to his cell until needed.

The narrative again returns to the frame, the man *on the bench* turning to the narrator, revealing why he, Raguel, could not leave Zephkiel just then, because things "fell into place," and he knelt before Zephkiel, calling him Father and Lord, recognizing Him, accusing Him of "pulling the strings," to create the circumstances leading to the murder: "Because nothing occurs without reason; and all the reasons are Yours. . . ." (163)

Saraquael kills Carasel, and Raguel kills Saraquael and demonstrates "to Lucifer the Injustice of the Lord," who has also created the Darkness and the voices within it.

The Creator offers to let Raguel forget this day, but if he remembers, and Raguel insists that he will, then he will not be able to speak of it to any other angel. The Creator then dismisses Raguel.

When we, the readers, read the first sentence of the next paragraph—"The man was silent, then." (164)—we know we are back in the narrative frame. The man finally gets up: "There you go, pal. That's your story. . . ."

And the narrator wants to know *what happened next.* But the night is leaving. Day is breaking. The man tells him that he left home, lost his way and "home's a long way back." That he moved on, coming to L.A.

There's a few more paragraphs as this part of the frame closes itself out, and the narrator is once again alone.

What was Gaiman's purpose for creating the outer portion of the frame: the narrator stranded in L.A., the old flame, her daughter? As we return to it, the narrator ponders the concepts of absolution and innocence, vaguely recalling a child's drawing of angels above a perfect city, thinking of this girl he once shared love with and of love's relationship to death.

The next day he flies back to England. On the plane he reads a newspaper account of the murder of two women and a child, then dreams of having sex with his old flame while she bleeds. He then stares at the clouds, imagining them in another land where "everyone knew how to get back where they started from," and thinks about the other reason he likes flying: "the proximity one feels to one's death."

In England, a blizzard causes a power failure at the airport, and our narrator ends up stuck in an elevator, staring at its walls, waiting for rescue, but confident that rescue will come and that he will soon go home.

Thus ends "Murder Mysteries," its construct as neatly arranged as Russian stacking dolls, one inside the other. The narrator and his life; the narrator and the shabby man who is Raguel. Flashback through the middle with bits of the outer frame interspersed within it. Logic and causality intact. The return to the final framework: the narrator and the shabby man who may very well be the angel Raguel, who has finally told his story, but not to another angel. And the conclusion: the narrator whose life and outlook has changed by events experienced himself and through the "false memory" experienced through the story teller who touched his life.

The careful structuring of frame and flashback in "Murder Mysteries" is a classic example of this story-telling technique.

Works cited:

Delany, Samuel R. *About Writing*. Middletown, CT: Wesleyan University Press, 1993.

Gaiman, Neil. "Murder Mysteries" in *Angels and Visitations, A Miscellany*. Minneapolis, MN. Dreamhaven Books, 1993.

CORALINE—A QUEST FOR IDENTITY

Mike Ashley

Like all good children's books, *Coraline* contains images and messages that will be interpreted on more than one level. And also like all good children's books, *Coraline* can be enjoyed as much by the adult reader as the child, each gaining something different.

It pays to read it twice, because the first reading allows you to enjoy the basic story, all the time knowing there is something dark and sinister playing with your senses under the surface, and it is only on a second reading that these start to show themselves.

The basic story is simple, as it should be, but also devastatingly dangerous. You find yourself being cautious about even thinking through the key images.

In the last week of her school holiday the young girl, Coraline, is still getting used to her new home, really an old house converted into several apartments, and her neighbours, old and rather unusual individuals. She is slightly frustrated that they can't get her name right, calling her Caroline instead, immediately creating an identity crisis.

The neighbours include an old, rather eccentric man who claims that he is training mice to play music. There are also two old actresses, rather like the two old women in Fawlty Towers, who are very friendly but also warn Coraline that she is in danger. They give her a stone with a hole in it as protection.

Though Coraline is clearly loved by her parents, her father is always busy and has little to do with her, whilst her mother is always getting her to do other things.

In the conversion of the house to apartments some old corridors and connections have been blocked off, but this doesn't stop Coraline's fascination with a door in the drawing-room which opens on to a brick wall. Rather mysteriously she is drawn to the door one night, summoned by moving shapes, but the door still opens on to the brick wall. It is only a day later, when Coraline is left alone and at a loose end, that she opens the door and finds it leads onto a passageway.

The passageway leads to an alternate house where Coraline

finds rather sinister versions of her father, her neighbours and most especially her mother. This "other mother" takes on a matriarchal creator role. It seems that she has created this whole alternate home, which is only as substantial as she has cared to imagine it. Within that home she has trapped individuals some of whom have been there for so long that they have faded away into ghost forms.

Coraline discovers that in order to get back to her own world she has to rescue these lost beings and find her real father and mother who have also become entrapped in this alternate world. To this end she is helped by the stone-with-a-hole from the two old ladies. Coraline also discovers that she can't trust her "other mother" to keep to her side of the bargain. Even after she feels she has succeeded, Coraline is haunted by the disembodied hand of the "other mother" that had become trapped in the door when Coraline made her escape.

Even on the first reading, despite the fascination with the story-line, the imagery of the "other mother" is disturbing and raises inevitable thoughts of children who, increasingly these days, are separated from their parents or shared between them and become torn between two alternate homes. Coraline's experiences must depict the fantasy equivalent of the broken home and split affections.

But there's far more to the story than that. It is much more about a quest for identity and understanding of the world, and may have reflected much of Gaiman's own uncertainties and trepidations. The book was started in 1991 but then lay abandoned for six years before Gaiman steadily returned to it, a fraction at a time before a final burst of activity in 2000 and some revision in 2001. The novel does not suffer from this piece-meal approach but there is a sudden shift from the present world to the alternate with a parallel psychological shift from reality to the uncertain. For well over half the story you have no idea what is around the next corner and the imagery—especially those of the deteriorated "other father" and the merged cocoon of the two old ladies in the alternate world—are both unexpected and shocking. Gaiman's approach to the novel suggests that these images must have burst unbidden from his subconscious and were doubtless as disturbing to him as they are to us.

This makes the book all the more personal and you start to see aspects of your own shadowy alternate worlds in Coraline's quest. How many of us have wondered from time to time what might have happened had we made other choices in life, and maybe in our imagination we have shifted to those worlds only to be unsure which one is for the best.

That is Coraline's problem. What should she do for the best? How does she come to terms with an "other mother" who professes her love for Coraline whilst at the same time is menacing and untrustworthy? Coraline's quest through this other world gradually gives her substance and meaning.

This problem over reality and identity hits you from the start of the book. It's not just that no one gets Coraline's name right, it's that the whole house is not a house. In moving to their new home part of Coraline's world has been shut off. She can venture into some of these other parts but there meets with strangeness and uncertainty. On one foggy day Coraline sees things only through a mist, and she admits she does not like the mist. Later she tries to draw the mist but all she can produce is a blank sheet of paper containing the letters

M S T
I

The 'I' of her own identity has removed itself from the surrounding mist and for the first time you realize that Coraline is trying to establish herself amongst her surroundings. It is only at that stage that she is ready to confront her "other mother."

At first in the "other world," things do seem exciting and fun, with wonderful food, plenty of toys and considerable attention from both parents. Coraline admits that "It's much more interesting than at home." More disturbing though is that both parents have black button eyes with no soul and their skin is like white paper. It is as if they are not quite real—not quite finished!

In this world the old man who trained mice, here trains rats. He actually gets her name right, as if this is the real world of Coraline and that Caroline is her other self in an unreal world. For some time Coraline struggles with these alternate identities. The one firm friend she gains in the other world, albeit somewhat capricious, is a cat that talks. It is the cat who has an understanding of things and spouts his own philosophy. The most pertinent arises when he tells Coraline that cats don't have names, only people do, adding:

> "That's because you don't know who you are. We know who we are, so we don't need names."

Coraline soon comes to realize that all is not well with this other world, and her quest to save herself, her family and the "lost children," allows her to distinguish between temptation and reality and come to terms with life. At the end the final way by which she can rid herself of the "other mother" is through deception and by creating an ersatz family of dolls. It is a true rite of passage and may likewise have been a rite of passage for the author.

This book will inevitably be compared to other children's classics, especially *Alice in Wonderland*, *Tom's Midnight Garden*, even *Peter Pan*. That is no mean achievement, and whilst there are obvious parallels and similarities, *Coraline* has much of its own creation. It is a powerful fable for the present day. Children and adults can relate to every aspect of it, and will doubtless continue to do so for many years to come. Coraline has to make decisions based on her own understanding of an uncertain world and trust to her instincts that they will be correct. In the end when she returns to her world she appreciates it so much more. Reality wins over imagination and temptation. Gaiman tells us "Nothing, she thought, had ever been so interesting."

What's more, her experiences have prepared her for life. She remains apprehensive but admits that, at least as regards school, nothing "could scare her anymore."

It is a parable that in this world of escape through drugs, computer games and virtual reality, reminds us that we have to face reality. Your world is what you make it.

Coraline could prove to be Gaiman's classic, a book that will be read and treasured for generations to come—his message for the future. It is a simple message—the grass is never greener—but one we are all prone to forget.

ANOTHER INTERVIEW
WITH NEIL GAIMAN

Darrell Schweitzer

Interviewer's note: This was recorded at the World Horror Convention in Denver, May 11-14 2000. Neil won a Stoker Award for the *Sandman* comics, but the real tribute to him and to his talent came the previous evening, when he conducted a *three hour* reading of the entirety of his new children's book, *Coraline,* about 28,000 words. It's a beautiful, eerie story, somewhat reminiscent of the best work of John Bellairs, author of *The Face in the Frost.* But what was most astonishing was that Neil, who is undeniably a good reader, held the audience for that long, completely spellbound, when they normally would have been at the Friday night parties. It was an amazing experience, comparable to the best Harlan Ellison readings, or the time Fritz Leiber read "The Haunter of the Dark" in Providence at the first World Fantasy Convention in 1975, only blocks away from where the events in the story "actually happened." Neil's three-hour reading is probably *not* going to start a tradition, because very few other people could actually do it.

This interview was recorded in the Green Room on Saturday afternoon, a much calmer and more ordinary time for such things.

Q: Our readers may know you less well than comic-book readers —

Gaiman: — the guy who wrote the introduction to the Lovecraft *Dream Cycle* book.

Q: Something like that. Or they've seen a pirated American tape of *Neverwhere* by now. So, could you give a brief outline of the high points of your career up to the moment?

Gaiman: My career to date, by Neil Gaiman, age thirty-nine and a half. I started out in England as a journalist. While working as a journalist, I collaborated with Kim Newman on a book called *Ghastly Beyond Belief,* a book of science fiction and fantasy quotations, the worst of. I then did a biography of Douglas Adams, while still supporting myself as a journalist, called *Don't Panic.* Then I threw my lot in for fiction, and did mainly graphic novels and comics for the next ten years. I started with a book called *Violent Cases,* then doing a monthly comic called *Sandman,* which won the World Fantasy Award and sundry other awards. But the best book I did during that time was one with Dave McKean called *Mr. Punch,* which is a fantasy about Punch and Judy and memory and childhood. I also wrote a bunch of short stories. I won the International Horror Critics Guild Award for *Angels and Visitations.* I have been nominated for various World Fantasy Awards and Stokers and suchlike along the way. I did a TV series called *Neverwhere,* then turned that into a novel in England and rewrote it as a novel for America. I then did a fairy story called *Stardust,* and am now hard at work on a novel called *American Gods,* which is late, and I just handed in a very, very creepy, scary children's story called *Coraline.* That's pretty much my career to date. I've done a few other things along the way.

Q: You may be the best-known comic book writer in the world. There aren't a lot of them who actually become *famous* in any case. So you must be doing something special.

Gaiman: I think Alan Moore may be the best known of us. I was very very lucky because the period in which I was writing mainstream comics happened to coincide with the period in which Alan Moore wasn't, which meant that I got to win every best-writer award in everything, which was great fun. But, yes, I suppose I am. The odd thing right now about being me is that there are people who have discovered me from different places and different directions. There are *Sandman* people who have no idea that I have done anything else. There are people who found me through *Neverwhere.* As far as they are concerned, that is my first novel. There are people who discover me from one place and not another. To some of them I am the guy who wrote the introductions to the Dunsany books, or who wrote *Stardust,* so to them I'm a Dunsanian scholar and fantasist.

Q: There are people who probably know you as a Lovecraftian humorist, for "Shoggoth's Old Peculiar."

Gaiman: That was so bizarre. It was nominated for a World Fantasy Award last year, which was very nice, albeit very, very puzzling. Luckily it was up against "The Specialist's Hat" by the lovely Kelly Link, which was a story I much preferred. I was very, very happy when it won. It was one of those nice occasions, because I couldn't think of what I'd do if I did get the award except get up and say, "I think this is really Kelly Link's" and hand it over to her.

Q: But yours is a story of great charm. Lovecraft somehow readily lends himself to humor.

Gaiman: Lovecraft was the inspiration for the very first piece of fiction I remember writing and being pleased with. I'm not saying that it was any good, but the first thing that I wrote that I was pleased with was an attempt to write Cthulhu's autobiography, as dictated to Mr. Whateley. I gave it to a fanzine called *Dagon* and they published it in the mid '80s.

Horror and humor are so close anyway, but Lovecraft lends himself because he takes it so seriously and his readers take it so seriously. You only have to twist half a turn to the left and the material becomes screamingly funny. Witness that wonderful —

Q: *Scream for Jeeves* by Peter Cannon?

Gaiman: No, I wasn't even thinking of *Scream for Jeeves*, which is also wonderful, and is based, oddly enough, on a gag that I must have come up with about the same time as Peter Cannon did. I'd written a letter to *Dagon* afterwards and said, "I'm glad people liked this Cthulhu biography so much. When I get around to it I will reveal the letters that have come into my possession, the Wodehouse-Lovecraft letters." I started talking about the musical they collaborated on, because Wodehouse actually was in New York and, I believe, a *Weird Tales* reader during the '20s. He was out there working on musicals. Wouldn't have been been fun if he'd written to Lovecraft and said, "Would you like to collaborate?" And I talked about "Cthulhu Springtime," which was the musical they collaborated on.

Let me see if I can remember some of the lyrics. I quoted a few:

> *Although I'm just a bird in a gilded cage,*
> *kept captive like some parakeet or love,*
> *when a maiden meets a giant lipophage,*
> *her heart gets chewed and broken like that old adage.*
> *I'm just a fool who thought that Cthulhu could fall in love.*

I explained how there was only one performance of the musical, the dreadful thing that happened to the theatre, and how nothing has ever been built there since. I had an enormous amount of fun with it.

I was going to say that coming into this convention [the World Horror Convention in Denver], there was that wonderful table in the dealers' room full of Cthulhupoid stuff, jokey stuff, including a Cthulhu to go on the back of your car instead of a Darwin or a fish, that sort of stuff. It's very Cthulhupoid.

Q: Were you warped by Lovecraft early in life like everybody else?

Gaiman: Oh yes. I was eleven or twelve. I was very lucky. Grafton books, or Granada Books had just brought the whole Lovecraft corpus back into print, about 1972 or 1973 in England. The first story of his I ever read was "The Outsider." That is such a great story. You know, the thing coming up into the light and then discovering it's the ghoul after scaring everybody.

But yes, I discovered HPL and thought he was great. And then I picked up Clark Ashton Smith and thought, I don't like you. You don't do it for me. Whatever it is I'm reading Lovecraft for and getting off on, I'm not getting from Clark Ashton Smith. It was really disappointing because the Smith books had these gorgeous covers. There was Averoigne and Zothique and all that. I'd buy all the Smith books and I loved the ideas behind them. A couple years later I discovered Jack Vance and *The Dying Earth* and thought, yes, this is better.

But probably I am a philistine. Probably if I went back and read Clark Ashton Smith now I'd go, oh what a fine and beautiful writer. I was missing it all. But possibly not.

Q: Other than to supply quotes for *Ghastly Beyond Belief,* did these inform your sensibility and influence what you wrote?

Gaiman: Definitely. Everything you read as a kid is important. Everything you read as a kid is shaping you, particularly if you're going to be a writer. When I look back now, there are some things that are just key books. Judy Merril's *SF 12.* It had "The Star Pit" by Delany. It had Lafferty's "Narrow Valley." It had Aldiss's "Confluence." It had some William Burroughs in it. I read that when I was 11 or 12. I didn't understand half of it. It didn't matter. It was shaping things inside my head. Running into Roger Zelazny mattered. Moorcock when I was nine was deeply, horribly important. Zelazny and Lafferty and Harlan Ellison and all those guys by the time I was ten or eleven, again, awfully, awfully important. I would be a very different writer without them.

What is odd is that I expected that I'd be a science fiction writer. When I was a kid, if you'd asked me what I was going to do, that's what I would have said. I expected to be Larry Niven. I figured I'd write cool, hard-science things, despite the fact that that was never what I actually wrote for pleasure. When I turned around somewhere in my early thirties and found that I seemed to be a fantasy and horror writer, I was almost surprised.

Q: I think that the reason for that, for most Baby-Boomers, is that when we were kids science fiction was much more predominant. There was very little fantasy and horror available. Therefore when you encountered fantastic fiction, it was under the umbrella of science fiction. I also thought I was going to be a science fiction writer, and look what happened.

Gaiman: I think that's exactly right. The stuff that actually was the drug we were responding to — not even that, the true awe. When you hit the true awe, it all came under the SF rubric. Books were packaged with spaceships on the cover. You go back and reread Zelazny now, and it's very obvious that he's not writing SF. He's writing fantasy. What is "A Rose for Ecclesiastes" anyway? It's a fine and beautiful fantasy.

Q: In those days, indeed, fantasy was something you had to sneak in, either as a children's book or as science fiction.

Gaiman: Yes.

Q: Now we may have the opposite problem. Not only is fantasy predominant, it's expected to be published in ten fat volumes. I wonder if somebody really could get a fine and beautiful *short* fantasy novel published now.

Gaiman: I don't know how fine and beautiful it is, but that was my intention with *Stardust*. The joy for me with *Stardust* was that it is a hair under 60,000 words. People say to me, "When you get to the end and you do that stuff where they're coming home, all of a sudden you take half a page and you list some of the cool things that happen to them. Why didn't you take five chapters to tell that?" And I reply that it would have turned it into a different book. I wanted to write a Dunsany book. I wanted to write something that came in at 60,000 words, that was a small, elegant book in which everything happened.

Q: I think the reason you got away with it is that you're

famous and you have clout. You have to have clout nowadays to get a short book into print. Anybody can have a long book, but if it's short, the publishers and bookstore buyers are going to have to be really convinced that it's going to sell, even if it doesn't weigh in by the pound.

Gaiman: Oh, I think so. And even then the publisher did some very peculiar things. And bless them. They want to maximize their sales and so forth. But they put this enormous typeface in, so they could get it to 350 pages instead of the 200 pages that it probably would have been much happier at.

Q: How did you make the transition from from writing comic scripts to writing novels? They are very different media, after all.

Gaiman: One of the things I did was, all the time while I was writing comics, I still kept a foot in the prose camp. I didn't get to write a lot of prose, but I wrote "Chivalry." I wrote "Troll Bridge." "Murder Mysteries." Some solid short stories that got anthologized and picked up for Year's Best anthologies, that kind of thing. So I was always writing the shorts. By the time I had finished *Sandman, Neverwhere* was happening. I had been working on that for five years, and I was then able to send the scripts off to Avon and say, "I'm going to be writing this novel. It's going to be based on these scripts." So I think that from that point of view, nobody was in any doubt.

But a lot of people have real problems moving from medium to medium. I don't know why that is, but I've watched it happen. There were some people, like Harlan Ellison, who are storytellers. If you say, "Tell it as a 30-minute episode for TV," and they can, and you say "Tell it as a big-budget movie" and they can. If you say "Tell it as a piece of stripped-down prose" and they can. You say "Tell it as a comic," and they can do it.

There are many, many more people who are fine novelists, but when you say, "Good, now write me a 15-page comic," and it's appalling. Or they cannot write screenplays. They cannot make the transition, or they cannot bring the magic from one medium to another.

Q: One of the differences might be — correct me if I'm wrong because you have written comics and I have not — that in a comic or a screenplay, you are expecting someone else to supply the visuals and much of the atmosphere, and therefore you concentrate on dialogue. By contrast, the worst screenplay writer ever would have been H.P. Lovecraft, because he was all visuals and atmosphere. He did, in his prose, all the things that art or photography would do, and less of what the script would do.

Gaiman: I disagree with you, and I think that one of the problems we get with people moving from one medium to another, especially into comics, is that's what they assume. They think that the artist is going to put in all the detaily stuff and all they have to do is worry about writing cool dialogue.

What you have in comics that you don't have in prose is control over how the information is received. You have control over the rhythm of the information, just putting it down beat by beat in panels. When I'm writing a script, I'm writing a letter to an artist, telling him what I want, what I'm trying to do, what I want in each panel, what effect we're trying to do. The thing that I miss in prose more than anything else, that is like a piece of the toolkit that you have in comics that you don't have in prose, is the silent panel. Just the beat after somebody says something, or you just pull back and somebody is standing there on their own without saying anything. You don't have to describe them anymore. You don't have to add anything else in. You just have a beat. I keep trying to do that in prose. How can I get that exact effect? I still haven't figured it out.

Q: You could skip a space. Or you could vary the rhythm of the prose drastically, as in a long, screaming tirade followed by a one-sentence paragraph that says, "Nothing happened."

Gaiman: It's one of those things that you can do in comics and you can approximate and move around it in prose. And there are things you can do in prose that you can't do in comics. You can really go into someone's head and start mucking around behind the eyes.

Q: I am reminded of a comment Lord Dunsany made. He saw a script which had a gorgeous description of a sun setting over a landscape, and this had to be crossed out, and it said, "Sun sets, left." This is what I mean by the visuals being supplied by somebody else, in that case the stage designer and the director.

Gaiman: Yes, that's very true. The advantage in doing a comic is that I can describe that sunset to an artist and see how close I can get it. If I just say, "Sunset," I might get anything. But one of the media that I love most is radio plays. There you can do both. You can do all the things you can do in prose and all the things you can do in comics, strangely. You have control over timing and beat, and you have the immediacy of films, but the audience is still building the pictures in their heads.

Q: You've got the visuals.

Gaiman: Exactly. I did a adaptation of my story "Murder Mysteries," which is about a murder committed in Heaven before the Fall, and about the angel investigating this murder. I adapted that for Sci Fi Channel, SciFi.Com. We put together a wonderful cast starring Brian Dennehy as the angel private eye. It is lovely listening to it because you can do things on the radio. At one point they're walking around this city of angels and they come into this hall in which the universe is being constructed. At one point the hero falls through the universe as it's being built. How many millions of dollars would it take to achieve that on the screen?

Q: Someone made the comment that there are some things you just can't do in any medium other than radio. It might have been Robert Bloch who said it. The example given was a scene in a radio play in which they filled up Lake Erie with whipped cream and a fleet of helicopters lowers a giant maraschino cherry on top. If you did that in a movie, it would just look silly, but the mind's eye can produce it effectively.

Gaiman: Exactly. You're doing it in people's heads. The one that really didn't work, I remember, was from *The Hitch-Hiker's Guide to the Galaxy*. When they did the line in the radio play, "Ford, you're turning into an infinite number of penguins," it was marvelous. But when they did the TV show and tried to show Ford turning into an infinite number of penguins, it was one of the most embarrassing moments in the whole show.

Q: Horror also works this way, and often does better on the radio.

Gaiman: Horror always exists as this wonderful balancing act between showing the monster and not showing the monster. What Clive Barker did that was so brilliant when the *Books of Blood* came out — it really felt like a breath of fresh air — was not only did he show the monster, but the monster that came on was cooler than the one that you'd imagined. That, I think, was lovely. Then everybody started showing the monster. Unfortunately their imaginations and their descriptive powers were not up to Clive's. I think that mostly monsters are best kept in the shadows.

Q: There is the basic aesthetic problem that once you've shown everything, you've shown everything and there is nothing more. I am sure we have all seen any number of movies that play all their cards early. Then, unless they have a strong plot, they're dead.

Gaiman: Completely. The weird thing right now about *American Gods*, my new novel, is that it is probably a fantasy novel. I don't think it is horror, though it has enough horror in it to upset some people. I got some lovely letters from ladies who were romance fans. They were big fans of *Stardust*. They have their newsletters and they have their websites, and they praised them to the heavens. And I cannot see them living *American Gods* at all. So word fifteen is "fuck." You're not through the first sentence before you get the word "fuck" because I just want to tell everybody that this is not a sweet book, and it's not a friendly book, and it's not a nice Victorian love story. If you have any trouble, *put it down now*. You have your out in the first sentence.

Q: So you'll get a different audience with every book. Do the *Neverwhere* readers like *Stardust*?

Gaiman: I don't think so. Some of them did and some of them didn't. The wonderful thing about my time in comics was that I did train a core readership in understanding that what I was going to do next was not what I did last. If you don't like it, that's probably okay, because there's a good chance you will like what I do after that. And I'm not going to do the same thing over and over and over again. So I trained people. Except, of course, that all the *Sandman* people went out and picked up *Neverwhere* and said, "Uh, it's not *Sandman*. We don't like this." The *Neverwhere* people said, "We love this. We've never read anything like it." Then they picked up *Stardust* and said, "Oh, this isn't *Neverwhere*. We don't know if we like this or not." Meanwhile, most of the people who picked up *Smoke and Mirrors*, my short-story collection, liked it, because even if there are short stories or whatever in there that you don't like, there's enough stuff in there that you probably would. It keeps them happy.

Q: Sooner or later you get the publisher offering you five million dollars for another *Neverwhere* sequel, and another, and another. You can get trapped that way, as Frank Herbert did with *Dune*. We all should hope to have this problem that people keep offering us millions . . . but what do you do in the face of this Faustian temptation?

Gaiman: I don't know. The big problem with me in *Neverwhere* is that I'd love to do another *Neverwhere* novel. I have at least two or three stories in the series going on in my head. But there are other things that I'd like to write first, which is why they aren't getting written. What I might do — I'm thinking that when the current novel is finished, I could do a book of three novellas. One would be a *Stardust* novella, one would be a *Neverwhere* novella, and one would be an *American Gods* novella. This is not an attempt to cash in on my audience, but because I have these bloody stories floating around in my head. The *Stardust* one is really peculiar because they get to go to Hell in a hot air balloon. There's a *Neverwhere* story called "How the Marquis Got His Coat Back." They're all nineteen to twenty thousand word stories, which is a really irritating length to write anything at, because nobody really wants that. So I will probably end up doing three in a book.

But, yes, the financial thing is horrible. You can really get trapped into what Joe Straczynski calls "the velvet trap," the Rod Serling thing. They give you an awful lot of money, and then your standard of living goes up to that awful amount of money, and then they've got you. Somebody who is earning 25,000 a year, go and offer them a million and they can turn you down with a clear conscience. I turned down a ten million dollar deal a few years ago with a clear and easy conscience, because I didn't want to do it. I didn't like the amount of things I'd have to give away to do it. Once you get trapped at a certain level, I can see how the whole *Dune* thing would come in. Roger writing more and more Amber books. You look at them, especially the last batch of Amber books, and they really weren't very good. They didn't read like he was writing them because he wanted to write them. Then all of a sudden he did *A Night in Lonesome October* which he really did want to write.

Q: Then someone could come to you and ask you to do an -

on-going weekly series of *Neverwhere*. Has that happened?

Gaiman: There's a movie that's happening right now, that is being directed by a guy called Richard Loncraine. I wrote about eight drafts of the script until I got very tired of writing drafts of the script, and I stepped aside, and I believe they've got Andrew Birkin writing the script. Then I will either come back or not come back at the end to give it a dialogue polish.

Q: To get back to an interesting comment you made before we started this interview . . . you said that one of the things you really wanted to read was all the works of Robert Aickman, cover to cover. This will probably surprise some of your fans. It's a different sensibility. What do you see in Robert Aickman that makes him essential?

Gaiman: I think that Aickman is one of those authors that you respond to on a very primal level. If you're a writer, it's a bit like being a stage magician. A stage magician produces coin, takes coin, demonstrates coin vanished. [Gaiman is doing this as he speaks, quite capably.] If you're a professional stage magician, you're not going, "Oh boy! He vanished the coin!" You're thinking that was a smooth or a not smooth French Drop. Or, "Look, he did that sleight. I haven't seen that one done in a while." Or, "Look, there's a reverse French Drop." That tends to be what you do as a fiction writer, reading fiction. You'll go, "Oh, look. He's setting that up." You're in the position of a stage magician in the audience. You may admire the way something is done, but you never worry if that woman is going to get cut in half. Reading Robert Aickman is like watching a magician work, and very often I'm not even sure what the trick was. All I know is that he did it beautifully. Yes, the key vanished, but I don't know if he was holding a key in the hand to begin with. I find myself admiring everything he does from an auctorial standpoint. And I love it as a reader. He will bring on atmosphere. He will construct these perfect, dark, doomed little stories, what he called "strange stories." I find the same with Lafferty. We were talking about Lafferty earlier as somebody who I'd love to read. I am hoping someone will do the complete short stories of R.A. Lafferty. What is interesting is that when you read the early Lafferty, the closer he comes to what one might consider a normal story, the less successful he is. I think that with Aickman, that the closer he comes to something that somebody else could have written, the less successful he is.

Q: What I find curious about both of these writers is that they are authors one admires very much but you don't really understand. Does anybody really understand either Lafferty or Aickman?

Gaiman: God? Certainly, if there is one. But no, I think that the joy of Lafferty and the joy of Aickman is the joy of people who exist completely independent of everything else.

I love Stephen King. I think that Steve is an astonishing storyteller. And I also think that he's a really good writer. I think that he's written books that were sloppy and I think that he's written books that were really good. But I think that he's a really good wordsmith. I think that he's a better wordsmith than he gives himself credit for. But Steve is comprehensible. That is one reason why he is a very popular writer, because you understand what he is talking about. You can connect to it. You can draw the dots. You can see where it works.

I can understand why Peter Straub responded to Robert Aickman, because Straub loves jazz. Steve loves rock. Stephen King is rock & roll. Aickman is jazz. And Lafferty is something played in an Irish bar on an instrument that you're not quite sure what it is and you're humming the tune but you don't remember the words as you walk out.

Q: Another thing about these writers is that you can tell they're not faking you out. There are many writers who will just plop down a mass of almost random words and say, "Well this is really very profound, and if you don't understand it you must be an ignoramus." You somehow know with Lafferty or Aickman that this is not the case.

Gaiman: Avram Davidson is another one of those. You're not being faked out. And Gene Wolfe. If you're going to put together four people who belong on the same page, I would have said Lafferty, Aickman, Gene Wolfe, and Davidson. If you don't get it, it's your fault somehow. Go back and read it again. You'll get there. I remember Aickman's "Mark Ingestre: The Customer's Tale." I wound up researching. Who was Lord Lovatt? What is his tie-in to Mrs. Lovett? What is the significance to all this stuff. How does it tie in to Sweeny Todd? I finally got to the point where I went, "You know, I do understand this." I don't think I've ever put as much effort into any other story by Aickman, but one assumes that it's there for the repaying, in the same way that a good Gene Wolfe story tends to return what gets put into it.

Q: These are all brave or oblivious writers. They are taking risks. If you do what they do, you run the risk that lots of lazy readers will take their money elsewhere, and lazy publishers will anticipate this and not publish you.

Gaiman: I don't think I am one of them. I may occasionally visit from time to time, but at the end of the day I am probably in the Stephen King camp. I'm a storyteller. The coolest thing for me is the telling of a story. The moments that matter are the moments when I get to surprise myself, the giving to people points of view they haven't had before.

A very strange thing caught me with *American Gods*, because I needed a prose style which was really meat-and-potatoes, very straightforward, very, very basic. And I got very tired of it very fast. So I started writing short stories to go into the body of the text, set in the past. For each of them I can write beautiful, elegant prose, and not to worry about the stripped-down, Elmore Leonard stuff that the novel is in.

Q: I think that you have to keep your readers in mind, but ultimately you have to take these risks for the sake of the book. But many people won't notice anyway. It's always been my theory that the reason that many really bad books get published is that a lot of readers are completely style-deaf. They just skim it. So somebody whose prose is like fingernails on the blackboard can get published and become a bestseller.

Gaiman: I think that's true. I'm not really one of those people. I tend to write for very small audiences. My audience can be me. If I am writing a short story, the audience can be the editor who solicited the story.

Q: The downside is that if most people are style deaf, they'll never know if you're writing beautifully.

Gaiman: That's very, very true. But I also figure that there are enough people out there who can tell the difference.

James Branch Cabell once said that a man crafts a beautiful sentence for the same joy you get from playing a good game of solitaire. You don't craft a beautiful sentence for the multitude. You craft a beautiful sentence for your own satisfaction.

Q: You've somehow managed to become very popular. You've had your cake and eaten it too.

Gaiman: I guess I have. I don't quite know how, and I don't necessarily want to investigate too hard. I think I'm very lucky. There are two kinds of saying "I think I'm very lucky." One is a self-deprecating way, and what you're actually saying is that I think I'm very clever and I think I'm very good, so I'm going to say I'm very lucky and you can all go, "No, no, no! He's not lucky. He's brilliant." I think I'm very lucky, just because the stories I like to tell happen to be the same stories that people like to read. I don't think I could change the kinds of stories I like to tell. So if public readership tastes did not happen to coincide with what I like to write, I would still be writing the same stuff, and I would simply not be selling anything. [Laughs.] I am fortunate that at this juncture, I'm telling stories people like to read. Whether or not this will continue or not I don't know. There is a wasteland in literature which is filled with authors, good authors and bad authors, who told the right story at the right time, and briefly were famous, briefly were popular.

Q: One example I can think of is Joseph Hergesheimer, who most people know from dedications and introductions in James Branch Cabell books. He woke up one morning in 1929 and he had no audience.

Gaiman: Completely. But Cabell himself was a minor writer, with some critical acclaim, who wrote *Jurgen,* had one line in some New York newspaper saying "This guy Cabell is getting away with murder; all the chorus girls are reading this filthy book he's written." The New York Society for the Suppression of Vice under Mr. Sumner busted *Jurgen,* took the plates, sued the publisher. Cabell and the publisher won the case, and Cabell was now a best-selling author. There was a line in *The New Yorker,* if memory serves saying that "while the literary laurels of the future are all in doubt, there is one name from our time that will ring out forever into the future and that is the name of James Branch Cabell." And by 1950, everything except *Jurgen* was out of print and he was writing for tiny university presses.

Q: Even now there are only occasional reprintings.

Gaiman: They reprint the fantasies, but there are Cabell books which are finer than some of his fantasies that have not been been back in print since 1929.

Q: Another one the critics of that era were certain would be one of the great novels, if not the greatest novel of the 20th century was Walter de la Mare's *Memoirs of a Midget*. It didn't happen.

Gaiman: It didn't happen, but that was the one they all pointed to. Like *Messer Marco Polo* by Donn Byrne. Yes, but tastes change. You write for your time. I write for me, at the end of the day. I am my audience. I write to amuse myself, in the very, very fundamental sense that it passes the time, it staves off boredom, and I don't know that there's anything else out in the world that I am actually any good at. And I have too much of a work ethic to sit and watch television all day, or else there isn't enough good TV, and I get bored. So I've got myself a little cabin now, twenty minutes from home, overlooking a lake. I get in my car and I drive my twenty minutes, and I settle down, and I write. There is no phone in there and there is no TV in there, and all the books are books that relate to whatever I am working on. And I write, or I make cups of tea.

Q: Thanks, Neil.

NEIL GAIMAN: AN INCOMPLETE BIBLIOGRAPHY

Davey M. Snyder

Updated and expanded from Lance "Squiddie" Smith's 1997 and 1999 editions by Davey Snyder, but still (and probably evermore) not quite caught-up. Grateful acknowledgement is made of the following additional sources: The *Locus* Index to Science Fiction[36], the Michigan State University Libraries Comic Art Collection index[37], Shield Albright[38] (for persnickety proofreading as well as source notes), Peter and Michael Karpas[39], and *the dreaming*[40]; and to Alice N.S. Lewis for style advice.

This bibliography is generously hosted online by DreamHaven Books & Comics at http://www.neilgaiman.net/bibliography.php, and is updated there as schedules allow.

Books, Graphic Novels, & Collections (including Films)

Adventures in the Dream Trade, NESFA Press, 2002 [*ADT*] ("Fan Letter," "Shameful Secrets of Comics Retailing: The Lingerie Connection" (introduction), "But What Has That to Do With Bacchus?" (introduction), "Breathtaker" (introduction), "Bratpack" (introduction), [Kurt Busiek's] "Astro City: Confession" (introduction), "300 Good Reasons to Resent Dave Sim," "Tantrum" (introduction), "The Dark Knight Returns," "Starchild: Crossroads" (introduction), "The Adventures of Professor Thintwhistle and His Incredible Aetheric Flyer" (introduction), "Of Time, and Gully Foyle" (introduction), "Concerning Dreams and Nightmares" (introduction), "The Einstein Intersection" (foreword),

36   The Locus Index to Science Fiction, http://www.locusmag.com/index/index.html

37   Michigan State University Libraries Comic Art Collection, http://www.lib.msu.edu/comics/index.htm

38   Shield Albright, http://www.neilgaimanbibliography.com/

39   Peter and Michael Karpas, http://www.enjolrasworld.com

40   the dreaming: the Neil Gaiman page, http://www.holycow.com/dreaming/

"The Swords of Lankhmar" (introduction), "The Screwtape Letters" (introduction), "The King of Elfland's Daughter" (introduction), "Curiosities: Lud-in-the-Mist," "From the End of the Twentieth Century" (introduction), "Jonathan Carroll" (introduction), "Roger Zelazny" (afterword to "Only the End of the World Again"), "The Beast That Shouted Love at the Heart of the World" (foreword), "Banging the Drum for Harlan Ellison," "After They've Brought on the Dancing Girls" (afterword), "A Writer's Prayer," "Neil's Thankyou Pome," "Sonnet," "How to Write Longfellow's 'Hiawatha'," "The Old Warlock's Reverie: A Pantoum," "In Re: Pansy Smith and Violet Jones" (afterword), "Banshee," "Post-Mortem on Our Love," "Personal Thing," "All Purpose Folk Song," "A Girl Needs a Knife," *American Gods* Web Log, "Hallowe'en," "December 7, 1995," "Good Boys Deserve Favours," "The Flints of Memory Lane," "Essay for Patti")

American Gods, HarperCollins/Morrow, 2001; Hodder Headline, 2001, 2002; 2005; SFBC, 2001; HarperTorch, 2002; HarperPerennial, 2003; Hill House Publishers (expanded, limited "Author's Preferred" edition), 2004

Anansi Boys, HarperCollins/Morrow, 2005; Hodder Headline, 2005; Review, 2005; Harper Audio (audio book), 2005

Angela, Image Comics, 1995 (Angela #1-3 (art by Greg Capullo), Image Comics, 1994-95); Image Comics/Todd McFarlane Productions, 1998 (as *Spawn: Angela's Hunt*); Image Comics, 2000

Angels & Visitations: A Miscellany, DreamHaven Books, 1993 [*AV*] ("The Song of the Audience," "Introduction," "Chivalry," "Nicholas Was . . .," "Babycakes," "Troll-Bridge," "Vampire Sestina," "Webs," "Six to Six," "A Prologue" (introduction to *Scholars and Soldiers*), "Foreign Parts," "Cold Colours," "Luther's Villanelle," "Mouse," "Gumshoe" (review), "The Case of the Four and Twenty Blackbirds," "Virus," "Looking for the Girl," "Post-Mortem on Our Love," "Being An Experiment Upon Strictly Scientific Lines," "We Can Get Them for You Wholesale," "The Mystery of Father Brown," "Murder Mysteries")

Black Orchid (with Dave McKean), DC Comics/Vertigo, 1991 (Black Orchid #1-3, DC Comics, 1988-89)

The Books of Magic, DC Comics/Vertigo, 1993 (The Books of Magic #1-4, DC Comics, 1990, 1991)

I: The Invisible Labyrinth (art by John Bolton)

II: The Shadow World (art by Scott Hampton)

III: The Land of Summer's Twilight (art by Charles Vess)

IV: The Road to Nowhere (art by Paul Johnson)

The Compleat Alice Cooper: The Last Temptation (art by Michael Zulli), Marvel Music, 1995; Dark Horse Comics, 2001 as *The Last Temptation* (*The Last Temptation #1-3*, Marvel, 1994)

Coraline, Harper Audio (audio book), 2002; Harper Children's Audio (UK) (audio book), 2002; HarperCollins, 2002 (also in special limited edition with additional material), 2003; Bloomsbury, 2002; SFBC, 2002

Creatures of the Night (art by Michael Zulli), Dark Horse Books, 2004 ("The Price," "The Daughter of Owls")

The Day I Swapped My Dad for Two Goldfish (with Dave McKean),

White Wolf/Borealis, 1997; HarperCollins, 2004; *The Neil Gaiman Audio Collection*, Harper Audio, 2004

Day of the Dead: Babylon 5 Script, DreamHaven Books, 1998; Babylon 5 v5.6 (video recording), Warner Home Video, 1999

Death: the High Cost of Living (art by Chris Bachalo, Mark Buckingham, and Dave McKean), DC Comics/Vertigo, 1994 (*Death: the High Cost of Living #1-3*, DC Comics, 1993; Death Talks About Life, DC Comics, 1993)

Death: the Time of Your Life (art by Chris Bachalo, Mark Buckingham, and Mark Pennington), DC Comics/Vertigo, 1997 (expanded version) (Death: the Time of Your Life #1-3, DC Comics, 1993, 1994)

Don't Panic: The Official Hitchhiker's Guide to the Galaxy Companion, Titan, 1988; Pocket, 1988; Titan 1993 (as *Don't Panic: Douglas Adams & The Hitch Hiker's Guide to the Galaxy*, with additional material by David K. Dickson); Titan UK, 2002 (as *Don't Panic: Douglas Adams & The Hitch Hiker's Guide to the Galaxy*, updated by M.J. Simpson); Titan Books US, 2003 (including Dickson 1993 and Simpson 2002 material, with new forward)

Duran Duran: The First Four Years of the Fab Five, Proteus, 1984

Dustcovers: The Collected Sandman Covers (with Dave McKean; includes "The Last Sandman Story"), DC Comics/Vertigo, 1997

Gods & Tulips, Westhampton House, 1999

Good Omens (with Terry Pratchett), Gollancz, 1990; Workman, 1990; Berkley, 1992; Ace, 1996; William Morrow, 2006

Green Lantern/Superman: Legend of the Green Flame (art by Michael D. Allred and Terry Austin, Mark Buckingham, John Totleben, Matt Wagner, Eric Shanower and Arthur Adams, Jim Aparo, Kevin Nowlan, Jason Little, Frank Miller), DC Comics, 2000

Harlequin Valentine (art by John Bolton), Dark Horse Books, 2001 [see also Short Fiction]

Marvel: 1602 (art by Andy Kubert and Richard Isanove), Marvel Comics, 2004 (1602 #1-8) [see also Short Fiction]

Melinda (art by Dagmara Matuszak), Hill House Publishers, 2005

Miracleman: Apocrypha (art by Mark Buckingham; includes "The Library of Olympus"), Eclipse Books, 1993 (Miracleman: Apocrypha #1-3, Eclipse Comics, 1991-92)

Miracleman Book 4: The Golden Age (art by Mark Buckingham), Eclipse Books, 1992 (Miracleman #17-22, Eclipse Comics, 1990-91)

MirrorMask (film; with Dave McKean), Sony Pictures, 2005

Mirrormask: A Really Useful Book, Dark Horse Books, 2005

Mirrormask Script Book (with Dave McKean), HarperCollins, 2005

Murder Mysteries, Biting Dog Press, 2001 (art by George Walker); Dark Horse, 2002 (art by P. Craig Russell) [see also Short Fiction]

The Neil Gaiman Audio Collection (audio recording), Harper Audio, 2004 [NGA] ("The Day I Swapped My Dad for Two Goldfish," "The Wolves in the Walls," "Cinnamon," "Crazy Hair")

Neil Gaiman: Live at the Aladdin (video recording), CBLDF, 2001

[*LA*] ("Chivalry," "Martha Soukup" (introduction to *The Arbitrary Placement of Walls*), "Being An Experiment Upon Strictly Scientific Lines," "The Price," "Locks," "Babycakes"; with audience questions and additional material)

Neil Gaiman's Midnight Days, DC Comics/Vertigo, 1999 ("Swamp Thing: Jack in the Green," "Brothers," "Shaggy God Stories," "Hold Me," "Sandman Midnight Theatre"; with introductory material)

Neil Gaiman's Only the End of the World Again (adapted by P. Craig Russell, art by Troy Nixey), Oni Press, 2000 [see also Short Fiction]

Neverwhere, BBC Books, 1996; BBC Video (with additional material), 1996; BCC Worldwide Ltd. (abridged audio books; CD set including additional material), 1996; Avon, 1997; Penguin, 1997; HarperTorch, 1998; HarperPerennial, 2003; A&E Home Video (DVD of original BBC television series; with additional material), 2003

On Cats & Dogs: Two Tales, DreamHaven Books, 1997 ("The Price," "Only the End of the World Again")

Outrageous Tales From the Old Testament, Knockabout Publications, 1987 ("The Book of Judges," art by Mike Matthews; "Jael and Sisera," art by Julie Hollings; "Jephthath and His Daughter," art by Peter Rigg; "Journey to Bethlehem," art by Steve Gibson; "The Prophet Who Came to Dinner," art by Dave McKean; "The Tribe of Benjamin," art by Mike Matthews)

The Quotable Sandman, DC Comics, 2000

The Sandman #1-75, DC Comics, 1989-1996

Preludes & Nocturnes, DC Comics/Vertigo, 1991 (#1-8; art by Sam Kieth, Mike Dringenberg, and Malcolm Jones III)

The Doll's House, DC Comics/Vertigo, 1991 (#8-16; art by Mike Dringenberg, and Malcolm Jones III, with Chris Bachalo, Michael Zulli, and Steve Parkhouse)

Dream Country, DC Comics/Vertigo, 1991 (#17-20; art by Kelley Jones, Charles Vess, Colleen Doran, and Malcolm Jones III)

Season of Mists, DC Comics/Vertigo, 1992 (#21-28; art by Kelley Jones, Mike Dringenberg, Malcolm Jones III, Matt Wagner, Dick Giordano, George Pratt, and P. Craig Russell)

Fables & Reflections, DC Comics/Vertigo, 1993 (#29-31, 38-40, 50, "Song of Orpheus," expanded "Fear of Falling"; art by Bryan Talbot, Stan Woch, P. Craig Russell, Shawn McManus, John Watkiss, Jill Thompson, Duncan Eagleson, Kent Williams, Mark Buckingham, Vince Locke, and Dick Giordano)

A Game of You, DC Comics/Vertigo, 1993 (#32-37; art by Shawn McManus, Colleen Doran, Bryan Talbot, George Pratt, Stan Woch, and Dick Giordano)

Brief Lives, DC Comics/Vertigo, 1994 (#41-49; art by Jill Thompson and Vince Locke)

World's End, DC Comics/Vertigo, 1994 (#51-56; art by Michael Allred, Gary Amaro, Mark Buckingham, Dick Giordano, Tony Harris, Steve Leialoha, Vince Locke, Shea Anton Pensa, Alec Stevens, Bryan Talbot, John Watkins, and Michael Zulli)

The Kindly Ones, DC Comics/Vertigo, 1996 (#57-69, "The Castle"; art by Marc Hempel, Richard Case, D'Israeli, Teddy Kristiansen, Glyn Dillon, Charles Vess, Dean Ormston, and Kevin Nowlan)

The Wake, DC Comics/Vertigo, 1997 (#70-75, plus material from The Dreaming #8; art by Michael Zulli, Jon J. Muth, and Charles Vess)

The Sandman: The Dream Hunters (with Yoshitaka Amano), DC Comics/Vertigo, 1999

The Sandman: Endless Nights (art by Frank Quitely, Milo Manara, Glenn Fabry, P. Craig Russell, Miguelanxo Prado, Barron Storey, and Bill Sienkiewicz), DC Comics/Vertigo, 2003

A Screenplay (limited edition), Hill House Publishers, 2004

Shoggoth's Old Peculiar (art by Jouni Koponen), DreamHaven Books, 2004 [see also Short Fiction]

A Short Film About John Bolton (film), SKA Films, 2003

Signal to Noise (with Dave McKean, expanded and revised), VG Graphics, 1992; Dark Horse Comics, 1992 [see also Short Fiction]

Smoke and Mirrors: Short Fictions and Illusions, Avon, 1998 [*SM*]; HarperPerennial, 2001; Hodder Headline, 2000 (expanded) [*SM (UK)*] ("Reading the Entrails: A Rondel," "An Introduction" (includes "The Wedding Present"), "Chivalry," "Nicholas Was . . .," "The Price," "Troll Bridge," "Don't Ask Jack," "The Goldfish Pool and Other Stories," "Eaten (Scenes from a Moving Picture)" (UK), "The White Road," "Queen of Knives," "The Facts in the Case of the Departure of Miss Finch" (UK), "Changes," "The Daughter of Owls," "Shoggoth's Old Peculiar," "Virus," "Looking for the Girl," "Only the End of the World Again," "Bay Wolf," "Fifteen Painted Cards from a Vampire Tarot" (UK), "We Can Get Them For You Wholesale," "One Life, Furnished in Early Moorcock," "Cold Colors," "The Sweeper of Dreams," "Foreign Parts," "Vampire Sestina," "Mouse," "The Sea Change," "How Do You Think It Feels?" (UK), "When We Went to See the End of the World by Dawnie Morningside, age 11¼," "Desert Wind," "Tastings," "In the End" (UK), "Babycakes," "Murder Mysteries," "Snow, Glass, Apples")

Snow, Glass, Apples: A Play for Voices, Biting Dog Press, 2002 (art by George Walker) [see also Short Fiction]

Speaking in Tongues (audio recording, with music by Adam Stemple), DreamHaven Inc., 2004 [*ST*] ("Daughter of Owls," "Instructions," "The Price," "The Sea Change," "The Facts in the Case of the Departure of Miss Finch")

Stardust (with Charles Vess), DC Comics/Vertigo, 1998 (Neil Gaiman & Charles Vess' Stardust #1-4); Avon/Spike, 1999 (expanded, unillustrated); Hodder Headline, 1999 (unillustrated); Titan, 1999; HarperPerennial, 2001; Avon, 2003

Telling Tales (audio recording, with percussion by Robin Adnan Anders), DreamHaven Inc., 2003 [*TT*] ("A Writer's Prayer," "Harlequin Valentine," "Boys and Girls Together," "The Wedding Present," "In The End," "Epilogue—Drums" by Robin Adnan Anders)

The Tragical Comedy or Comical Tragedy of Mr. Punch (with Dave McKean), VG Graphics, 1994; DC Comics/Vertigo, 1994

Two Plays for Voices, Harper Audio (audio book), 2002 ("Snow, Glass, Apples," "Murder Mysteries")

Violent Cases (with Dave McKean), Titan/Escape, 1987; Tundra, 1991; Kitchen Sink Press, 1994, 1997

A Walking Tour of the Shambles (with Gene Wolfe), American Fantasy Press, 2002

Warning: Contains Language (audio recording, with Dave McKean and The Flash Girls), DreamHaven Inc., 1995 [*WCL*] ("The Song of the Audience," "Nicholas Was . . .," "Babycakes," "Cold Colours," "The White Road," "Banshee," "Chivalry," "Troll Bridge")

The Wolves in the Walls (with Dave McKean), HarperCollins, 2003; Bloomsbury, 2003; *The Neil Gaiman Audio Collection*, Harper Audio, 2004; HarperTrophy, 2005

Edited

Ghastly Beyond Belief (with Kim Newman), Arrow, 1985

Now We Are Sick: An Anthology of Nasty Verse (with Stephen Jones), DreamHaven Books, 1991

The Sandman: Book of Dreams (with Ed Kramer), HarperPrism, 1996; HarperCollins Voyager, 1996; HarperTorch, 2002

co-editor, co-plotter, and co-creator: *The Totally Stonking, Surprisingly Educational and Utterly Mindboggling Comic Relief Comic*, Fleetway, 1991

created with Mary Gentle, *Villains*, Roc, 1992

devised with Mary Gentle and Roz Kaveney

- *The Weerde*: Book I, Roc, 1992
- *The Weerde*: Book II, Roc, 1993

devised with Alex Stewart

- *Eurotemps*, Roc, 1992
- *Temps*, Roc UK, 1991

Short Fiction, Comics, & Poetry (including Lyrics)

(abbreviated references: **ADT** *Adventures in the Dream Trade*; **AV** *Angels & Visitations*; **LA** *Live at the Aladdin*; **SM** *Smoke & Mirrors*; **ST** *Speaking in Tongues*; **TT** *Telling Tales*; **WCL** *Warning: Contains Language*; **TYBFH** *The Year's Best Fantasy & Horror* [edition], ed. Ellen Datlow and Terri Windling [#1-16], ed. Ellen Datlow and Kelly Link & Gavin J. Grant [#17-current], St. Martin's Press)

The owners of all URLs included here have Neil's permission

to publish his work in that format.

"All Purpose Folk Song (Child Ballad #1)," The Magian Line v1.4, 1994; recorded by The Flash Girls on *Play Each Morning Wild Queen*, Fabulous Records, 2001; http://apoca-lypse.org/pub/flash/lyrics/AllPurposeFolkSong.html; *ADT*

"Anansi Boys Chapter 1" (excerpt, draft), *Mythcon 35 Program Book*, The Mythopoeic Society, 2004

Ancient Emperor, Hill House Publishers, 2003 (limited-edition chapbook, story originally written as part of *American Gods* but never used)

". . . And Eyes of Flame" (the 'Ifrit' section of *American Gods*), *Necon XX: the Twentieth Anniversary Commemorative Volume*, Necon Committee, 2000

"Angela" (art by Todd McFarlane), *Spawn #9*, Image Comics, 1993; *Spawn: Book Two*, Image, 1998

"Babycakes," *Taboo #4* (art by Michael Zulli), 1990; *Born to be Wild* (art by Michael Zulli), Eclipse Comics, 1990; *AV*; *WCL*; *SM*; *LA*

"Banshee," recorded by The Flash Girls on Maurice and I, Fabulous Records, 1995; *WCL*; *ADT*

"Bay Wolf," *SM*; *Dark Detectives*, ed. Stephen Jones, Fedogan & Bremer, 1999

"Being an Account of the Life and Death of Emperor Heliogabolus," *Cerebus #147*, Aardvark-Vanaheim; limited edition chapbook, 1992; http://www.holycow.com/dreaming/helio/index.html; 24 Hour Comics, ed. Scott McCloud, About Comics, 2004

"Bitter Grounds," *Mojo: Conjure Stories*, ed. Nalo Hopkinson, Warner Aspect, 2003

"A Black and White World" (art by Simon Bisley), Batman Black and White #2, DC Comics, 1996; *Batman Black and White*, DC Comics, 1997

"Blood Monster" (art by Nancy J. O'Connor), *Taboo #6*, Spiderbaby Graphics/Tundra, 1992

"Boys and Girls Together," *Black Heart, Ivory Bones*, ed. Ellen Datlow and Terri Windling, Avon, 2000; http://www.endicott-studio.com/jMA0301/boysGirls.html, 2002; *TT*

"Brothers" (art by Richard Piers Rayner, Mike Hoffman, and Kim De Mulder), *Swamp Thing Annual #5*, DC Comics, 1989; *Neil Gaiman's Midnight Days*

"The Butterfly Road," recorded by Folk UnderGround on *Buried Things*, Happyfun! Records, 2003

"The Case of the Four and Twenty Blackbirds," *Knave v16 #9*, 1984; *AV*; *The Mammoth Book of Comic Fantasy II*, ed. Mike Ashley, Robinson, 1999; *Horrible Beginnings*, ed. Steven H. Silver & Martin H. Greenberg, DAW Books, Inc., 2003 (with additional introduction); http://www.neilgaiman.com/exclusive/4&20.asp

"The Castle" (art by Kevin Nowlan), *Vertigo Jam #1*, DC/Vertigo, 1993; *Sandman: The Kindly Ones*

"Celebrity Rare Bit Fiends" (with Rick Veitch), *Roarin' Rick's Rare Bit*

Fiends #2, #3, King Hell, 1994

"Changes," *Crossing the Border: Tales of Erotic Ambiguity*, ed. Lisa Tuttle, Gollancz, 1998; *SM*

The Children's Crusade #1 (art by Chris Bachalo and Mike Barreiro), DC Comics/Vertigo, 1993

The Children's Crusade #2 (with Alison Kwitney and Jamie Delano; art by Peter Snejbjerg), DC Comics/Vertigo, 1994

"Chivalry," *Grails: Quests, Visitations and Other Occurrences*, ed. Richard Gilliam, Martin H. Greenberg and Edward E. Kramer, Unnameable Press, Atlanta GA, 1992; *Advance Comics #58*, 1993; *AV*; *Grails: Quests of the Dawn*, ed. Richard Gilliam, Martin H. Greenberg and Edward E. Kramer, Penguin/Roc, 1994; *WCL*; *SM*; *Cicada v1 #1*, 1998; *LA*; *A Quest-Lover's Treasury of the Fantastic*, ed. Margaret Weis, Warner/Aspect, 2002; *New Magics*, ed. Patrick Nielsen Hayden, Tor Teen 2004

"Cinnamon," *Overstreet's FAN v1 #4*, 1995; http://www.neilgaiman.net/cinnamon/page1.htm, 2002; *The Neil Gaiman Audio Collection*, Harper Audio, 2004

"Closing Time," *McSweeney's Quarterly*, Issue 10, Winter 2002-03; *McSweeney's Mammoth Treasury of Thrilling Tales*, ed. Michael Chabon, Vintage Books, 2003; *The Mammoth Book of New Terror*, ed. Stephen Jones, Robinson, 2004; *Year's Best Fantasy 4*, ed. David G. Hartwell and Kathryn Cramer, HarperCollins/Eos, 2004

"Cold Colours," *Midnight Grafitti #6*, Winter 1990; Future Comics, 1993; *Time Out Book of London Short Stories*, ed. Maria Lexton, Penguin, 1993; *AV*; *WCL*; *SM* (as "Cold Colors")

"Comix Ecsperiense," *Comics Experience 5th Anniversary Ashcan*, Comix Experience, 1994

"Conversation Piece!" (art by David Wyatt), *2000AD #489*, Fleetway, 1986; *2000AD 1994 Yearbook*, Fleetway; *Time Twisters #17*, Quality Comics, 1989

"The Court" (art by Warren Pleece), *It's Dark in London*, Serpent's Tail, 1996; rewritten as "Keepsakes and Treasures: A Love Story"

"Cover Story" (art by Kelley Jones), *AI Book 5*, Atomeka Press, 1991

"Culprits or, Where Are They Now?" (with Eugene Byrne and Kim Newman), *Interzone #40*, 1990

"Crazy Hair," *The Neil Gaiman Audio Collection*, Harper Audio, 2004

"The Daughter of Owls," *Overstreet's FAN v1 #9*, 1996; *Tales of the Unanticipated #18*, Rune Press, 1997; *SM*; *Creatures of the Night* (art by Michael Zulli), Dark Horse Books, 2004; *ST*

"Deady and I," *Deady the Evil Teddy v3*, Sirius Entertainment, 2004

"Death: A Winter's Tale" (art by Jeffrey Jones), *Vertigo: Winter's Edge #2*, DC Comics/Vertigo, 1999

"December 7, 1995," *Tori Amos Dew Drop Inn Tour* souvenir book, 1995; *ADT*

"Desert Wind," liner notes for *Omaiyo* (recording) by Robin Adnan Anders, Rykodisc, 1998; *SM*

"Desire: How They Met Themselves" (art by Michael Zulli), *Vertigo:*

Winter's Edge #3, DC Comics/Vertigo, 2000

"Diseasemaker's Croup," *The Thackery T. Lambshead Pocket Guide to Eccentric & Discredited Diseases*, ed. Jeff VanderMeer and Mark Roberts, *World Fantasy 2002 Medical Sampler* (chapbook), 2002; Night Shade Books, 2003; Bantam, 2005

"Don't Ask Jack," *Overstreet's FAN v1 #3*, 1995; San Diego Comic Con poster, 1995; *SM*

"Eaten (Scenes from a Moving Picture)," *Off Limits: Tales of Alien Sex*, ed. Ellen Datlow, St. Martin's Press, 1996; *TYBFH 10th*, 1997; *SM* (UK); *World Horror Convention 2002 Souvenir Book*, 2002

"The Facts in the Case of the Departure of Miss Finch," *Frank Frazetta Fantasy Illustrated v1 #3* (illustrated by Tony Daniel), Fall 1998; Rune Press, 1999; *SM* (UK); *ST*

"The Faery Reel," *The Faery Reel: Tales from the Twilight Realm*, ed. Ellen Datlow & Terri Windling, Viking, 2004

"The False Knight on the Road" (art by Charles Vess), *The Book of Ballads and Sagas #1*, Green Man Press, 1995; *Sing Out! v40 #4*, 1996; Ballads, Green Man Press, 1997; The Book of Ballads, Tor, 2004

"Fear of Falling" (art by Kent Williams), *Vertigo Preview #1*, DC/Vertigo, 1992; *Sandman: Fables & Reflections*

"Featherquest," *Imagine #14*, 1984

"Feeders and Eaters" (art by Mark Buckingham), *Revolver Horror Special*, Fleetway, 1990; *Asylum #2*, Millennium, 1993; *The Best of Asylum Volume 1*, Millennium, 1994; *Keep Out the Night*, ed. Stephen Jones, PS Publishing, 2002 (rewritten, unillustrated); *TYBFH 16th*, 2003

"Fifteen Painted Cards from a Vampire Tarot," *The Art of Vampire the Masquerade*, White Wolf Publishing, 1998; *SM* (UK); *The Mammoth Book of Vampires*, ed. Stephen Jones, Carroll & Graf, 2004 (as "Fifteen Cards from a Vampire Tarot")

"The Flints of Memory Lane," *Dancing with the Dark*, ed. Stephen Jones, Vista, 1997; *ADT*

"The Flowers of Romance" (art by John Bolton), *Vertigo: Winter's Edge #1*, DC Comics/Vertigo, 1998

"Folk UnderGround" http://www.folkunderground.com/songs.html, recorded by Folk UnderGround on demo disk, 2003; recorded by Folk UnderGround on *Buried Things*, Happyfun! Records, 2003

"Forbidden Brides of the Faceless Slaves in the Nameless House of the Night of Dread Desire," *Gothic! Ten Original Dark Tales*, ed. Deborah Noyes, Candlewick, 2004; *Fantasy: the Best of 2004*, ed. Karen Haber and Jonathan Strahan, ibooks, 2005

"Foreign Parts," *Words Without Pictures*, ed. Steve Niles, Arcane/Eclipse Comics, 1990; *Fantasy Tales v12 #6*, ed. Stephen Jones and David A. Sutton, Robinson, 1991; *AV*; *The Giant Book of Fantasy Tales*, ed. Stephen Jones and David Sutton, The Book Company, 1996; *SM*

"Fragments" (art by S.M.S. and Fox), *Redfox #20*, Valkyrie, 1989

"From Homogenous to Honey" (art by Bryan Talbot and Mark Buckingham), *AARGH! (Artists Against Rampant Government Homophobia)*, Mad Love, 1988

"A Girl Needs A Knife," recorded by The Flash Girls on *Maurice and I*, Fabulous Records, 1995; *ADT*

"The Girls," *Tori Amos Strange Little Girls Tour* souvenir book, 2001; http://www.hereinmyhead.com/neil/slg.html

"Going Wodwo," *The Green Man: Tales From the Mythic Forest*, ed. Ellen Datlow and Terri Windling (art by Charles Vess), Viking Childrens Books, 2002; recorded by Folk UnderGround on *Buried Things*, Happyfun! Records, 2003

"The Goldfish Pool and Other Stories," *David Copperfield's Beyond Imagination*, ed. David Copperfield, Janet Berliner and Martin H. Greenberg, HarperPrism, 1996; *SM*

"Goliath," http://whatisthematrix.warnerbros.com/cmp/comic_index.html, 1999; *The Matrix Comics* (art by Bill Sienkiewicz and Greg Ruth), ed. Spencer Lamm, Burlyman Entertainment, 2003

"Good Boys Deserve Favours," *Overstreet's FAN v1 #5*, 1995; *ADT*

"The Great Cool Challenge" (art by Shane Oakley), *BLAAM! #1*, Willyprods, 1988

"Hallowe'en," *Time Out #1397*, 1996; *ADT*

"Harlequin Valentine," *World Horror Convention 1999 Program Book*, 1999; *TYBFH 13th*, 2000; *The Mammoth Book of Best New Horror: Volume Eleven*, ed. Stephen Jones, Robinson, 2000; *Strange Attraction*, ed. Edward E. Kramer, Shadowlands, 2000; *TT* [see also Books]

"The Herring Song" (with Lorraine Garland), recorded by The Flash Girls on *The Return of Pansy Smith and Violet Jones*, Spin Art, 1993; http://apocalypse.org/pub/flash/lyrics/herringsong.html

"Hold Me" (art by Dave McKean), *Hellblazer #27*, DC Comics, 1989; *Neil Gaiman's Midnight Days*

"An Honest Answer" (art by Bryan Talbot), *Eastercon Programme Book*, British Science Fiction Society, 1994; *Vogarth v2 #1*, Vogarth Comix, 1994; *The Magian Line v2.1*, 1994; *Wiindows #21*, Cult Press, 1994; *Ex-Directory: The Secret Files of Bryan Talbot*, Knockabout Comics, 1997; *Unknown Quantities*, Funny Valentine Press, 1999

"How Do You Think It Feels?," *In the Shadow of the Gargoyle*, ed. Nancy Kilpatrick and Thomas S. Roche, Ace, 1998; *SM* (UK); *Bento Story Art Box*, Allen Speigel Fine Arts, 2001

"How to Sell the Ponti Bridge," *Imagine #24*, 1985

"How to Write Longfellow's 'Hiawatha'," *ADT*

"I, Cthulhu, or, What's a Tentacle-Faced Thing Like Me Doing in a Sunken City Like This (Latitude 47° 9'S Longitude 126° 43'W)," *Dagon #16*, 1987; http://www.neilgaiman.com/exclusive/essay07.asp, 2003

"I'm A Believer" (art by Massimo Belardinelli), *2000AD #536*, Fleetway, 1987 ["Published story was significantly rewritten by the 2000AD staff to the point that Gaiman no longer claims it as his."]; *Time Twisters #18*, Quality Comics, 1989

"In the End," *Strange Kaddish: Tales You Won't Hear from Bubbie*, ed. Clifford Lawrence Meth and Ricia Mainhardt, Aardwolf Publishing, 1996; *SM* (UK); *TT*

"The Innkeeper's Soul" (art by Larry Welz), *Cherry Deluxe #1*, Cherry Entertainment, 1998

"Instructions," *A Wolf at the Door and Other Retold Fairy Tales*, ed. Ellen Datlow and Terri Windling, Simon & Schuster, 2000; http://www.endicott-studio.com/cofhs/cofinstr.html, 2000; *TYBFH 14th*, 2001; *Fantasy Readers Wanted—Apply Within*, ed. Nick Aires and James Richey, Silver Lake Publishing, 2003; [*ST*

"Inventing Aladdin," *Swan Sister: Fairy Tales Retold*, ed. Ellen Datlow and Terri Windling, Simon & Schuster, 2003

"It Was A Dark and Silly Night . . ." (art by Gahan Wilson), *Little Lit: "It Was A Dark and Silly Night . . .," ed. Art Spiegelman and Françoise Mouly, HarperCollins/Joanna Cotler, 2003*

"Keepsakes and Treasures: A Love Story" (originally "The Court"), *999: New Stories of Horror and Suspense*, ed. Al Sarrantonio, Avon, 1999; *TYBFH 13th*, 2000

"The Light Brigade, Chapter 1: The Path of the Just" (with Nigel Kitching, art by Nigel Kitching), *Trident #1, Trident Comics*, 1989

"The Light Brigade, Chapter 2: Take Five" (art by Nigel Kitching), *Trident #1, Trident Comics*, 1989

"Locks," *Silver Birch, Blood Moon*, ed. Ellen Datlow and Terri Windling, Avon, 1999; http://www.endicott-studio.com/cofhs/coflocks.html, 1999; *LA*

"Looking for the Girl," *Penthouse* (UK) v20 #10, 1985; *AV*; *Demon Sex*, ed. Amarantha Knight, Knight, Rhinoceros, 1998; *SM*

"Luther's Villanelle" (art by Dave McKean), *The Adventures of Luther Arkwright #10 "ARKeology"* (as "Villanelle"), Valkyrie, 1989; *The Crystal Palace Exhibition of 1990* (art by Ali Clark), Propaganda; *AV*; Wiindows #16, Cult Press, June 1994 (adapted by Tommy Berg); *Heart of Empire #5*, Dark Horse Comics, 1999

"Manuscript Found In A Milkbottle," *Knave v17 #8*, 1985

"A Meaningful Dialogue," recorded by The Flash Girls on *Play Each Morning Wild Queen*, Fabulous Records, 2001; http://apocalypse.org/pub/flash/lyrics/AMeaningfulDialogue.html

Miracleman #23: The Silver Age Book One "The Secret Origin of Young Miracleman!" (art by Mark Buckingham), Eclipse Comics, 1992

Miracleman #24: The Silver Age Book Two "When Titans Clash!" (art by Mark Buckingham), Eclipse Comics, 1993

"Mister X: Heartsprings and Watchstops" (art by Dave McKean), *AI Book 1*, Atomeka Press, 1989; The Edge, Vanguard, 2003

"The Monarch of the Glen," *Legends II*, ed. Robert Silverberg, Voyager, 2003; Del Rey, 2003

"Mouse," *Touch Wood: Narrow Houses II*, ed. Peter Crowther, Little, Brown, UK, 1993; *AV*; *SM*

"Murder Mysteries," *Midnight Grafitti*, ed. Jessica Horsting and James Van Hise, Warner, 1992; *TYBFH 6th*, 1993; *AV*; *SM*; http://www.scifi.com/set/playhouse/murder/, 2000: *Murder Most Divine: Ecclesiastical Tales of Unholy Crimes*, ed. Ralph McInerny and Martin H. Greenberg, Cumberland House Publishing, 2000; *Two Plays for Voices* [see also Books]

"My Life," *Sock Monkeys* (200 out of 1,863), Arne Svenson and Ron Warren, Greybull Press/Ideal World Books (through Distributed Art Publishers), 2002

"Nicholas Was . . .," *Drabble II: Double Century*, ed. Rob Meades and David B. Wake, Beccon Publications, 1990; *AV*; *WCL*; *SM*; *A Yuletide Universe*, ed. Brian Thomsen, Warner Aspect, 2003

"Nightfall," http://www.scifi.com/tribute/nightfall.html, 2001

"Now We Are Sick" (with Stephen Jones), *Now We Are Sick Sampler*, ed. Neil Gaiman and Stephen Jones, [publisher not noted], 1986; *Now We Are Sick*, ed. Neil Gaiman and Stephen Jones, DreamHaven Books, 1991

"October in the Chair," *Conjunctions: 39—The New Wave Fabulists*, guest ed. Peter Straub, ed. Bradford Morrow, Bard College (also through Distributed Art Publishers), 2002; *Year's Best Fantasy 3*, ed. David G. Hartwell, HarperCollins/Eos, 2003; *The Mammoth Book of Best New Horror: Volume 14*, ed. Stephen Jones, Carroll & Graf, 2003

"The Old Warlock's Reverie: A Pantoum," *Once Upon A Midnight*, ed. James A. Riley, Michael N. Langford and Thomas E. Fuller, Unnameable Press, 1995; *Negative Burn #50* (art by Guy Davis), Caliber Press, 1998; *ADT*

"On The Wall," recorded by One Ring Zero on *As Smart As We Are* (audio CD and companion book), Soft Skull Press, 2004

"One Life, Furnished in Early Moorcock," *Elric: Tales of the White Wolf*, ed. Edward E. Kramer, White Wolf, 1994; *Elric #0* (art by P. Craig Russell), Topps, 1996; *Stranger Kaddish*, ed. Jim Reeber and Clifford Lawrence Meth, Aardwolf Publishing, 1997; *SM*; *Elric: Stormbringer*, Dark Horse Press, 1998

"Only the End of the World Again," *Shadows Over Innsmouth*, ed. Stephen Jones, Fedogan & Bremer, 1994; *On Cats & Dogs: Two Tales*, DreamHaven Books, 1997; *Lord of the Fantastic: Stories in Honor of Roger Zelazny* (with Afterword), ed. Martin H. Greenberg, Avon Eos, 1998; *Oni Double Feature #6-8*, Oni Press, 1998 (adapted by P. Craig Russell, art by Troy Nixey); *SM*; *ADT* (only Afterword) [see also Books]

"Original Sins" (art by Mike Hoffman and Kevin Nowlan), *Secret Origins Special #1*, DC Comics, 1989; *Batman Featuring Two-Face and The Riddler*, DC Comics, 1995

"Orphée," liner notes for *Orphée* (recording, by various artists), Projekt Records, 2000

"Other People," *The Magazine of Fantasy & Science Fiction*, Oct/Nov 2001

"Pages from a Journal Found in a Shoebox Left in a Greyhound Bus Somewhere Between Tulsa, Oklahoma, and Louisville, Kentucky," *Tori Amos Scarlet's Walk Tour* souvenir book, 2002; TYBFH 16th, 2003

"Pavane" (art by Mark Buckingham), *Secret Origins #36*, DC Comics, 1989

"Personal Thing," recorded by The Flash Girls on *Play Each Morning Wild Queen*, Fabulous Records, 2001; http://apocalypse.org/pub/flash/lyrics/PersonalThing.html; *ADT*

"Post-Mortem on Our Love" (with Lorraine Garland), *AV*; *The Magian Line v1.2*, 1993; recorded by The Flash Girls on *The Return of Pansy Smith and Violet Jones*, Spin Art, 1993; http://apocalypse.org/pub/flash/lyrics/postmortemonourlove.html; *ADT*

"A Prayer and Hope . . ." (script of *Miracleman #17*), *Panel One: Comic Book Scripts by Top Writers*, ed. Nat Gertler, About Comics, LLC, 2002

"The Price," *On Cats & Dogs: Two Tales*, DreamHaven Books, 1997; *Dark Terrors 3: The Gollancz Book of Horror*, ed. Stephen Jones and David Sutton, Gollancz, 1997; *SM*; *LA*; *Creatures of the Night* (art by Michael Zulli), Dark Horse Books, 2004; *ST*

"The Problem of Susan," *Flights: Extreme Visions of Fantasy*, ed. Al Sarrantonio, Roc, 2004

"Queen of Knives," *World Horror Convention 1995 Program Book*, 1995; *Tombs*, ed. Edward E. Kramer and Peter Crowther, White Wolf, 1995; *TYBFH 9th*, 1996; *The Mammoth Book of Best New Horror: Volume Seven*, ed. Stephen Jones, Raven, 1996; *SM*

"Reading the Entrails: A Rondel," *The Fortune Teller*, ed. Lawrence Schimel and Martin H. Greenberg, DAW, 1997; *SM*

"The Return of Mink Stole" (art by Eddie Campbell), *The Spirit: The New Adventures #2*, Kitchen Sink Press, 1998

"Riding the Flame / Little Beggarman," recorded by The Flash Girls on *The Return of Pansy Smith and Violet Jones*, Spin Art, 1993

Sandman Midnight Theatre (with Matt Wagner; art by Teddy Kristiansen), DC Comics/Vertigo, 1995; *Neil Gaiman's Midnight Days*

"The Scorpio Boys in the City of Lux Sing Their Strange Songs," *Alan Moore: Portrait of an Extraordinary Gentleman*, ed. Gary Spencer Millidge, Abiogenesis Press/Top Shelf Productions, 2003

"Screaming" (art by Mark Buckingham), *Total Eclipse #4*, Eclipse Comics, 1989; *Miracleman #21*, Eclipse Comics, 1991; *Miracleman Book Four: The Golden Age*

"The Sea Change," *Overstreet's FAN v1 #6*, 1995; *SM*; *[ST*

"Shaggy God Stories" (art by Mike Mignola), *Swamp Thing Annual #5*, DC Comics, 1989; *Neil Gaiman's Midnight Days*

"Shoggoth's Old Peculiar," *The Mammoth Book of Comic Fantasy*, ed. Mike Ashley, Robinson, 1998; *SM*; *TYBFH 12th*, 1999; *Acolytes of Cthulhu*, ed. Robert M. Price, Fedogan & Bremer, 2001; chapbook (art by Jouni Koponen), DreamHaven Books, 2004 [see also Books]

"Signal to Noise," *The Face v2 #9-15*, June-December, 1989; BBC3 radio drama performance, 1996; audio play CD, Allen Spiegel Fine Arts, 2000 [see also Books]

1602 #1-8 (art by Andy Kubert and Richard Isanove), Marvel, 2003-04 [see also Books]

"Sloth" (art by Bryan Talbot), *Seven Deadly Sins*, Knockabout Publications, 1989; *Ex-Directory: The Secret Files of Bryan Talbot*, Knockabout Comics, 1997

"Snow, Glass, Apples," DreamHaven Books (limited-edition chapbook), 1994; http://www.holycow.com/dreaming/stories/snow.html; TYBFH 8th, 1995; *Love in Vein II*, ed. Poppy Z. Brite and Martin H. Greenberg, HarperPrism, 1997; *SM*; http://www.scifi.com/set/playhouse/snowglassapples/, 2001; *Two Plays for Voices* [see also Books]

"The Song of the Audience," *AV*; *WCL*

"The Song of the Lost" (art by Jae Lee), *Heroes*, Marvel, 2001

"Song of Orpheus" (art by Bryan Talbot and Mark Buckingham), *Sandman Special #1*, DC, 1991; *Sandman: Fables & Reflections*

"Sonnet," *ADT*

"Sonnet in the Dark" (with Lorraine Garland), recorded by The Flash Girls on *The Return of Pansy Smith and Violet Jones*, Spin Art, 1993

"A Study in Emerald," *Shadows Over Baker Street*, ed. Michael Reaves and John Pelan, Del Rey, 2003; *Science Fiction: the Best of 2003*, ed. Karen Haber and Jonathan Strahan, ibooks, 2004; *TYBFH 17th*, 2004; http://www.neilgaiman.com/exclusive/StudyinEmerald.asp

"Swamp Thing: Jack in the Green" (art by Steve Bissette and John Totleben), *Neil Gaiman's Midnight Days*

"Sweat & Tears" (with Faye Perozich; art by Yanick Paquette and Michael Lacombe), *Blood Childe #4*, Millennium Publications, 1995

"Sweeney Todd: The Demon Barber of Fleet Street" (art by Michael Zulli), *Taboo #6 Sweeney Todd Penny Dreadful*, *Taboo #7*, *Spiderbaby* Graphix/Tundra, 1992

"The Sweeper of Dreams," *Overstreet's FAN v1 #8*, 1996; *SM*

"Tastings," *Sirens and Other Daemon Lovers*, ed. Ellen Datlow and Terri Windling, HarperPrism, 1998; *SM*

"Tea and Corpses," recorded by The Flash Girls on *The Return of Pansy Smith and Violet Jones*, Spin Art, 1993; http://apocalypse.org/pub/flash/lyrics/teaandcorpses.html

"Train." (art by Ben Black and Carsten Bradley, music by Jason Seigler), narrated and animated dream, The Dream Project, http://www.thedreamproject.org/dream_ii.html, 2002 (originally posted in NG web site Journal http://www.neilgaiman.com/journal/2002_09_15_archive.asp#854 70702)

"Troll Bridge," *Snow White, Blood Red*, ed. Ellen Datlow and Terri Windling, AvoNova, 1993; *AV* (as "Troll-Bridge"); *Previews vIII #8*, 1993; *Comic World #30*, 1994; *TYBFH 7th*, 1994; *Realms of Fantasy v1 #1*, 1994; *WCL*; *Fantasy Stories*, ed. Mike Ashley, Robinson Children's Books, 1996; *The Random House Book of Fantasy Stories*, ed. Mike Ashley, Random House, 1997; *SM*; *A Distant Soil #25* (art by Colleen Doran), Image Comics, 1998; *Cicada v1 #6*, July-August, 1999; *The Prentice Hall Anthology of Science Fiction and Fantasy*, ed. Garyn G. Roberts, Prentice-Hall, 2001

"True Things" (art by Mark Buckingham), *The Extraordinary Works of Alan Moore*, ed. George Khoury, Twomorrows Publishing, 2003

"Vampire Sestina," *Fantasy Tales v10 #2*, ed. Stephen Jones and David A Sutton, Robinson, 1989; *The Mammoth Book of Vampires*, ed. Stephen Jones, Robinson, 1992 (removed from the 2004 edition);

AV; *The Giant Book of Fantasy Tales*, ed. Stephen Jones and David Sutton, The Book Company, 1996; *Book of Vampires*, ed. Stephen Jones, Barnes & Noble, 1992; *SM*

"Vier Mauern" (art by Dave McKean), *Breakthrough*, ed. P. Christin and A.C. Knigge, Catalan Communications, 1990

"Virus," *Digital Dreams*, ed. David V. Barrett, New English Library, 1990; *AV*; *SM*

"The Wake: Chapter 1, Which Occurs in the Wake of What Has Gone Before" (Sandman #70) script, *Fiddler's Green: A Sandman Convention Souvenir Book*, 2004

"Wall, A Prologue" (art by Charles Vess), *A Fall of Stardust* portfolio chapbook, Green Man Press, 1999

"We Can Get Them For You Wholesale," *Knave v16 #7*, 1984; *Winter Chills #3*, 1989; *AV*; *Negative Burn #11*, Caliber Press, 1994 (adapted by Joe Pruett and Ken Meyer, Jr.); *Negative Burn: Best of Year One*, Caliber Press, 1995; *SM*; *Bangs & Whimpers: Stories About the End of the World*, ed. James Frenkel, Lowell House/Roxbury Park Books, 1999

"Webs," *More Tales from the Forbidden Planet*, ed. Roz Kaveney, Titan, 1990; *Comics Scoreboard #48*, 1993; *AV*

"The Wedding Present," *Dark Terrors 4: The Gollancz Book of Horror*, ed. Stephen Jones and David Sutton, Gollancz, 1998; *SM*; *The Mammoth Book of Best New Horror: Volume Ten*, ed. Stephen Jones, Robinson, 1999; *TT*

"What's in a Name?" (art by Steve Yeowell), *2000AD #538*, Fleetway, 1987

"The Wheel" (art by Chris Bachalo), *9-11: September 11th 2001, Volume 2*, DC Comics, 2002

"When is a Door" (art by Bernie Mireault and Matt Wagner), *Secret Origins Special #1*, DC Comics, 1989; *Batman Featuring Two-Face and The Riddler*, DC Comics, 1995

"When We Went to See the End of the World by Dawnie Morningside, age 11¼," *SM*; *Scary! 2: More Stories to Make You Scream!*, ed. Peter Haining, Souvenir Press, 2002

"The White Road," *Ruby Slippers, Golden Tears*, ed. Ellen Datlow and Terri Windling, Morrow AvoNova, 1995; *WCL*; TYBFH 9th, 1996; *SM*

"Wordsworth" (art by Dave McKean), *Clive Barker's Hellraiser #20*, Epic, 1993; *Clive Barker's Hellraiser: Collected Best*, Checker Book Publishing Group, 2002

"A Writer's Prayer," *ADT*; *TT*

"Yeti," recorded by The Flash Girls on *Maurice and I*, Fabulous Records, 1995 ["The author points out that he wrote this when he was seventeen, and is thus absolved of all responsibility. Not according to the laws of the State of Minnesota, mister."]

"You're Never Alone With a Phone!" (art by John Hicklenton), *2000AD #488*, Fleetway, 1986; *Time Twisters #17*, Quality Comics, 1989

Other Works

The owners of all URLs included here have Neil's permission to publish his work in that format.

Afterword,

- "A Book Review," *The Lord of Castle Black* by Steven Brust, Tor, 2003
- "(After They've Brought on the Dancing Girls)," *Images of Omaha #1*, ed. Reed Waller and Kate Worley, Kitchen Sink Press, 1992; *ADT*
- "Epilogue: The Lady and/or the Tiger: II" (with Roz Kaveny), *Weerde: Book 1*, ed. Mary Gentle and Roz Kaveny, Roc UK, 1992
- "In Re: Pansy Smith and Violet Jones," liner notes for The Flash Girls: *The Return of Pansy Smith and Violet Jones* (recording), Spin Art, 1993; http://apoca-lypse.org/pub/flash/lyrics/pansyandviolet.html; ADT
- *Nameless Sins* by Nancy A. Collins, Gauntlet Publications, 1994

American Gods Web Log, February-September 2001, http://www.neilgaiman.com/journal_archives/archive.asp; *ADT*

"Anthony Boucher—The Compleat Werewolf, and Other Stories of Fantasy and SF," *Horror: The 100 Best Books*, ed. Stephen Jones and Kim Newman, Xanadu Publications Ltd., 1988, Carroll & Graf, 1988

"Banging the Drum for Harlan Ellison," *Readercon 11 Souvenir Book*, 1999; *AggieCon 31 Program Book*, 2000; *ADT*

"Being An Experiment Upon Strictly Scientific Lines," *20/20 #11*, 1990; *AV*; *LA*

"Books Have Sexes; or to be more precise, books have genders," http://www.powells.com/features/gaiman.html, 2001; http://www.neilgaiman.com/exclusive/essay02.asp (as "All Books Have Genders"), 2002

(cover art) *But I Digress* by Peter A. David, Krause Publications, 1994

"Close Encounters: R.A. Lafferty" (article section), *The Washington Post* Book World Section, April 7, 2002

Comic Book Superheroes Unmasked, video documentary interview, A&E Home Video, 2003

"The Craft," *James Herbert: By Horror Haunted*, NEL, 1992

"Curiosities":

- *The Manuscript Found at Saragossa* by Count Jan Potocki, *The Magazine of Fantasy & Science Fiction*, Sept 1998
- *Lud-in-the-Mist* by Hope Mirrlees, *The Magazine of Fantasy & Science Fiction*, July 1999; *ADT*

Dark Dreamers photo accompaniment, *Dark Dreamers: Facing the Masters of Fear*, Cemetary Dance, 2001

"The Dark Knight Returns," *Foundation: The International Review of Science Fiction #38*, Winter 1986/87; *ADT*

"Dead Write," *Skeleton Crew v2 #1*, July 1990

Death entry (art by Mike Dringenberg), *Who's Who in the DC Universe #8*, DC Comics, 1991

"Discworld leaves its black hole," FT.com *Financial Times*, July 12, 2002

"Douglas Adams: An Appreciation," *Locus #485*, June 2001

"Drawn in Darkness," *Bolton: Haunted Shadows* by John Bolton, Halloween Artworks, 1998

Eisner Keynote Speech 2003, presented at Eisner Awards ceremony, San Diego Comic Con; http://www.neilgaiman.com/exclusive/EisnerKeynotespeech.asp, 2003

Essay for Patti, *The Faces of Fantasy*, Tor, 1996; *ADT*

Faeries: a musical companion to The Art of Brian Froud liner notes (recording, by various artists), Windham Hill Records, 2002

Fan Letter, *Overstreet's FAN v1 #11*, 1996; *ADT*

"Flame On!," *Clive Barker's Shadows in Eden*, ed. Stephen Jones, Underwood-Miller, 1991

Foreword,

- *100 Graphic Novels for Public Libraries*, Kitchen Sink Press, 1996
- *The 101 Best Graphic Novels Supplement for Libraries* by Stephen Weiner, NBM Publishing Inc., 2001
- *The Beast That Shouted Love at the Heart of the World* by Harlan Ellison, Borderlands Press, 1994; *Edgeworks 4*, White Wolf, 1997; *ADT*
- *The Compleat Alice Cooper: The Last Temptation*, Marvel Music, 1995
- *The Complete Bone Adventures v2* by Jeff Smith, Cartoon Books, 1994
- *Doctor Who: Eye of the Tyger* by Paul McAuley, Telos Publishing, 2003
- *The Einstein Intersection* by Samuel R. Delany, Wesleyan University Press, 1998; *ADT*
- "Foreword: What Was He Like, Douglas Adams?," *The Ultimate Hitchhiker's Guide to the Galaxy* by Douglas Adams, Del Rey/Ballantine Books, 2002
- *Hitchhiker: a Biography of Douglas Adams* by M. J. Simpson, Justin, Charles & Company, 2003
- *Lucifer: Devil in the Gateway* by Mike Carey, DC Comics/Vertigo, 2001
- *Rising Stars #1* by J. Michael Straczynski, Keu Cha, and Jason Gorder, Image/Top Cow, 1999; Rising Stars: Born In Fire, Image Comics/Top Cow, 2001
- The Solomon Kane Sketchbook by Gary Gianni et al, Wandering Star, 1997

Gaiman, Neil (Richard) entry (with Ron Tiner), *The Encyclopedia of Fantasy*, ed. John Clute and John Grant, St. Martin's Press, 1997

"Gene Wolfe: Be Willing To Learn," *World Horror Convention 2002 Souvenir Book*, 2002

Graphic Novel entry (with John Clute), *The Encyclopedia of Science Fiction* updated edition, ed. John Clute and Peter Nicholls, St. Martin's/Griffen, 1995

"Harlan & Me . . .," *Guest of Honor: Harlan Ellison*, Chicago ComicCon, 1994

"How Dare You?," Borders.com, 2001 (as "In Search of America"); http://www.neilgaiman.com/exclusive/essay01.asp, 2002

"Identity Crisis," *Punch v296 #7744*, 1989

Interview in

- *The Neil Gaiman Audio Collection*, Harper Audio, 2004
- *Writers on Comics Scriptwriting*, ed. Mark Salisbury, Titan UK, 1999; Titan Books Ltd., 2002

Interview with,

- Alan Moore, *American Fantasy v2 #2*, Winter 1987
- The Hernandez Brothers, *The Comics Journal #178*, July 1995
- Lou Reed, "Waiting for the Man," *Reflex #26*, July 26, 1992
- Gene Wolfe, "The Knight at the Door," *The New York Review of Science Fiction #186*, February 2004; http://www.bordersstores.com/features/feature.jsp?file=gaimanwolfe

Introduction,

- "About Kim Newman, with notes on the creation and eventual dissolution of the Peace and Love Corporation," *The Original Dr. Shade and Other Stories*, Pocket UK, 1994
- *The Adventures of Professor Thintwhistle and His Incredible Aetheric Flyer* by Dick Lupoff and Steve Stiles, Fantagraphics Books, 1991; *ADT*
- *Angels & Visitations: A Miscellany*, DreamHaven Books, 1993
- *The Arbitrary Placement of Walls* by Martha Soukup, DreamHaven Books, 1997; *LA*
- *Biten* by Yoshitaka Amano, Asahi Sonorama, 1999
- *Blake's 7: The Inside Story* by Joe Nazzaro & Sheelagh Wells, Virgin, 1997
- "The Books of Magic: An Introduction," *The Books of Magic: the Invitation*; *The Books of Magic: Bindings*; *The Books of Magic: The Children's Crusade*, by Carla Jablonski, Eos, 2003
- *Brat Pack* by Rick Veitch, King Hell-Tundra, 1992; *ADT*
- "Breathtaker: An Introduction," *Breathtaker* by Mark Wheatley and Marc Hempel, DC Comics/Vertigo, 1994; *ADT*

- "But What Has That To Do With Bacchus?," *Deadface: Immortality Isn't Forever* by Eddie Campbell with Ed Hillyer, Dark Horse Comics, 1990; *Eddie Campbell's Bacchus #1*, Eddie Campbell Comics, 1995; *ADT*
- "The Cartoonist—An Introduction," *The Cartoonist v1 #1* by Teri Sue Wood, Dogstar Press, 1997
- *The Collected Omaha, Volume 5* by Reed Waller and Kate Worley, Kitchen Sink Press, 1993
- "Concerning Dreams and Nightmares," *The Dream Cycle of H.P. Lovecraft*, Ballantine Del Rey, 1995; *ADT*
- *A Death Gallery*, DC Comics/Vertigo, 1994
- "A Distant Soil: An Introduction," *A Distant Soil: The Gathering* by Colleen Doran, Image Comics, 1997
- "Dori Seda: An Introduction," *Dori Stories: The Complete Dori Seda* by Dori Seda, Last Gasp of San Francisco, 1999
- "The Endless," *The Endless Gallery*, DC/Vertigo, 1995
- "Four Bookshops," *Shelf Life: Fantastic Stories Celebrating Bookstores*, ed. Greg Ketter, DreamHaven Books, 2002, 2005
- *From the End of the Twentieth Century* by John M. Ford, NESFA Press, 1997; *ADT*
- "Growing Pains" (as Gerry Musgrave), *Swamp Thing v5* by Alan Moore, Titan Books, 1988
- *Hanging Out With the Dream King* by Joe McCabe, Fantagraphics Books, 2005
- "'How Do You Baffle A Vegetable?' and Other God Jokes," *Swamp Thing v8* by Alan Moore, Titan, 1988
- "Intro From the Heart," *Hearts of Africa* by Cindy Goff, Rafael Nieves, and Seitu Hayden, Slave Labor Graphics, 1994
- Jonathan Carroll website http://www.jonathancarroll.com/introduction.html; *ADT*; **Gods & Monsters: World Fantasy Convention 2002 Souvenir Book**, 2002 (as "One of the Brotherhood")
- *The King of Elfland's Daughter* by Lord Dunsany, Del Rey/Impact, 1999; Millennium Books, 2001; *ADT*
- *Kurt Busiek's Astro City: Confession* by Kurt Busiek, Brent Eric Anderson, and Will Blyberg, Homage Comics, 1997; *ADT* (as "Astro City: Confession")
- *Lud-In-The-Mist* by Hope Mirrlees, Millennium Books, 2000
- "Me and my Dadd and Mark Chadbourn," *The Fairy Feller's Master Stroke* by Mark Chadbourn, PS Publishing, 2002
- *Noodles: Sketchbook Stuff, Random Drawings and Telephone Squiggles* by Michael Zulli, Tundra, 1991
- "Of Blood and Bad Craziness . . .," *Swamp Thing v2* by Alan Moore, Titan Books, 1987
- "Of Time, and Gully Foyle," *The Stars My Destination* by Alfred Bester, Random House/Vintage Books, 1996; *ADT*

- "On Barron Storey: An Introduction," *W.A.T.C.H. v2 #1*, Vanguard Productions, 1996

- "On Spares: A Short, Formal Introduction, with Additional Theory," *Spares: Special Edition* by Michael Marshall Smith, Overlook Connection Press, 1998

- "Original Synners: An Introduction to the Tenth Anniversary Edition," *Synners* by Pat Cadigan, Four Walls Eight Windows, 2001

- "Prologue: The Lady and/or the Tiger: I" (with Roz Kaveney), *Weerde: Book 1*, ed. Mary Gentle and Roz Kaveney, Roc UK, 1992

- *The Sandman: King of Dreams* by Alisa Kwitney, Titan, 2003; Chronicle Books, 2003

- *Saviour Book One* by Mark Millar, Daniel Vallely, and Nigel Kitching, Trident Comics, 1990

- *Scholars and Soldiers* by Mary Gentle, Macdonald & Co., 1989; Orbit, 1990; *AV* (as "A Prologue")

- "*The Screwtape Letters*: An Introduction," *The Screwtape Letters* by C.S. Lewis, adapted by Charles E. Hall and Pat Redding, Marvel, 1994; *ADT*

- *Shadows of Light and Dark* by Jo Fletcher, Airgedlámh Publications/The Alchemy Press, 1998

- "Shameful Secrets of Comics Retailing: The Lingerie Connection," *How to Get Girls (Into Your Store)*, ed. Deni Loubert, Friends of Lulu, 1997; http://www.friends-lulu.org/handbook.html; *ADT*

- *Smoke and Mirrors*, Avon, 1998

- *Sonovawitch! And Other Tales of Supernatural Law* by Batton Lash, Exhibit A Press, 2000

- *Starchild—Crossroads* by James A. Owen, Coppervale Press, 1998; *ADT*

- "The Swords of Lankhmar," *Return to Lankhmar* by Fritz Leiber, White Wolf, 1997; *ADT*

- *The Tale of One Bad Rat, Book One* by Bryan Talbot, Dark Horse Comics, 1994

- *Tantrum* by Jules Feiffer, Fantagraphics Books, 1997; *ADT*

- "Trifles Light as Air and Otherwise," *Swamp Thing v4* by Alan Moore, Titan Books, 1987

- *The Vertigo Tarot* by Rachel Pollack, DC/Vertigo, 1995

- *Voice of the Fire* by Alan Moore, Top Shelf Productions, 2003

- *What I Thought I Saw* by Kelli Bickman, Yatra Publications/11:11 Studio, 1996

- "What This Book is Really About," *The Worm: the Longest Comic Strip in the World*, Slab-O-Concrete Productions, 1999

- "Why Dead Birds Move and Flowers Go to Hell," *Swamp Thing v3* by Alan Moore, Titan Books, 1987

- "The Wound That Never Heals: An Introduction," *The Man in the Maze* by Robert Silverberg, ibooks, 2002

Introduction to "In Our Block" by R.A. Lafferty, *My Favorite Fantasy Story*, ed. Martin H. Greenberg, DAW, 2000

Introduction to "Seven Nights in Slumberland" by George Alec Effinger, *George Alec Effinger Live! From Planet Earth*, Golden Gryphon Press, 2005

Introduction to "Warning: Death May Be Injurious to Your Health" (with Stephen Jones), *Robert Bloch: Appreciations of the Master*, ed. Richard Matheson and Ricia Mainhardt, Tor, 1995

"Jack Kirby Tribute," *The Comics Journal #167*, April 1994

"James Herbert: Growing Up in Public," *Gaslight & Ghosts*, ed. Stephen Jones and Jo Fletcher, 1998 World Fantasy Con/Robinson Publishing, 1988

Jones, Diana Wynne entry (with John Clute), *The Encyclopedia of Fantasy*, ed. John Clute and John Grant, St. Martin's Press, 1997

"King of the Gory Tellers," *Today*, Oct 19 1986; *Clive Barker's Shadows in Eden*, ed. Stephen Jones, Underwood-Miller, 1991

Lafferty, R(afael) A(loysius) entry (with John Clute), *The Encyclopedia of Fantasy*, ed. John Clute and John Grant, St. Martin's Press, 1997

Life, the Universe, and Douglas Adams, video narration (by Joel Greengrass and Rick Mueller), Greater Talent Network Inc., 2002

"Looking Back at the King of the Comics," *Hogan's Alley v1 #1*, Autumn 1994

"Love and Death: Overture," *Swamp Thing: Love and Death* by Alan Moore, Stephen Bissette, John Totleben, and Shawn McManus, DC Comics/Vertigo, 1990

"A Modest Proposal," *Free Speeches*, Oni Press, 1998

"The Murders on the Rue Morgue" (with Alan Moore), *Negative Burn #13*, Caliber Press, 1994; *Alan Moore's Songbook*, Caliber Press, 1998

"The Mystery of Father Brown," *100 Great Detectives*, ed. Maxim Jakubowski, Xanadu, 1991; *AV*

"Neil's Thankyou Pome," *The Magian Line v2.2*, 1994; *ADT*

"On Cities" (embedded essay), *SimCity 2000* computer game, Electronic Arts, 1993; http://www.neilgaiman.com/exclusive/Simcity2000.asp

"On Discovering Diana Wynne Jones," *Boskone 32 Program Book*, NESFA, 1995

"Preamble and Bits" (with Sergio Aragones), *Welcome Back to the House of Mystery*, DC Comics/Vertigo, 1998

Princess Mononoke, English-translation screenplay (original by Hayao Miyazaki), Miramax Films, 1999; Miramax Home Entertainment, 2000

"A Recognition," *Echoes: The Drawings of Michael William Kaluta*, Vanguard Publishing, 2000

"Reflections on Myth (with digressions into Gardening, Comics and Fairy Tales)" in *Columbia: A Journal of Literature and Art #31*,

Winter 1999

Sex, Lies, and Superheroes, video documentary interview, Prince Street Films, 2003

"Six to Six," *Time Out*, 1990; *AV*

Sketchbook, Negative Burn #25, Caliber Press, 1995

"Something About Collaborating with Artists," *Locus #510*, July 2003

"Spadework: Punch Book Review of Josiah Thompson's Gumshoe," *Punch v297 #7749*, 1989; *AV* (as "Gumshoe")

"300 Good Reasons to Resent Dave Sim," Comic Buyer's Guide #977, 1992; *Feature Magazine v3 #4*, Winter 1997; *ADT*

"Team Spirit: Summerland by Michael Chabon" (book review), *The Washington Post* Book World Section, October 6, 2002

"Terry Pratchett: An Appreciation," *Noreascon 4 Souvenir Book*, Massachusetts Convention Fandom, Inc., 2004

"They Were Probably Just Being Polite," *Gods & Monsters: World Fantasy Convention 2002 Souvenir Book*, 2002; http://www.neilgaiman.com/exclusive/essay08.asp (as "Neil Gaiman on Dave McKean"), 2003

untitled (Robert Bloch appreciation), *Robert Bloch: Appreciations of the Master*, ed. Richard Matheson and Ricia Mainhardt, Tor, 1995

"Where Do You Get Your Ideas?," IBS.com, 1997; http://www.neilgaiman.com/exclusive/essay03.asp, 2002

"Writing and Werewolfing," *Waterstone's Guide to Science Fiction, Fantasy & Horror*, ed. Paul Wake, Steve Andrews and Ariel, Waterstone's, 1998

Interviews (print): *FA #109*, Jan 1989; *Fear!* Feb 1990; *Skeleton Crew* Nov 1990; *Fear!* June 1991; *Locus #362* (with Terry Pratchett), Mar 1991; *Visions* Fall 1991; *The Comics Journal #155* (with Dave McKean), Jan 1993; *The Comics Journal #163*, Nov 1993; *The Comics Journal #169*, July 1994; *IT Magazine & Comics #1*, Sept 1994; *Aberrations #35*, 1995; *The Comics Journal #188*, July 1996; *Interzone* Feb 1997; *Westwind #232-235*, Aug-Dec 1998; *Locus #459*, Apr 1999; *Gauntlet #17 & 19*, 1999, 2000; *Weird Tales*, Summer 2000; *Sketch #14*, 2002; *Locus #500* (with Gene Wolfe), Sept 2002; *The Third Alternative #32*, Fall 2002; *Chronicle #229*, Oct 2002; *Vertigo X Preview*, 2003; *Locus #528*, Feb 2005

Selected Secondary Bibliography

Hanging Out With the Dream King by Joe McCabe, Fantagraphics Books, 2005

The Library of Graphic Novelists: Neil Gaiman by Steven P. Olson, Rosen Publishing Group, 2005

Neil Gaiman's The Sandman and Joseph Campbell: In Search of the Modern Myth by Stephen Rauch, Wildside Press, 2003

The Sandman Companion by Hy Bender, DC Comics, 1999, 2000

The Sandman: King of Dreams by Alisa Kwitney, Titan, 2003; Chronicle Books, 2003

Additional Sources

The *Locus* Index to Science Fiction,
http://www.locusmag.com/index/index.html

Michigan State University Libraries Comic Art Collection,
http://www.lib.msu.edu/comics/index.htm

Shield Albright, http://www.neilgaimanbibliography.com/

Peter and Michael Karpas, http://www.enjolrasworld.com

the dreaming: the Neil Gaiman page,
http://www.holycow.com/dreaming/

CONTRIBUTOR NOTES

Bethany Alexander lives in Gaithersburg, Maryland. She is currently en route to an M.Ed. in early childhood education, eagerly working towards the day when, speckled with paint in primary colors, she can say, "No, dear, that doesn't go in your mouth" with some authority.

William Alexander's critical credits include working as an assistant editor for *Weird Tales* and *Women's Worlds: The McGraw-Hill Anthology of Women Writing in English*, and lecturing at the University of Vermont's peer-reviewed Tolkien conference. He spent a semester in Ireland pretending to be Canadian (which helped him write about Mad King Sweeny for this collection), and has written fiction for *Weird Tales*, *Zahir*, *The SiNK* and *Seven Days*. He is currently earning an M.A. in English Literature at UVM.

Mike Ashley is a leading British anthologist and scholar, editor of the long series of *Mammoth* anthologies for Robinson and Carroll & Graf, such as *The Mammoth Book of New Jules Verne Adventures*, *The Mammoth Book of Sorcerers' Tales*, several Arthurian anthologies, and much more. With Frank Parnell, he compiled the important index *Monthly Terrors*, and has more recently published a definitive biography, *Algernon Blackwood, An Extraordinary Life*.

Mary Borsellino is an Australian writer and researcher who only bothers to seek out traditional publication for her work because it means she can afford to keep buying comics. She has been interested in studying cultural production since a young age, which made her somewhat unique amongst her class of aspiring marine biologists. In hindsight, this strikes her as slightly odd, as she was very fond of dolphins at the time.

Marilyn "Mattie" Brahen is the author of seven published stories, some of which have appeared in *The Ultimate Halloween*, *Crafty Cat Crimes*, *Fantastic*, *Scheherezade*, and *Marion Zimmer Bradley's Fantasy Magazine*. Her first novel, *Claiming Her*, appeared in 2003 and was favorably reviewed in *Publishers Weekly*.

She is at work on her second, while also reviewing for *The New York Review of Science Fiction.*

Chris Dowd is currently completing a Ph.D. in literature at the University of Connecticut, where he also teaches composition and creative writing. His research and teaching interests include Irish literature, contemporary drama, and the graphic novel. In addition, he works as a freelance writer.

Robert K. Elder writes about film and culture for the *Chicago Tribune.* His work has appeared in *The New York Times*, *Premiere*, *The Los Angeles Times*, salon.com, and many other publications. Rob recently released the book *John Woo: Interviews*, the first oral history of the director's life, movies and legacy. Rob has also contributed to books on poker, comic books and visual design. A member of the Chicago Film Critics Association, Rob teaches journalism at Columbia College Chicago. The Montana native graduated from the University of Oregon's School of Journalism and Communication. His website is: www.robelder.com.

It is a little known fact that he survived a Snuffleupagus encounter in the wild. He reports this but does not elaborate.

Rob has been known to carry a tape recorder.

JaNell Golden lives in Knoxville, Tennessee.

Ben P. Indick spent a lifetime as a pharmacist but also has written plays for children and adults, many of which have been performed. Of note are half a dozen fantasy stories, and numerous essays, as well as two books on science fiction authors. He is particularly proud of having appeared in all of Darrell Schweitzer's studies of authors of fantastic literature. He currently reviews books and interviews authors for *Publishers Weekly.*

Jason Erik Lundberg has had fiction and nonfiction published in over twenty venues, including *The Third Alternative*, *Strange Horizons*, *Fantastic Metropolis*, *Infinity Plus*, *The Green Man Review*, *Escape Pod* and *Electric Velocipede*. His short fiction has been nominated for the Fountain Award and honorably mentioned in *The Year's Best Fantasy and Horror.* With his wife, artist-writer Janet Chui, he runs Two Cranes Press, a critically-acclaimed independent publisher out of North Carolina. He is a graduate of the Clarion Writers' Workshop and the M.A. program in Creative Writing at North Carolina State University, and currently teaches English at Saint Augustine's College in Raleigh. Lundberg maintains a website and blog at jasonlundberg.net, and a literary podcast called *Lies and Little Deaths: A Virtual Anthology*.

Stephen Rauch is the author of *Neil Gaiman's 'The Sandman' and Joseph Campbell: In Search of the Modern Myth*, the first book-length criticism of Gaiman's work. He has written a forthcoming book about Garth Ennis' and Steve Dillon's *Preacher*, also from Wildside Press. Stephen firmly believes that popular culture criticism can be intelligent and well-written, and still appeal to people everywhere, not just a small group of academics. His interests include comics, science-fiction/fantasy/horror, mythology, religion, psychology, and pop music, and wherever else people find meaning, with a special eye towards long serial narratives. He was born in Florida in 1979, but now lives in Philadelphia. Visit Stephen on the web at www.stephenrauch.com.

Peter S. Rawlik, Jr. is an ecologist whose technical work has been published in the *Journal of the North American Benthological Society*, and *Hydrobiologia*. An avid collector of Lovecraftian material, he has contributed fiction to *Crypt of Cthulhu* and *Talebones*. He resides in South Florida, between hurricanes.

Julie Myers Saxton lives in California.

Darrell Schweitzer is the author of three novels, *The White Isle*, *The Shattered Goddess*, and *The Mask of the Sorcerer*. His more than 250 short stories have appeared in a variety of publications, including *Realms of Fantasy*, *Interzone*, *Twilight Zone Magazine*, *Amazing Stories*, and elsewhere. He has published books on H.P. Lovecraft and Lord Dunsany, and edited such critical symposia as *Discovering H.P. Lovecraft*, *Discovering Modern Horror Fiction*, *Discovering Classic Horror Fiction*, and *Exploring Fantasy Worlds*. He has been co-editor of *Weird Tales* since 1987 and has been nominated for the World Fantasy Award four times (winning once, with George Scithers, for editing *Weird Tales*).

Baba Singh works out of San Francisco, writing on varied subjects from psychology to linguistics to critical theory. Having studied rhetoric and semiotics, he ventures into the world of fantasy, science fiction, and even soap operas with an eye toward meaning and identification in narrative. Currently in the works is a science fiction novel, a treatise on *Days of Our Lives*, and a doctorate in psychology.

Davey (Deborah M.) Snyder compiled the first version of this bibliography several years ago for a convention program book because none of the then-available resources were quite what was needed, and hasn't been able to stop—or keep up with Neil—since. She's been a science fiction and fantasy fan and convention runner for over twenty-five years, and a reader much longer than that. She is a member of the New England Science Fiction Association and a NESFA Press worker, and sits on the World Fantasy Board of Directors. In 2004 she ran Fiddler's Green, a *Sandman*-focused convention that raised over $50,000 for the Comic Book Legal Defense Fund. As 'Office Archaeology,' she's a professional organizer and assistant, with several genre writers among her clients.

INDEX

Note: In this index, an entry for the title a book or other longer work appears in italic, with the author's name in parentheses, as in *A Midsummer Night's Dream* (Shakespeare). The titles of volumes of the Sandman series as collected in book form appear thus: *Preludes and Nocturnes* (Sandman). Individual episodes within the series appear thus: "A Midsummer Night's Dream" (Sandman). References to Sandman alone refer to either the periodical (the original comic books) or the series as a whole. A page number with a letter after it, like 135n, means the reference is in a footnote.